Consumption and Public Life

Series Editors: **Frank Trentmann** and **Richard Wilk**

Titles include:

Mark Bevir and Frank Trentmann (*editors*)
GOVERNANCE, CITIZENS AND CONSUMERS
Agency and Resistance in Contemporary Politics

Daniel Thomas Cook (*editor*)
LIVED EXPERIENCES OF PUBLIC CONSUMPTION
Encounters with Value in Marketplaces on Five Continents

Nick Couldry, Sonia Livingstone and Tim Markham
MEDIA CONSUMPTION AND PUBLIC ENGAGEMENT
Beyond the Presumption of Attention

Kate Soper and Frank Trentmann (*editors*)
CITIZENSHIP AND CONSUMPTION

Forthcoming:

Jacqueline Botterill
CONSUMER CULTURE AND PERSONAL FINANCE
Money Goes to Market

Roberta Sassatelli
FITNESS CULTURE
Gyms and the Commercialisation of Discipline and Fun

Consumption and Public Life
Series Standing Order ISBN 1–4039–9983–X Hardback 1–4039–9984–8 Paperback
(*outside North America only*)

You can receive future titles in this series as they are published by placing a standing order. Please contact your bookseller or, in case of difficulty, write to us at the address below with your name and address, the title of the series and the ISBN quoted above.

Customer Service Department, Macmillan Distribution Ltd, Houndmills, Basingstoke, Hampshire RG21 6XS, England

Citizenship and Consumption

Edited by

Kate Soper
London Metropolitan University

Frank Trentmann
Birkbeck College, University of London

First published 2008 by
PALGRAVE MACMILLAN
Houndmills, Basingstoke, Hampshire RG21 6XS and
175 Fifth Avenue, New York, N.Y. 10010
Companies and representatives throughout the world

PALGRAVE MACMILLAN is the global academic imprint of the Palgrave
Macmillan division of St. Martin's Press, LLC and of Palgrave Macmillan Ltd.
Macmillan® is a registered trademark in the United States, United Kingdom
and other countries. Palgrave is a registered trademark in the European
Union and other countries.

ISBN-13: 978–0–230–55346–0 hardback
ISBN-10: 0–230–55346–X hardback

This book is printed on paper suitable for recycling and made from fully
managed and sustained forest sources. Logging, pulping and manufacturing
processes are expected to conform to the environmental regulations of the
country of origin.

A catalogue record for this book is available from the British Library.

A catalog record for this book is available from the Library of Congress.

10   9   8   7   6   5   4   3   2   1
17   16   15   14   13   12   11   10   09   08

Printed and bound in Great Britain by
CPI Antony Rowe, Chippenham and Eastbourne

Contents

Part 3   Prospects

List of Plates

List of Figure and Table

Figure

Table

Acknowledgements

This volume developed out of a two-day international workshop on "Citizenship and Consumption" held at Cambridge, England, in spring 2006. Each of these two subjects has attracted a large and ever-growing body of work, but the relationship between the two has received surprisingly little attention. The aim of the meeting was simple: to bring together scholars from their different intellectual homes to explore points of contact and discuss agency, norms, mediations, and the spaces in which citizens and consumers come together. For their contributions to the discussion, we are very grateful to Clive Barnett, John Clarke, John Keane, Catherine Needham, Janet Newman, Martin Powell, and Tine Rostgaard. Many thanks also to Stefanie Nixon for administrative support and to Laura Bevir for the index. Trinity Hall, Cambridge, provided an ideal setting for stimulating talk, and we should like to thank the Master, Martin Daunton, for his generous hospitality. The meeting was made possible by co-funding from the Economic and Social Research Council and from the Arts and Humanities Research Council, which is gratefully acknowledged.

The author and publishers have made every attempt to contact copyright holders. If any have inadvertently been overlooked, the publisher will be pleased to make the appropriate arrangements at the first opportunity.

Notes on Contributors

Zygmunt Bauman is Emeritus Professor of Sociology at Leeds University, UK. Having served as Professor of Sociology and, at various times, Head of Department at Leeds from 1972 until his retirement in 1990, he is known throughout the world for works such as *Legislators and Interpreters* (1987), *Modernity and the Holocaust* (1989), *Modernity and Ambivalence* (1991) and *Postmodern Ethics* (1993).

Mark Bevir is Professor of Political Science at the University of California, Berkeley, USA. He is author of *The Logic of the History of Ideas* (1999) and *New Labour: A Critique* (2005), and co-author, with R.A.W. Rhodes, of *Interpreting British Governance* (2003), and *Governance Stories* (2006). He is co-editor, with Frank Trentmann, of *Critiques of Capital in Modern Britain and America* (2002) and *Markets in Historical Contexts* (2004), and, with Robert Adcock and Shannon Stimson, of *Modern Political Science* (2007).

Nick Couldry is Professor of Media and Communications and Culture at Goldsmiths College, University of London, UK. He is the author or editor of six books: *The Place of Media Power* (2000), *Inside Culture* (2000), *Media Rituals: A Critical Approach* (2003), *Listening Beyond the Echoes: Agency and Ethics in a Mediated Age* (2006) (co-edited with James Curran), *Contesting Media Power* (2003), and *MediaSpace* (2004) (co-edited with Anna McCarthy).

Michelle Everson is Professor of Law at Birkbeck College, University of London, UK. She researches and publishes widely in the fields of European public law, European economic law and European regulatory law. Her recent publications include *The Making of a European Constitution: Judges and Lawyers Beyond Constitutive Power* (2007).

Karl Gerth is a University Lecturer in Modern Chinese History at Oxford University, UK, and Fellow of Merton College. In 2003, Harvard University Press published his book on the role of nationalism in forming a consumer culture in modern China, *China Made: Consumer Culture and the Creation of the Nation*. His current research projects examine consumerism in contemporary China and the dismantling of market culture in the early People's Republic of China.

Ferenc Hammer is Assistant Professor at the Institute for Art Theory and Media Studies at Eötvös Loránd University in Budapest, Hungary. He researches in the field of material culture and media studies. His recent work includes *Communication and Social Justice: On Poverty Portrayals in Current Affairs TV* (2006, in Hungarian); 'Strange but Responsive Bedfellows: Single-issue Activism and the Media', *Eastbound*, 2006/1; and 'A Gasoline Scented Sindbad: The Truck Driver as a Popular Hero in Socialist Hungary', *Cultural Studies*, XVI (1), 2002.

Matthew Hilton is Professor of Social History at the University of Birmingham, UK. He is the author of *Smoking in British Popular Culture* (2000) and *Consumerism in Twentieth-Century Britain* (2003). He has co-edited *The Politics of Consumption* (2001) and *Au nom du consommateur* (2005). His history of global consumer politics, *The Poverty of Choice: Consumer Activism in an Era of Globalisation* is forthcoming.

Christian Joerges is Professor of Economic Law at the European University Institute in Florence, Italy. His recent publications deal with the Europeanization of Economic and Private Law, transnational risk regulation at European and international level, and compliance and legitimacy problems of transnational governance arrangement. They include, edited with Paul Blokker, *Confronting Memories: European 'Bitter Experiences' and the Constitutionalisation Process*, Special Issue of the *German Law Journal* (6:2, 2005), and, edited with Michael Zürn, *Law and Governance in Postnational Europe: Compliance Beyond the Nation-State* (2005).

Sonia Livingstone is Professor in the Department of Media and Communications at the London School of Economics, UK. She is author or editor of nine books and 100+ academic articles and chapters in the fields of media audiences, children, and the Internet, domestic contexts of media use and media literacy. Recent books include *Young People and New Media* (2002), *The Handbook of New Media* (edited, with Leah Lievrouw, 2006), *Audiences and Publics* (edited, 2005), and *Media Consumption and Public Engagement: Beyond the Presumption of Attention* (with Nick Couldry and Tim Markham, 2007).

Tim Markham is Lecturer in Media (Journalism) at Birkbeck College, University of London, UK. Before joining Birkbeck, Tim worked as the research officer on the 'Media Consumption and the Future of Public Connection' research project at the London School of Economics. The book on the project, *Media Consumption and Public Engagement: Beyond the Presumption of Attention*, co-authored with Nick Couldry and Sonia Livingstone was published by Palgrave Macmillan (2007).

Michele Micheletti is Professor of Political Science at Karlstad University, Sweden. Her recent publications include 'Mobilizing Consumers for Global Social Justice Responsibility-Taking', *Annals of the American Academy of Political and Social Science* (2007), with Dietlind Stolle; *Politics, Products, and*

Markets: Exploring Political Consumerism Past and Present, with Andreas Follesdal and Dietlind Stolle (2006); and the monograph *Political Virtue and Shopping: Individuals, Consumerism, and Collective Action* (2003). She was the guest editor of the special issue 'Shopping for Human Rights', *Journal of Consumer Policy* (2007), with Andreas Follesda.

Bronwen Morgan is Professor of Sociolegal Studies at the University of Bristol, UK. Her recent publications include 'The Politics of Necessity', edited with Frank Trentmann, Special Issue of *Journal of Consumer Policy*, 29(4) (2006); 'The North-South Politics of Necessity: Regulating for Basic Rights Between National and International Levels', *Journal of Consumer Policy*, 29(4) (2006); 'Turning Off the Tap, Urban Water Service Delivery and the Social Construction of Global Administrative Law', *European Journal of International Law*, 17 (2006), pp. 215–247; and *Social Citizenship in the Shadow of Competition: The Bureaucratic Politics of Regulatory Justification* (Ashgate Press, 2003).

John O' Neill is Professor of Political Economy at Manchester University, UK. He has written widely on the philosophy of economics, political theory, environmental policy, ethics and the philosophy of science. His books include *Markets, Deliberation and Environment* (2007), *The Market: Ethics, Knowledge and Politics* (1998), and *Ecology, Policy and Politics: Human Well-Being and the Natural World* (1993). He has co-authored a book *Environmental Values* (forthcoming) with Alan Holland and Andrew Light.

Kate Soper is Professor of Philosophy in the Institute for the Study of European Transformations at London Metropolitan University, UK. Her publications include *On Human Needs* (1981); *Humanism and Anti-Humanism* (1986); *Troubled Pleasures: Writings on Politics, Gender and Hedonism* (1990); *What is Nature? Culture, Politics and the Non-Human* (1995); *To Relish the Sublime? Culture and Self-Realisation in Post-Modern Times* (2002) (with Martin H. Ryle); and *Counter-Consumerism and its Pleasures* (edited with Lyn Thomas and Martin Ryle) (forthcoming 2007).

Frank Trentmann is Professor of History at Birkbeck College, University of London, UK. His recent publications include the volumes of essays *Consuming Cultures, Global Perspectives* (2006) (with John Brewer) and *The Making of the Consumer: Knowledge, Power and Identity in the Modern World* (2006). He is the author of *Free Trade Nation: Commerce, Consumption and Civil Society in Modern Britain* (2007).

1

Introduction

Kate Soper and Frank Trentmann

Consumption today is an established part of political life, perhaps more than ever before in human history. Its sphere of influence ranges from ethical consumerism in civil society to the fostering of 'choice' in government policies, all the way to a micropolitics of everyday life, for example a person's purchase of a Fairtrade product or the pursuit of a simpler, less-resource-intensive lifestyle. What does it mean to be a consumer for our role as citizen? Is consumption itself a dimension of citizenship? Wherever we look, these questions have moved to the forefront of public debate. Choice and desire, our material lifestyle and use of things are at the heart of the discussion about well-being, happiness, and sustainability.

What is surprising, therefore, is how little serious attention the literature on citizenship has accorded to the diverse practices, values, and objects involved in consumption. Texts on citizenship have plenty to say about citizens in relation to the state, nationality, rights and freedoms, the equality of sexes, and the environment, but consumption tends to receive short shrift. If it figures at all, it is as an awkward topic quickly passed over. The consumer appears only as an individuated figure of a neo-liberal world of markets challenging the citizen.[1] The consumer here is located within the domain of the market, distinct from that of the state and its citizens.

Conversely, the enormous boom of interest in consumer culture in the last two decades initially developed largely in isolation from questions of citizens and their political institutions. Spectacle and image, taste and identity, these were at the forefront of enquiries into how consumption was remaking modernity. Consumption in this conception might at times offer individuals a way to resist and retreat from mainstream politics, for example through the creation of subcultures and transgressive identities that challenged conventional norms and lifestyles.[2] But if in this limited sense it could be said to have sponsored a new kind of personal politics, the connections to citizenship more generally were left implicit.

This theoretical divide between public (citizenship) and private (consumption), however, always had difficulty accounting for the advancing

1

complexity of consumer cultures. In recent years, it has been visibly challenged by a whole range of social, cultural, and political developments. At both local and global levels, consumption has become a principal source of political engagement for many citizens, in campaigns for better working conditions, animal welfare, and global fair trade. Consumerism, too, has spurred discussion about the appropriate balance between market and non-market systems of provision, and, most fundamentally, about the nature of the 'good life' and of our obligations to present and future generations.

These recent developments invite us to place consumption and citizenship in a shared framework of analysis. This is the main aim of this volume. We ask about their interaction over time, giving due attention to different traditions in the past, to the dialogue between the two in rhetoric and practice today, and to possible combinations in the future.

This collection of essays is designed to broaden the terms of debate, to allow for a more nuanced and wide-ranging consideration of the ways in which consumption and citizenship shape each other. It extends the ideological frame of reference to think about how different traditions of citizenship and consumption have come together. It gives greater consideration to the variety of consumption practices and norms. And, finally, it looks above and below the level of the state to include local and global spheres of politics. Together, these perspectives highlight the diversity of consumption and its political dynamics. The essays, therefore, do not postulate a singular model. Rather they have been chosen and organised as a set of pathways, giving the reader a chance to engage with diverse political traditions, to ponder on the political implications of different consumption practices, and to reflect on competing visions of the place of consumption in the good life.

The currently dominant debate, at least in Western Europe and North America, has been in terms of a sharp divide between community and choice. Most often, citizenship and consumption have been located on opposite sides of a divide between public and private. In part, this constellation reflects the impact of neo-liberalism in the 1990s, with its strategies of privatisation and consumerisation of public services. For its champions, a market mechanism like choice promises to empower citizens as consumers and make public services more efficient and accountable. For its critics, choice stands condemned as an individuating ploy that would further erode people's already thinning engagement with the public world, destroying citizenship in any meaningful sense of the world.[3]

In the last decade, amidst concerns over growing political apathy, these two sides of the debate have tended by their nature to reinforce each other. This confrontation has been especially pronounced in Britain, where consumerism became a litmus test for competing world views and policies. For the New Labour government, contemporary society had become a consumer society, a transformation that amounted to a historic caesura with a more producer-oriented welfare state model of the 1945 settlement. Public services and public life needed to adapt to a more consumerist outlook. Citizens, it argued, wanted choice. The government's role was to break down paternalist hierarchies and encourage citizens to become more demanding, assertive, and informed. Critics, by contrast, blamed consumerism for promoting individualisation, a selfish and materialist culture of spend-now worry-later which undermined people's sense of civic belonging and their ability to care for present and future generations. Bringing the mentality of shopping to public services threatened to convert public hospitals and schools into virtual supermarkets. These broader fears are well captured in Chapter 9 by Zygmunt Bauman in this volume. Consumption, in this view, is somehow less authentic than other social activities. It is seen as solitary and wasteful. And its rise is connected to a decline of politics: a once-shared public domain administered by the state shattered into little shards of life politics individually run by consumers themselves. Consumerism leaves behind a void.

Such anxieties about consumerism are, it should be stressed, not without their precedents. They do not arise only in response to a recent era of affluence and the new type of 'consumer society' that emerged in the decades after the Second World War. Behind them lies a far older clash of beliefs, anxieties, and prejudices. Fears of what consumption might do to a political community and to the public good are as old as consumption itself.[4] Anxieties have found expression through a variety of ideological traditions – from conservatism and Protestantism to Marxism.[5] Their core values, however, can be traced to one particular tradition of citizenship: republicanism. It provides a source for much contemporary communitarianism and post-Marxist disaffection with commercial society. Looking back to an ideal citizen in ancient Athens and Rome, the republican vision of citizenship regained prominence in early modern Europe. Citizenship here was an all-encompassing identity (although one, of course, restricted in practice to a male elite). It involved active participation in the affairs of the community, its defence, laws, and government.[6] Citizens were in principle free and equal. They bore arms and literally had a stake in the country. A true citizen was a soldier, councillor, landowner, and father rolled into one. Republican virtue and self-government were fit for small political communities like city-states and republics. This view of citizenship could not deal with a rapidly expanding world of goods and commerce in the eighteenth century. Material riches and temptations, along with new demands for political inclusion, put to the test the republican idea of virtue with its vision of active citizenship.

The more transnational and fluid forces of consumption and commerce ran directly counter to the organising principles and mentality of republican citizenship with its organic social and territorial outlook. Public spirit and action, it appeared, required austerity. Jean-Jacques Rousseau was typical in his admiration of the simple lifestyle of Roman citizens. The desire for new goods, their trade, and their growing importance in peoples' lives, all these seemed to him to explode the organic identity of the republican citizen into many smaller competing identities. The acquisitive spirit, he feared, could encourage the pursuit of more personal pleasures and fulfilments rather than participation in public life. This new, more commercial society promoted a more privately accented understanding of freedom rather than virtue – citizenship now came to have less to do with active involvement and more with virtual representation by vote and parliamentary assembly. Politics, in the liberal tradition, was about guarding individuals' freedom from the state as much as about giving them the freedom to be active in the state.

This eighteenth-century watershed, between republican virtue and liberal freedom, has been the defining moment for modern debates about consumption and citizenship. Arguably, at least in Europe and the United States, these two traditions continue to provide protagonists with their main vocabularies in debating whether consumption is good or bad for public life. For those in the communitarian tradition, consumption is less authentic, its engagements more superficial, fluid, and less real than a simpler, more earthy, and anchored involvement in the community. Consumers are driven by self-interest, a set of motivations that limit reflexivity, social accountability, and public engagement, if they do not exclude them altogether. The yearning for material comfort and 'physical gratification', Alexis de Tocqueville warned in the 1830s, made Americans 'restless in the midst of abundance'. The prospect of new possessions made people lose their 'self-restraint' and 'lose sight of the close connection that exists between the private fortune of each and the prosperity of all'.[7] De Tocqueville hoped that religion and a democratic spirit might contain the corrosive force of materialism. Critics of mass consumption have regularly voiced similar anxieties about the need to protect communal life against the restless, selfish, and privatising force of materialism – and continue to do so in our own times.[8] For neo-liberals, by contrast, choice is an instrument of freedom that releases the individual citizen from the hierarchical, paternalist influence of the welfare state, and makes public bodies more accountable to the wishes of the people.

This is not the place for a technical investigation of how consumerist reforms of public services have worked out.[9] What deserves emphasis, however, is how narrow and self-limiting these terms of debate have become. The dualism between community and choice has been one important feature of the history of this subject, but it has not been the only one. There are other fruitful ways of looking at the relationship between consumption and citizenship.

This volume suggests three correctives. First, it offers a more open-ended, ecumenical approach to traditions of citizenship and consumption. Republicanism is not the only tradition of citizenship. A consideration of the place of consumption in civic life needs to give consideration to other traditions of citizenship.

Second, we take a broader look at the material, social, and institutional terrains of consumption. Communitarianism has offered an ideological critique of consumption rather than a description of consumption in everyday life. Much of it focuses on shopping as individuating, but consumption involves a diversity of practices, norms, and systems of provision – from eating out to taking a bath, from basic goods to conspicuous consumption, and from public swimming pools to private gyms. Anthropological, sociological, and historical research has shown how buying and using things is also a resource for shared identity, communication, and social practice; commercial and caring relations often complement each other.[10] Even shopping can be less self-centred than its reputation.[11] Consumption is not just a market phenomenon. It is also shaped by laws and institutions that deserve greater attention than they have received in studies in consumer culture.

A final, and related, corrective, therefore, is to look above as well as beneath the nation state. The republican tradition was preoccupied with small political communities. Yet, consumption has many transnational dynamics. Today, it is shaped by international organisations like the World Trade Organisation and the European Union as well as by individual states. This supranational realm is also shaped by civil society. International consumer movements have played a historic role in this widening sphere, from transatlantic boycotts of slave-grown sugar two hundred years ago to Fairtrade movements in recent years. To approach the subject with a simple dichotomy between state and market, where people are either citizens or consumers, risks missing the mediating domain of civil society, which with its own networks of activism and normative processes of deliberation overlaps with both.

Traditions

There is no self-evident reason to adopt this tradition of citizenship as a natural starting point of enquiry. In fact, to do so is to overlook the diversity of citizenship traditions. Putting these back into the story shows how consumption has also nurtured civic life at key moments in modern history.

Other languages of citizenship flourished alongside republicanism. These have included more authoritarian models of obedient subjects (Hobbes) and projects of fusing national and civic identity (the nation state), but there have also been traditions that have been less exclusively state-centred and more open to the contribution of civil society.[12] In this latter view, plural identities are far less of a problem than in the other traditions. Citizenship, here, is about living with difference. Political power is not anchored in the state but shared between government and non-governmental organisations, and it is this overlapping arrangement that protects citizens from despotism. Politics, in other words, comes from below as well as from above.

The communitarian critique of consumerism sits uneasily alongside the historical record of the growth of civil society with increasingly vocal and active citizens in the modern period. It was, arguably, no coincidence that civil society expanded alongside consumption in the transatlantic world of the eighteenth century. Civil society was nurtured by sociability. Sociability, in turn, was nurtured by the spread of new consumer goods (china, cutlery, tea, and sugar), new public spaces of consumption (coffee houses), and new media consumption (novels and newspapers). To what degree this new culture of consumption ever really produced a deliberative public sphere in Jürgen Habermas' famous account is debatable.[13] What is clear, however, is that it opened up new social spaces for women and encouraged new networks of clubs and associations – 'nurseries of democracy' as Tocqueville famously called them. We do not need to idealise the democratic practices of these new bodies – some were exclusionary, others were rife with conflict. What matters here is to recognise that the spread of consumption coincided in important ways with emerging challenges to social hierarchies, and thus contributed to a considerable expansion of the social terrain of citizenship. Communitarian attacks on consumerism sometimes forget the extent to which Republicanism was inward-looking, patriarchal, and socially exclusive. The relevance of this tradition of active citizenship is doubtful in a more global age of large-scale organisations and democratic mass politics.

A more pluralistic perspective on consumption and citizenship suggests the dangers of contrasting simple 'passive' and 'active' modes of public engagement. In the nineteenth century, liberalism and radicalism did indeed champion new, more representative types of citizenship, but these also continued to encourage active forms of civic engagement at the local level.[14] Rather than distracting from civic life, consumption in fact helped to energise it in fresh ways. Most directly, liberal and radical politics generated a new sense of consumer rights. Political battles over Free Trade and local provision of water, gas, and other services generated a new identity of the consumer. Far from being a private, self-seeking, identity, this consumer became fused with the citizen: a citizen-consumer, who had rights to be heard and consulted. Attention to this particular 'consumer' identity of the citizen may have marked an infringement of the organic, landed unit of the citizen in the republican tradition, but for the majority of people it meant a greater voice and inclusion in the body politic than ever before. Initially, the consumer was a male, middle-class point of reference of the local taxpayer, but the universal gravity of the new identity was impossible to contain. The consumer interest became the public interest and, as such, also became a source of legitimation for groups formally excluded from citizenship, like women and many members of the working class. At the turn of the nineteenth to the twentieth century, social movements on both sides of the Atlantic invoked the language of the 'citizen-consumer' in battles over political emancipation and social equity. Indirectly, too, the expansion of commercial spaces, like department stores, opened up public spheres and communication for women in unprecedented ways. Consumption was a conduit for citizenship more than a check upon it.[15]

This volume adds to this revisionist literature by expanding the scope of citizenship and civic traditions further to include non-European traditions of citizenship and the material politics in socialist societies as well as progressive ideals of choice in liberal democratic societies.

Choice has been at the heart of the current debate over consumerism and stands as a symbol for the individualist and economistic working of the market. Most scholars working in the humanities and social sciences, including some economists, have turned away from 'choice' as a satisfactory unit of analysis, emphasizing instead the role of habits and routines, socially embedded values and preferences, and institutions and systems of provision in shaping consumption. There is a risk, however, of throwing the baby out with the bathwater. As Mark Bevir and Frank Trentmann show in Chapter 2, 'choice' did not always have the individualist and materialist associations it later acquired in mainstream economics after the Second World War.[16] For the fathers of modern liberal economics, like Alfred Marshall in the late nineteenth century, choice went hand in hand with altruism and a commitment to a civil society of self-governing citizens. Choice, too, was at the centre of John Dewey's progressive democratic vision in inter-war America – as a mode sponsoring constant reflection and re-evaluation in everyday life, choice helped people to develop personal ethics and social awareness, critical for a full civic life. In reclaiming choice for civic consumption we need, it is true, to be open to the ways in which the choices of some frequently pre-empt or diminish the choices available to others. We need to acknowledge that people's choices in the present might bring short-term satisfaction but reduce their own well-being in the future; and we need also to recognise the co-option of consumption choices within market relations and the ways these come to define the norms of the 'good life' itself.[17] But it is certainly not necessary to start out with a sharp divide between individual choice and civic life. Liberal and democratic societies developed alternative traditions of choice and citizenship that deserve recognition.

These alternative traditions are a reminder that even within Europe and the transatlantic world it is problematic to presume one tradition of citizenship as a natural starting point to think about consumption, or to presume a natural progression from rights and liberties to participatory citizenship and then to social citizenship, made famous by T. H. Marshall. The transatlantic world always contained competing traditions of citizenship, some more symbiotic with consumption, some more antagonistic. The contrast becomes even starker when we look beyond republican and liberal Europe. In China, the sequence has been the reverse of Marshall's progression. A notion of social rights developed prior to a political sense of liberty and civic participation. The rights of citizens were intimately tied to the interests of the state. Citizenship, a concept introduced towards the end of the Qing dynasty, here concerned rights, but they were rights given by the state to the individual to enhance the power of the state, not inalienable rights protecting the individual from the state. As Karl Gerth emphasizes in Chapter 3, this tradition had fundamental implications for the ways consumption was politicised in the course of the twentieth century.[18] Consumption, and consumer movements aiming at the boycott of alien products, became a vehicle of nation-state building. Consumption was not a 'private' but a 'public' affair. As Gerth suggests, the legacy of this patriotic appropriation of consumption continues to be felt to this day.

It is not only in capitalist democracies that consumption is politicised, Indeed, it could be argued that it has a more extensive and complex political role in the lives of people in societies that seek to limit and regulate commodity culture or overcome it altogether. Particular commodities can become symbols of freedom, both of personal self-expression and of a potential critique of public hierarchy. In the 1960s–1970s, it was jeans perhaps more than any other commodity that symbolised this dual function. The sartorial politics of jeans, therefore, offer a convenient case study to test how public and private norms of consumption became embodied in the material politics of everyday life. As Ferenc Hammer shows in his contribution, the arrival of jeans prompted a whole series of complex and contradictory responses by public authorities, parents, and socialist firms.[19] Jeans were not just symbols of resistance. Wearing jeans could challenge authority, but acquiring jeans might also necessitate collusion with an uncle or a family friend sufficiently wellplaced with the regime to obtain them in the first place. The socialist regime, in turn, developed a pragmatic approach to the new world of youthful goods and desires, appropriating jeans as a sign of Hungary's cultural openness and economic modernity. By the 1970s, the government had a manufacturing agreement with Levi Strauss. Politically, jeans were migrating. Initially a sub-cultural form, it became incorporated in the regime's own cultural politics of power.

Norms and practices

If goods are politically mobile and flexible, easily travelling across a public/private divide, their movements in everyday life and political discourse are also a reminder that consumption is ultimately about process and practices not just signs or representation. Of course, there are connections between the two – if we were not made aware of a new technological product, for example, and did not have money or access to it, we would not be able to use it. But our practice of consumption is not exhausted in the act of purchase or the signs of advertising, even if these usually play a mediating role. Consumption is a social practice. It has to do with using things, and is not simply about commodities as such.

A shift in perspective from object to practice entails looking differently at a fundamental question: what is consumption for? Alongside Marxism and

Marxist-inspired critics, most notably the Frankfurt school, the second most influential critique of consumerism's impact on community and public virtues is that of writers who have targeted its conspicuous nature and status-oriented function. Today associated with Thorstein Veblen's path-breaking *The Theory of the Leisure Class*, published just over a century ago, and with Pierre Bourdieu's study of *Distinction* (1979), but located in far deeper and long-standing moral anxieties, this approach emphasises the socially wasteful role of consumption in reinforcing and recreating social hierarchies. Instead of contributing to social cohesion and well-being, consumption becomes a wasteful and self-defeating quest to keep up with the Joneses, leading to a spiral of ever-bigger houses, cars, and yachts.[20]

Once more, to avoid misreading, we are not arguing that consumption has nothing to do with status competition. Yet we perhaps also need to look at its significance and its impact on civic culture in a wider historical context. Writing two hundred and fifty years ago, in the midst of an earlier wave of expanding consumer culture, Adam Smith suggested that the alternative could be worse. People, by nature, he argued, were vain and yearning for distinction, so it was far better they poured their energies into collecting and showing off with objects than, following feudal custom, into building up a retinue of retainers.[21] Possessing things was preferable to possessing people. As Smith in effect acknowledges here, gratification of *amour propre* is an important aspect of human satisfaction, and some conduits for its expression will always be sought. But these do not necessarily have to involve possession of either goods or persons, and a major concern for us today must be how to provide for the pleasures of display and distinction in socially just and sustainable ways. That said, we should also not overstate the centrality of status consumption in people's lives. Individuals with means to do it may on occasion buy a Ferrari or a yacht or go to Monte Carlo to keep up with the Joneses, but for the majority of people at most times consuming has little to do with 'luxury fever'. A lot of consumption is ordinary and mundane, not conspicuous – listening to the radio over breakfast, taking a bath, commuting by car or train, gardening and doing home improvement, watching one's favourite sport team, and surfing the net. All of these, of course, are influenced in the forms they take and the instruments they use by market provision, and they all have their specific environmental impacts. But if viewed purely as practices, these consumption activities are about people performing certain tasks with the help of things. Some of these activities will indeed have implications for status or can be appropriated for status-seeking purposes. But, if there is a dynamic driving them, it is about accomplishment and the pursuit of competences and habitual pleasure and comfort rather than signalling superior status to the rest of society.

Sociologists of practice have in recent years made considerable progress in unravelling the practices involved in such consumption activities as eating, bathing, and driving.[22] The main focus has been on the rhythms and evolution of these practices, how they come together, change, and (sometimes) die. At first sight, this may look esoteric. What is so interesting about how people shower? But such practices, of course, become hard-wired into the material, technological, and institutional make-up of our societies, and understanding lifestyle changes involves a knowledge of their evolution. Similarly, we need to focus more on habitual and ordinary consumption and identify the implications of different practices for civic life and public engagement.

If there has been one culprit that has been blamed more than any other for the public disengagement in 'consumer society' it has been television. Television has been blamed for everything from dumbing down to the erosion of associational life; both theses have been subjected to equally strong critiques.[23] But while we know a good deal about programming, advertising, and viewing hours, we know far less about the impact that watching television has on people's sense of themselves as members of the public and on their sense of public connection. This is the aim of enquiry in Chapter 7 by Nick Couldry, Sonia Livingstone, and Tim Markham.[24] Media consumption, they show, is a quintessential consumption practice. For most people, it is one of the most habitual parts of everyday life. To understand it, we need to look at the details of the routine. What they find runs counter to the dominant story of public apathy or growing disengagement with national issues. Most people watch the news as a matter of habit. They remain concerned about national issues more than about local or international ones. In the United Kingdom, Internet use has remained less salient than in the United States. Watching television has not made people feel disconnected. Rather, people feel connected to public life but feel they are ignored by politicians or lack the opportunity to put their concerns into action. In other words, the much-decried decline in civic action and political engagement may have less to do with consumption per se and more with the erosion of opportunities for political intervention.

Even when the sociological focus is on the everyday practices of consumption, and its more mundane pursuits, it is important to recognise the wider economic and political structures by which these practices are shaped, and to which they are responding. If markets, as Michelle Everson and Christian Joerges (following Karl Polanyi) remind us in this volume, are always socially embedded, the cultures of consumption are likewise always influenced and, in many ways, constrained by the market context. For Bauman, this has indeed resulted in a heightened political apathy and erosion of the space of citizen action and republican concern. In the 'liquid modern' society, he argues, the gratifications of private consumption have been all too successfully substituted for the more onerous responsibilities of citizenship, and it is only in the ephemeral 'swarms' of World Cup patriotism and suchlike that we are witness to any manifestation of collective behaviour in a society otherwise given over to excess, waste, deception, and absorption of all dissent and resistance.

Other contributors to this book, however, would reject the implication that affluence has finally put an end to the politics of consumption. Rather, as conflicts over needs and necessity played a critical role in widening the arena of popular politics, from boycotts and riots in the run-up to the American War of Independence and the French Revolution in the eighteenth century to battles over Free Trade in Great Britain and fair prices in the United States in the early twentieth century, so today, they would argue, ordinary consumption remains a vital source for political action.[25] If few people in the North fight over 'the cheap loaf' these days, many certainly continue to agitate over water, utilities, housing, food safety, and pollution.[26] In Chapter 6, Matthew Hilton highlights the contribution of ordinary, 'banal' consumption to a pragmatic form of international consumer politics in the 1970s and 1980s.[27] The new form of consumer-testing agencies, first pioneered in the United States in the inter-war years before becoming an established feature across the globe, has mostly come in for criticism as actively feeding a more self-centred materialist culture bent on acquiring ever-faster, cheaper, and better goods. As a movement, consumerism, in this view, was actively complicit in reducing politics from a public-oriented to a private-centred affair. As Hilton shows, this is at best a partial view and ignores much of the political work performed by consumer agencies especially in international politics. It was often testing activities that first catapulted problems with products and market failures into the arena of politics. Consumer protection concerned questions of life and death, from baby food to unsafe cars, from healthcare to housing. The third wave of consumerism was about the poor, impoverished, and excluded, as much as about the well-fed middle classes with their shiny white consumer durables.

The spill-over from issues and campaigns relating to consumer protection on safety and pricing to the broader ethical concerns with the conditions of manufacture of goods sets the context for Michele Micheletti's presentation of the contemporary anti-sweatshop movement as directly comparable to earlier campaigning for the abolition of slavery.[28] There are parallels in the scandals and abuses suffered in both cases, she suggests, as also in the reliance of both on cheap labour to provide readily affordable goods to Western consumers. In both cases, too, she argues – in a dialectics of optimism much at odds with Bauman's pessimism – capitalism encouraged the sensibility that has revolted against these outrages, and has thus itself created the conditions of humanitarian dissent to such types of exploitation.[29]

Consumer movements are not progressive in and of themselves, and we must guard against creating pure or ideal types; groups supporting the abolition of slavery did not have a problem with Empire as such, and there were 'buy empire goods' campaigns as well as radical and social justice movements.[30] In general, however, Micheletti's argument raises interesting questions about the defining features and ideological commitments of the market economy, and the extent to which neo-liberalism today might be said to have exceeded or offended against these. In a context where deregulated global capitalism blocks legislation against sweatshops as a barrier to free trade, humanitarian concern for this contemporary form of slave labour must look elsewhere for representation or political take-up. It is in this context that campaigners have appealed to the accountability of consumers for the exploitative practices involved in the production of their commodities (a fostering of global solidarities theorised in the so-called 'social connection model of political responsibility').[31] Where this has happened, movements of consumer resistance forged through communicative action (consciousness raising and opinion formation) take on a more openly contestatory role.

Comparable concerns with the fluid and shifting boundaries between consumption and citizenship in the global context today lie at the heart of Bronwen Morgan's engagement with the complex relations between law and civil disobedience actions over provision and access to water.[32] The focus here is on a new type of 'political consumerism' of payment boycotting, or 'disloyal exit', where we have unusual consumer behaviour implicating what it is to 'act as a citizen' or display republican virtue. Drawing on studies of protests in South Africa and New Zealand, Morgan shows how illegal moves to secure vital needs can count as legitimate acts of 'political consumerism' (and may seek, and even find, defence in human rights law and other jurisdiction) while simultaneously confounding ideas about what is 'proper' to the exercise of lawful and responsible citizenship. In the case of normal 'ethical' consumption, where consumers choose to pay for an alternative product, the 'tacit' cultural contract of exchanges is secured and routinely observed. But this contract breaks down where no alternative choice of an essential product is available or affordable. As Morgan says, civil disobedience from this angle challenges the link between consumption and production on much more structural terms than law-abiding ethical consumption (although, as Micheletti and Soper both indicate, the latter might come over time to have that effect), since it demands a say in drawing the contours of the political community in which production and consumption take place. From this optic, we need to understand the boundaries between citizen and consumer as intimately caught up in the drawing of a number of others, notably those between consumer/criminal and consumer/subject of human rights.

Some similar issues, we might note, are raised in respect of critical mass bike-rides and illegal protests against road and airport expansion in the United Kingdom and other countries in Europe. Clearly, these are not directly comparable to protests over a provision that is, like water, essential to life, but they are often motivated by a sense of the foreclosing of choices for the future and by concern for the promotion of forms of consumption that may ultimately have significant impact on the quality of life of future generations. Social norms are also clearly operating in their case to determine the propriety of certain consumer conducts, to create 'insiders' and 'outsiders', and to pose questions about whether the protesters should be regarded as delinquents or as representatives of civic virtue.

Looking ahead: Global challenges and perspectives

Such issues connect with broader ones concerning the spatial and temporal relations and responsibilities of the 'consumer-citizen' in the contemporary 'global' world. As production has become dominated by transnational corporations and thus relatively removed from the legislation of national governments, it has brought about new conditions, both constraining and enabling, on the exercise of consumer politics. The power of transnational giants to set the agenda on modes of production and consumption has been hugely extended, particularly within the neo-liberal economic regime of recent decades; but so, too, has their dependency on continued consumer spending, brand loyalty, and insatiability in an era in which consumers, at least in the richer societies, have become both more knowledgeable and more concerned about the social and environmental impacts of their own 'consumerist' affluence. At the same time, in the post–Cold War period, we have seen the emergence and development of new forms of civil society in Central and Eastern Europe, the growth and expansion of the European Union itself, and significant evolution and complexification of transnational institutions, protocols, and legal processes. All this has had significant impact on the forms and terrain in which a citizenship dimension of consumption might be exercised and on the range of its possible accountability. Whereas, traditionally, the citizen aspect of consumption had proceeded from (and been associated with) a territorially defined community or nation state, this conception no longer applies, or is at best partial. A key question is how far the less routinised and more parochial bonds cemented through particular consumer protests and campaigns can be translated into more far-reaching and effectual forms of transnational agency. In this connection, Morgan suggests that the law can have positive impact in furnishing courts and tribunals that amplify and help to legitimise consumer protests, thus enlarging the space for the political participation of ordinary citizens in policy making.

The law, however, as Everson and Joerges point out in their contribution, is a social institution or system that is invoked in the pursuit of various and often-conflictual interests and agendas on consumption, and subject to many tensions between its more purely procedural functions and its more material, or socially integrative roles.[33] What is more, as markets, political systems, and consumers have broken free from national communities to act upon regional and global stages, so have the legal encounters with the consumer grown evermore numerous and complex. Today, for example, law is not only expected to ensure that the practices of consumption adhere to ethical standards or issue in 'good' normative institutions, but also immensely complicated and hampered in any such tasks by the de-politicisation of the global market and the regulatory frameworks introduced to guarantee free trade and commercial choice. And this is especially so in cases where the safety, morality, and social rationale of marketing specific products or processes remain highly contested. The quality of these tensions and the predicaments posed for lawyers are illustrated by reference to the recent decision of a WTO Panel on the conflict between the United States and the European Union on import restrictions placed on Genetically Modified Organisms (GMOs). Although in this case, Everson and Joerges argue, it is relatively clear that the global legal order has allowed itself to be colonised by the logic of 'sound science' in its encounters with the consumer, this situation may itself change over time if 'enabled' consumers become more vociferous than before in demanding a political re-structuring of the market.

Already an influence on consumer responses in this respect, the environmental impact of consumption is likely to play an even more critical role in the future. Environmental considerations are clearly very much at issue in the building of transnational solidarities and promotion of cosmopolitan democracy. They are also already shifting and complicating the parameters of thinking about the 'citizen–consumer' coupling. For example, new questions are posed in this context about the criteria of civic 'altruism' and the definition of the 'caring' consumer. It may be true that the conventional picture of the 'selfish' consumer is confounded in the evidence that consumers are hugely concerned with the welfare of family and friends, and that their consumption in this sense takes place as part of a 'caring' ethic. But the 'altruism' of a parent who buys expensive brand trainers to please their child must be distinguished from that of those who inconvenience themselves (for example, by refusing to fly) for the sake of the larger public good. What is more, even the most ordinary or routine forms of consumption, such as driving, are now complicit in environmental degradation – and may be no more innocent in this respect than more spectacular or ostentatious consumer behaviour. Quite often, in fact, it is the more unconscious and everyday 'forms of life' that preclude the imagining and development of more sustainable alternative sources of pleasure and fulfilment.

Questions about such alternatives, the quality of the 'good life', and the possible agents of any redirection of consumption along more sustainable routes move to the centre in the contributions from John O'Neill and Kate Soper.[34] Both authors write in awareness of the current debates about the ways of countering environmental degradation and the trust that has been placed in science and technology to offer a corrective for this. In both cases, however, the focus is less on how to sustain the 'consumerist' lifestyle than on the quality and conditions of the 'good life' itself, and how these might be better secured through altered work and life priorities and differing patterns of consumption. O'Neill's point of departure is the claims of the recent hedonic research and the so-called 'happiness' economists such as Layard that increasing life satisfaction does not entail increased levels of consumption.[35] Sympathetic though he is to the general suggestion that well-being involves much more than high levels of material consumption, he is also sceptical of the subjective bias in the assessments of the hedonic tradition, and he himself favours instead a more objective Aristotelian approach. The eudaimonic tradition, he argues, offers a more satisfactory account of citizenship across generations, and thus provides a surer basis for understanding – and assuming – commitments to those yet to be born. The problem today, however, is that the market imperative towards increased labour mobility and the production of non-durable articles has undermined social and material continuity and thus discouraged the provision of the kind of human and environmental goods associated with this vision of the 'good life'. O'Neill, however, is at the same time sensitive to the very considerable difficulties of constructing any such communal identity and continuity in ways that are consistent with respect for individual autonomy and independence.

Here, then, we have a temporal register of the dilemma or debate between liberal and communitarian tendencies, and one that connects to issues raised by other authors about how to sustain the civic potential of consumer agency across the dispersed and disaggregated activities of individual consumers. Addressing the issue from a different angle, Soper theorises the ways in which emergent forms of disaffection with the 'consumerist' lifestyle and revisions of thinking about the 'good life' may now be providing a distinctive rationale for adopting more civically oriented attitudes to consumption. The egoism or self-interest of the consumer may in this sense already comprise for some (and potentially for many more in the future) an interest in consuming in a more collectively sensitive and environmentally friendly fashion. 'Alternative hedonist' responses on this account – and Soper insists she is hypothesising a possible form of political evolution rather than predicting it – could therefore in coming decades reinforce, and even trump, other pressures for the promotion of more sustainable consumption. The moral and material dissatisfactions generated by the affluent lifestyle itself would then acquire a definite political dimension and contribute to other grounds surveyed in this volume on which consumption has come to figure as a 'level' or space of resistance to the dominance of corporate capitalism.

It will be clear from this introductory survey that the perspectives on citizenship and consumption included in this volume are diverse in their coverage and message. As indicated earlier, the primary aim here is to provide a forum for an expanded and more nuanced debate rather than to prescribe its terms or defend a paradigm of thinking in this complex area. Such links as there are between contributors are therefore of a fairly general kind: a concern to develop a more qualified view of the relations between 'citizen' and 'consumer' and to explore the political potential (if any) of the often complex concerns, duties, motives, and pleasures caught up in contemporary consuming. For some the priority is to correct simplistic and historically distorting theories of the inherently private and 'selfish' consumer, and/or to challenge the traditions of citizenship that have most usually been opposed to consumption. The 'citizen-consumer' here figures as a hybrid to be unpacked in order to discover a more ramified understanding of both consumption and politics than is offered in much economic and social theory. For others, the interest in the actual or potential 'civic' dimensions of consumption is linked to the erosion of other sources of political empowerment and contestation in the globalized era, and consumption here figures as a site of newly emerging forms of social and environmental responsibility and political agency. Most contributors here, however, despite their different levels and types of engagement are sensitive to the current 'fluidity' and normative complexity of the coupling of two concepts so long viewed as opposed. They recognise, that is, how readily the rhetoric of the 'citizen-consumer' lends itself to projects of privatisation and disempowerment, even as they seek to retain the term as a more positive tool of analysis of some emerging and relatively under-theorised aspects of consumption. Most would accept, too, that the current dependency of the globalized economy on the promotion of a 'consumerist' way of life that is at once so closely associated with 'freedom and democracy' and at the same time so socially and ecologically damaging is emerging as a significant source of tension for our times. In this context, the various perspectives opened up in this volume offer a timely engagement with currently evolving forms of opposition and synthesis between citizenship and consumption.

Part 1
Retrieval

2

Civic Choices: Retrieving Perspectives on Rationality, Consumption, and Citizenship

Mark Bevir and Frank Trentmann

The current debate about consumption and citizenship is often conducted in two opposed languages: choice/consumerism versus community/citizenship. This chapter is an attempt at disturbing this simple polarity. Much of the recent scholarly and critical political engagement with consumption has developed as a reaction to neoliberalism. Choice has become tightly associated with consumerism and markets. For its advocates, choice is equivalent to individual freedom for active citizens in a world of demanding consumers. For its communitarian critics, choice is equivalent to the erosion of shared civic values. For other critics it acts as a key vehicle of governmentality in the construction of 'advanced liberal' subjects.[1]

Of course, the dichotomy between choice/consumerism and community/ citizenship rests on strong ideal-typical abstractions. In the field of consumption studies, the main response has been to question the association between choice and consumption. Historians have emphasised how consumer advocacy and the discourse of the consumer have played a vital role in expanding citizenship and civic life, offering a kind of parallel politics for disenfranchised groups as well as advancing the voice and claims of enfranchised citizens. Against long-standing charges of the selfish qualities or conspicuous nature of modern consumption, anthropologists have retrieved the role of consumption in creating, recycling, and adapting sociality, family, and ethnic networks and cultural bonds. Economic sociologists have shown that there is no inherent conflict for most people to have choice and spend money on parts of emotional life – such as childcare – and at the same time have strong feelings for community and family. Sociologists of ordinary consumption have directed attention to the ongoing routines of consumption that continue to take up a major slice of time and money in modern societies, such as washing, cooking, or reading, all of which tend to go unnoticed in the popular association of consumption with individual choice or shopping. And theorists and philosophers have wondered whether the hedonistic qualities often associated with modern consumption may not be a source of alternative political and lifestyle projects. In short, a lot of consumption fits badly within a simple characterisation of consumerism and choice.[2]

These critical projects deserve recognition, but by joining in one overall direction (away from choice) they also risk evacuating the debate about choice, reinforcing a sense that choice is a monopoly of neoliberals. This is a mistake. In this essay, we want to take the debate in a different direction, re-examining and reclaiming aspects of choice for a more pluralistic understanding of consumers and consumption in civic life. Champions and critics of consumerism alike, we argue, have left behind an impoverished understanding of the rationalities at work when consumers exercise choice. The task now is not to take sides but to step outside this limited and distorted frame of discussion. Instead of leaving choice and rationality to the enemy and focusing on other dimensions of consumption, scholars of consumption should re-engage with what has been and continues to be a major phenomenon in modern societies. The purpose of this paper is to chart some of the possible directions, historically and theoretically. We begin with acts of retrieval. The current debate amounts to a considerable narrowing of a broader terrain of choice and rationality. Retrieving some of the altruistic, ethical, and civic dimensions of choice in the late 19th and early 20th centuries, we then proceed to suggest a view of local reasoning that recognises both the creative role of consumers as actors and the contribution of local knowledges. Together, the historical and theoretical reflections point to the potential of a more pluralistic view of consumers to transcend the bi-polar contrasts between consumerism and communitarianism.

It is tempting to place our current fixation with choice alongside an earlier historical moment. In the late 19th and early 20th centuries too, questions of individual choice, consumers, and citizenship moved to the public and academic fore. That period too saw a pronounced acceleration in globalisation and major debates about the place of consumption in public life. Rational choice, currently dominant in the human sciences, can be traced to the founding moments of what is frequently termed 'neoclassical economics', in the 1870s–1890s, with its new, mathematical analysis of individual utility functions and a focus on the individual as a unit of analysis. But such parallels also hide important differences, not least by reducing neoclassical economists into rather simple-minded forefathers of a currently popular economistic mindset. Let us therefore begin by demolishing such a linear genealogy.

Alfred Marshall (1842–1924) was one of the doyens of the new economic science, and is as good a starting point as any of his contemporaries to question the popular equation of neoclassical economics with a commitment to individual choice, and materialistically minded, self-maximising *homo oeconomicus*. Marshall was among those late Victorian and Edwardian thinkers who pioneered a move away from diachronic approaches to the human sciences such as those associated with romantic, organic, evolutionary, and historical themes; he began to introduce more synchronic, modernist modes of knowing such as those associated with atomisation, analysis, models, and correlations. Nonetheless, the shift from historicism to modernism was not a sudden epistemic rupture. At first these two different modes of knowing often cohabited. Marshall attempted to locate the new economic science within larger historical and ethical frameworks. Even as he established the teaching of economics as a distinct subject, he characteristically emphasised, on the first page of his seminal *Principles of Economics* (1st edn 1890), that

> ethical forces are among those of which the economist has to take account. Attempts have indeed been made to construct an abstract science with regard to the actions of an 'economic man', who is under no ethical influences and who pursues pecuniary gain warily and energetically, but mechanically and selfishly. But they have not been successful.[3]

Far from being selfish, man endured 'toil and sacrifice with the unselfish desire to make provision for his family'. But if familial affections were recognised, Marshall asked, why should economists not also include other 'altruistic motives' as part of 'normal action'? Marshall saw his main contribution as giving scientific attention to all those actions which had regular qualities, including ethical qualities. Similarly, Léon Walras, who at the time introduced the mathematical modelling of competitive general equilibrium, was keen to emphasise the role of love, charity, and other 'disinterested emotions' in economic life.

The growing dominance of neoclassical economics with its interest in the individual consumer since the Second World War makes it easy to forget that 'the consumer' was not the discovery let alone the monopoly of Marshall and Jevons. 'The consumer' had powerful supporters in alternative traditions, such as historical economics and heterodox underconsumptionism. Indeed, if Marshall had been a historical economist writing on the European continent, he would have emphasised the spread of national and social feelings of solidarity as one of the main effects of advancing consumption. Equally it has been argued that the mathematical revolution masked a great deal of continuity between the so-called 'classical' and 'neoclassical' generations, especially with a shared interest to protect the consumer against monopoly. A keen interest in social solidarity, altruism, and civil society was a shared, cultural context of the late 19th and early 20th centuries.[4]

At that time social, national, and organic conceptions of consumption circulated widely in radical, feminist, historical, and institutional approaches. The idea of the citizen-consumer became an increasingly central aspect of popular politics on both sides of the Atlantic, in battles for (not against) Free Trade (freedom of trade created democratic government, social justice, and international peace), the vote for women (if women showed their competence as voters in the marketplace, they should also be able to cast their vote at the ballot box), and against sweating and cruel working conditions (morally just and other-regarding consumers could raise the social conditions of exploited workers). All these cases are reminders that consumption and citizenship can have positive affinities; they cast doubt on the assumption that there is some inherent tension between the two.[5] It might be argued that such synergies may have existed at the progressive margins of public discourse, and that what mattered in the long run was a different, more individualist logic that was pouring forth from a new more instrumentalist economic mindset. So let us advance a little further into the orthodox heart of what is often believed to have sponsored an individual selfish consumer whose pursuit of choice is seen to threaten community and civic life: neoclassical economics.

Marshall vehemently rejected charges, brought by John Ruskin and Thomas Carlyle, of promoting a 'dismal science' of man as a selfish beast. Much of the misunderstanding, he argued, could have been avoided if only classical economists had more precisely stated that money was simply a convenient measure of a person's motives, not the primary motive. Man, to Marshall, was 'a man of flesh and blood', pursuing business affairs but also sacrificing himself for his family and country – 'a man who is not below the love of a virtuous life for its own sake'. Few were more Victorian than Marshall in warning contemporaries about the abuses of wealth and the moral dangers of wasteful display; he was rather 'too anxious to do good', as John Maynard Keynes would later put it.[6] Much of economic life was about giving greater scope and energy to this virtuous life, strengthening the bonds of community and civil society.

What was the role of the consumer in the dynamics of economic and public life? Marshall and contemporaries followed the earlier generation of John Stuart Mill in viewing the consumer as vulnerable and in need of public protection against monopolistic firms and other abuses in the market place. Both generations shared an optimistic belief in the emancipatory powers of the cooperative movement. Far from succumbing to selfish interests or being steamrolled and seduced by emerging brands and department stores, liberal economists had a strong (perhaps even overly optimistic) belief in consumer self-organisation: gradually, through the spread of cooperative culture, consumers would free themselves from abuse and powerlessness and advance into socially responsible proto-citizens. Associational life would thus promote more 'noble' economic habits.

The active, creative role of the consumer in this public arena deserves emphasis because it can be seen to echo Marshall's view of the consumer as innovator more generally. Much of the critique of consumerism is based on an idea of the consumer as a servile end-user, a passive person swamped by mass-produced goods designed and engineered and made attractive by producers, advertisers, and marketers. J. K. Galbraith has, perhaps, provided the most-influential picture of this servile consumer for social critics of consumption since the Second World War.[7] Anthropologists, like Mary Douglas and Baron Isherwood, by contrast, have presented choice over goods as a secondary expression of the social dynamics, inclusion, and exclusion that operates in families, communities, and networks.[8] For Marshall, meanwhile, it was activities and practices that shaped a consumer's wants and desires – not the other way around. Consumers themselves were a dynamic force in wanting better quality and more diverse and distinguished goods and services. There are six stages in what has been called the 'Marshallian ladder of consumption': increased quantity, increased quality, increased variety, the satisfaction of new wants, a demand for distinction, and a demand for excellence.[9]

Consumers, then, were not so much dragged up a ladder of consumption: they walked up freely and in their own fashion, adding new steps as they did so. Much of this upward momentum was driven by an innate desire for distinction. But this did not lead to a fixed hierarchy of distinct status groups. Rather, for Marshall, the active pursuit of new wants and consumer practices made consumers seek out new social associations. Choice, in other words, was a mechanism through which consumers changed their identity and personal desire, and their social practices and affiliations; the recent 'practice turn' in the social sciences which has led sociologists to focus on the active role of consumers in shaping, developing, adapting, or terminating practices of consumption (like home improvement or new leisure practices) can be seen as a modified version of this view.[10]

All this is very different from what became standard modern consumer theory. The consumer for Marshall was a social actor, shaping demand, and responsible for co-evolving products and services and their uses. This view of the consumer as an active and creative human agent points to an open, fluid social life, and away from a conception of community as fate. Put differently, Marshall's trust in the new science of economics was not as a neutral recording device capturing people's pursuit of self-interest; it was as a key to unlock an upward drive in human desire, practice, and sociality.

The pleas for a new economic science by Marshall and contemporaries like the Austrian economist Eugen von Böhm-Bawerk were not merely theoretical interventions in a secluded ivory tower. Economic science provided consumer leagues with much-needed scientific authority and debating power in their battle for 'white lists' and against socially degrading products and working conditions. Before he became a darling of neoliberal think tanks like the Ludwig von Mises Institute in the late 20th century, Eugen von Böhm-Bawerk, Carl Menger's successor at Vienna University and one of Ludwig von Mises' last teachers, was used by the Christian Social Union (CSU), a social movement of some 5000 members with plenty of connections and ambition: the CSU used his theories of capital and rent to justify the claim that consumers had the power to transform capitalism by moralising their consumption behaviour.[11]

Historically, Marshall's attempts to correct a mistaken view of economics as a science about selfish material motives proved just as unsuccessful as he was successful in establishing the professional credentials of the new science over less mathematical and more institutional models. It would be wrong, however, to think that critics of neoclassical economics simply accepted defeat and had nothing interesting or positive to say about choice. Far from it, the debate about the limits of utilitarian and mathematical models led to significant attempts to reclaim choice from the bosom of the new economic science and for progressive politics. Let us look at one key moment in this development: the debate about ethics and choice amongst consumer advocates and theorists in inter-war America.

Alongside consumer-testing agencies, the Home Economics movement established itself in inter-war America as a popular national network of consumer education and advocacy. Founded in 1899, the American Home Economics Association had by the 1930s over 12,000 members. Already by 1928 there were 322 four-year degree-granting programmes that produced 27,619 majors. Home economics courses became established parts of secondary school teaching and further education and of discussion outside schools such as in women's clubs. Courses on 'consumer buying' taught students about prices and product quality, and ranged from health and home to banking and art. The main mission of the movement was to create a nation of discriminating consumers who would both reflect on their individual needs and desires and thereby cultivate social values and responsibilities. Hazel Kyrk, the influential home economist at the University of Chicago, explained how consumption combined an exercise of choice with the creation of new, higher needs and values. Individuals combined the identities of a 'buyer' and a 'consumer', she wrote in *Economic Problems of the Family* (1929).[12] Buying was about the 'technologies of consumption', practising efficient purchasing decision, concerned with fair prices, and saving money and time. The 'consumer' was about the normative and ethical universe in which such purchasing decisions took place. Consuming involved the evaluation of choices and the setting of standards. It affected 'questions of motives, of values, of ends'. Fostering 'wise consumption choices' – the project of the home economics movement – therefore involved attention to material needs and to moral values, cultivating an individual who not only could make shrewd decisions in the marketplace, but also chose forms and practices of consumption that would stimulate the mind and create bonds of affection and social networks.

American historians have recently retrieved the political dimensions of an advancing citizen-consumer in the era of the New Deal. This new consumer power operated via new institutional linkages and open encouragement by the state, such as the exposure of profiteering, an attack on producer oligopolies, and an attempt to secure 'fair prices'.[13] The ethical revaluation of choice was a second important source of this vigorous embrace of the consumer as citizen. Kyrk, for example, had little sympathy (or patience) with a mathematical, neoclassical understanding of the individual as someone maximising utility: her prize-winning *Theory of Consumption* (1923) began as a demolition job of marginal utility theory, especially of W. S. Jevons. A theory of economics as a mere theory of exchange value, she argued, failed to offer any understanding of the attitudes that shaped choice. Instead of leaving choice to neoclassical economists and moving on, however, Kyrk went out to reclaim choice for a view of civic consumption.[14]

It was John Dewey's philosophy of knowledge through practice that provided the framework for an expanded appreciation of choice. Dewey attacked the 'false psychology' underlying a marginal theory of choice. The idea that knowledge originated in sensations and was composed of cost–benefit calculations, he argued, dangerously ignored the influence of habits, customs, and impulses.

> The baby does not move to the mother's breast because of calculation of the advantages of warmth and food over against the pains of effort. Nor does the miser seek gold, nor the architect strive to make plans, nor the physician to heal, because of reckonings of comparative advantage and disadvantage. Habit, occupation, furnishes the necessity of forward action in one case as instinct does in the other.[15]

Marginalists got the nature of the deliberation that preceded choice wrong. 'Deliberation is not calculation of indeterminate future results. The present, not the future, is ours', as Dewey neatly put it. When deliberating about choices, individuals did not calculate future events, but applied memory and experience in 'constructive imaginative forecasts of the future'. Life was all about choosing and developing a reflective habit that helped individuals to make sense of, assess, and order an otherwise messy set of probable actions.

> The moral is to develop conscientiousness, ability to judge the significance of what we are doing and to use that judgement in directing what we do, not by means of direct cultivation of something called conscience, or reason, or a faculty of moral knowledge, but by fostering those impulses and habits which experience has shown to make us sensitive, generous, imaginative, impartial in perceiving the tendency of our inchoate dawning activities.

Deliberating choices required people to reflect upon their impulses and habits. 'Therefore', Dewey concluded, 'the important thing is the fostering of those habits and impulses which lead to a broad, just, sympathetic survey of situations.'[16]

Choice looks very different in Dewey's presentation from how it appears in the current debate. Today choice typically appears either as an instrument of maximising future satisfaction or as a terrifying ordeal that swamps individuals with too many self-centred decisions and distracts them from a world of values and commitments that is seen to lie outside the mechanical, narrow arena of choice in the marketplace. For Dewey, choice appears, in contrast, as a wonderful, lifelong opportunity for individuals to practise, revise, and perfect their own habits of reflection, keeping activity alive well beyond the instant in which a decision was taken. In other words, it allows individuals to connect past and present, to search, experiment, and reflect – to play a role in actively shaping their own destiny and identity. It raises the human self above the level of animal and machine, for reflection and '[i]maginative forethought of the probable consequences of a proposed act keeps that act from sinking below consciousness into routine habit or whimsical brutality. It preserves the meaning of that act alive, and keeps it growing in depth and refinement of meaning.'[17]

Whatever we think today of Dewey's instrumentalist version of pragmatism, this approach to deliberation, choice, and practical reasoning highlights the possible alternative meanings of choice that have been lost as the circle of debate has narrowed into a bi-polar battle between consumerism and communitarianism. It also points to the different avenues available to citizen-consumers. It is no coincidence that Dewey became one of the founders of the League for Independent Political Action, a third party movement set up in the United States in 1929. Dewey was no friend of the New Deal. But his view of practical reason, of seeing, knowing and doing as one inseparable process, clearly favoured a view of the choosing consumer as someone who by trial and error established ways of coping with experiences and challenges and of developing more enlightened paths of action. It was lack of choice, mindless routines, or rigid hierarchies that stifled the experimental freedom through which individuals attained their humanity. To limit choice was like chaining an individual to a pole of fixed habits or expectations kept in place by others. Though from a very different starting point, Dewey, like Alfred Marshall, arrived at an account of the consumer as a creative individual.

We do not need to follow all of Dewey's ideas to appreciate one important insight. Choice is not only about markets. It is part of human nature. While choice changes in scope and function across time and cultures, there is choice in everyday human life in all systems of provision. Just as neoliberal champions of choice would do well to interrogate their market-oriented version of choice by remembering the workings of choice outside the market, so communitarian critics would do well to recall the local reasoning involved in choices in everyday life, a local reasoning that is all too easily forgotten in attacks on choice in public services or the shopping mall.

The older perspectives of the late 19th and early 20th centuries offer an interesting challenge to an instrumentalist view of choice. Consumers appear less as responding to external stimuli and more as changing the stimuli and future sensations through their actions. These older perspectives also raise intriguing implications for more recent sociological and anthropological enquiries into consumption. Sociologists currently engaged in a 'practice turn', interested in the formation, revision, and termination of routine consumption practices, might benefit from considering the role of local reasoning and reflexivity at work. Equally when anthropologists explore the place of morals and sociality within shopping and other consumption 'choices', they might benefit from playing more attention to the Deweyan notion of that actions are coordinated through an evolving and reflexive arch of deliberation.

There are implications for economists, too. In the last 30 years, some economists have used psychophysics to question the standard model of economic utility with its strong assumptions of coherent preference curves and matching decision and experience values; preferences are here replaced by a concern with attitudes, most famously in Kahneman and Tversky's prospect theory with its emphasis on risk aversion and on the centrality of gains and losses, not states of wealth. Dewey and, since, Rorty have levied some powerful criticisms against cognitive psychology that, as far as we can make out, have not been adequately taken on board in recent psychological-economic approaches to deliberation.[18] To the contrary, psychological-economic approaches still seem to replicate many synchronic, modernist tropes. They concentrate on offering formal models – often legitimated by statistical correlations or purportedly universal cognitive theories – of widespread human 'errors' or other departures from a fixed rationality. They certainly do not offer us contingent narratives of the local reasoning and situated agency of individuals who remake themselves and their environments against the background of specific traditions and practices.

These are potential avenues of enquiry, but here we would like to unpack some of the more general implications for our view of rationality and relate these to the troublesome mix of consumption and citizenship. We will do so by, first, clarifying a different version of rationality that allows for creative and local reasoning vis-à-vis dominant, conventional assumptions of rationality. This requires breaking free from dominant frames associated with modernist modes of knowing with their emphasis on the synchronic, atomisation, and analysis, and, instead, a retrieval of alternative forms of reasoning that emphasise the local circulation of reasoning, the active role of agents in constituting decisions and norms, and a recognition of the presence of incommensurate and conflicting values. Instead of dumping rationality altogether, we would suggest a presumption of consistency that appears in the local reasoning of situated agents. We would thereby be led to a more pluralist conception of the civic demands and qualities of consumption in local, everyday life.

Defining rationality in terms of consistency allows us to hold onto a version of rationality while staying outside the problematic world-views of neoclassical economics and their modernist sociological critics. Neoclassical economics with its axiomatic view of rationality in terms of individual utility-maximising actions and objectively valid beliefs (or perfect information) has been subjected to a range of criticisms, both from within the economics profession – such as Simon's concept of 'bounded rationality' in the 1950s or, more recently, from writers influenced by cognitive psychology – as well as by anthropologists and others. For our purposes, the main defect in neoclassical economics is that it elides the local and contingent nature of reasoning and decision making that informs human actions. Actions and individuals are decontextualised – a defect also found in Simon's concept of 'bounded rationality'.[19]

By contrast, a presumption of consistency would accommodate the local and diverse nature of preferences, beliefs and reason. We have discussed the presumption of consistency at greater length elsewhere.[20] Here we want just to mention briefly how it differs from both the economic (choice/consumerism) and the sociological (community/citizenship) perspectives that we have been discussing. Unlike contemporary economic views of choice, a presumption of consistency does not require anything like autonomy or self-reflexivity. Consistency allows, to the contrary, that people accept a large number of beliefs on the authority of others and that they hold yet others only sub-consciously. More generally still, a presumption of consistency makes rationality a feature of webs of beliefs, rather than a personal disposition or a feature of actions. We should also stress here that we are invoking a presumption, not an axiom. We do not rule out that people might be irrational. We merely start out by looking for a consistent pattern among people's beliefs before declaring them inconsistent.

Our emphasis on local reasoning and situated agency also places us outside what has been the main critique of the utility-maximising individual in the last century, that of modernist sociologists. This critique has come in two main forms. On the one hand, there is a prominent tradition of sociologists expressing fear over an almost totalitarian spread of selfish, acquisitive, and instrumental reasoning and action in modern, capitalist, consumerist societies: Max Weber, Herbert Marcuse, Michel Foucault, and others have contributed to this tradition. On the other, an equally prominent tradition finds sociologists insisting that individuals are not utility-maximisers; rather, individuals follow social norms or act out established social roles. At times, these two traditions combine in broad condemnations of modernity, capitalism, or consumerism for spreading selfish and instrumental norms and thereby wrecking elder forms of solidarity and community. Recently, communitarians have made much of the idea that the spread of instrumental rationality, a rights mentality, and also consumerism have undermined community and democracy.[21]

It is worth noting that these sociological traditions, with their alternative concept of rationality, often date, like neoclassical theory, from the late-nineteenth-century shift away from romanticism, with its emphasis on the organic, and towards modernism, with its emphasis on the synchronic, atomisation, and analysis. The proponents of sociological rationality reject the idea of using axioms to construct deductive models. However, they too compartmentalise aspects of social life so as to manage and explain facts.

They too seek to make sense of the particular not by locating it within a temporal narrative but by reducing it to mid-level or even universal generalisations that typically operate across time and space. They replace narratives, not with deductive models, but with appeals to classifications, correlations, functions, or perhaps ideal types – hence the popularity of all-round critiques of 'conspicuous consumption' and fears of a universal materialistic 'consumerism' or the advancing dependence of modern or late-modern societies on utilitarian, market-based systems of order and coercion.

A reliance on modernist modes of knowledge means that these accounts in the tradition of Max Weber, Emile Durkheim, and Bronislaw Malinowski have problems allowing adequately for agency. Classifications, correlations, and functions generate forms of explanation that reduce individual choices and actions to social facts. So, when sociologists appeal to rationality as appropriateness, they usually argue that individual actions are governed by social norms or social roles in a way that appears to neglect situated agency.[22] Crucially, if norms or roles explain people's actions, then the implication is that they somehow fix the content of people preferences, beliefs, or reasoning; if they did not do so, we would presumably need to explain people's actions by reference to their preferences, beliefs, or reasoning, not social norms and social roles. The idea of situated agency, by contrast, implies that although people set out against the background of traditions and practices, they are capable of reasoning and acting in novel ways so as to modify this background. In other words, consumers, like all human beings, are creative individuals actively engaged in shaping their environment, norms, and practices.

Just as sociological traditions have often struggled to allow adequately for local reasoning and situated agency, so they have often inspired overly simplistic dichotomies between self-interest and altruism or mass consumer societies and traditional societies. They treat self-interest and social norms alike as being fixed and defined against each other. Such dichotomies arise in part because social scientists are committed to modernist modes of knowing that require them to hide agency within monolithic – even reified – concepts defined by apparently fixed essences or properties, which then explain other features or effects. They thereby elide the different and contingent patterns of belief and desire that lead people to act in overlapping ways so as to create the social institutions and practices to which these concepts refer.

It is true, of course, that some sociologists have argued that consumption has become, in the late twentieth century, about services, experiences, and identities. Yet, these sociologists all too often then locate their ironic, postmodern consumers and their postmodern social formations as the historical successors of the utility-maximiser and mass consumption, which in turn are supposed to have replaced pre-modern peoples and traditional societies.[23] For example, the strong thesis in recent writings on governmentality – that the 'advanced liberalism' of the last few decades has hollowed out citizenship by constructing the persona of the active, self-reliant consumer – presumes, indeed requires, a strong view of an earlier time when citizens were active, and consumers passive or altogether absent.[24] As historical research and political theory suggests, such monolithic, historical contrasts tend to reify concepts and so to ignore the historical circulation, modification, and contestation of plural rationalities and diverse cultures of consumption.[25] Their totalising assumptions about a new consumer discourse are also, of course, at odds with the multiple, conflicting identities that continue to circulate in everyday life in defiance of the discourse of 'advanced liberalism' championed by governments, business, and media.[26]

One reason to defend a presumption of rationality is, therefore, to draw attention to agency and the way it unsettles the dichotomies associated with much sociological theorising, allowing us to recognise major questions about the emergence, development, and contestation of diverse practices. The local quality of reasoning deserves emphasis. Local reasoning typically consists in people pushing and pulling at their existing beliefs and a new experience or idea so as to bring them into some kind of coherent relationship. The new set of beliefs then appears in their decisions and actions as their situated agency. This agency embodies people's capacities for creativity. People reason creatively in that there is no rule defining how they will modify their prior beliefs so as to accommodate a new experience or idea.[27] The creative nature of local reasoning is, of course, precisely what prevents our offering formal models of it. Instead of fixed models or outcomes, we have diverse, contingent outcomes. Instead of a formal analysis of a fixed rationality, we require complex accounts of the circulation of diverse rationalities.

So, the concepts of local reasoning and situated agency enable us to step outside the needlessly self-imprisoning frame of analysis which has almost instinctively led many social scientists and commentators to cast civic life and consumer culture as mutually exclusive systems, locked in a struggle of survival. Questioning the dominant narrative of a transition from passive to active consumers does not need to involve suspending critical moral or political properties. A recovery of organic and historical themes from previous centuries need not lead to a Whiggish celebration of progress. Far from it, attention to the many complex, shifting relationships between consumption and citizenship highlights the different moral and political positions that consumers have occupied in the past but that have effectively been written out of the canon of the modern social sciences fixated with the selfish, acquisitive, and ultimately anomic qualities of modern life. Consumption could be a kind of parallel politics for groups formally excluded from citizenship, such as the many women's consumer leagues and cooperatives on both sides of the Atlantic in the late 19th and early 20th centuries. But the appeal to an 'active consumer' could also be tied to the cultivation of an imperially minded shopper, who built the empire by consuming imperial products, as in inter-war campaigns for imperial development in Britain.[28]

Nor should we presume some kind of ethnocentric Western monopoly for such political incursions into the mental and material landscape of consumption – the enormous national product exhibitions in China, after the 1911 revolution, which sought to foster a patriotic culture of consumption,[29] easily dwarfed the projects possible in the British empire, where the metropolis still adhered to Free Trade. Instead of some grand global historical transition from citizenship and community to consumption and individuation, we should recognise that these co-existed in different combinations at the same time in modernity.

The concepts of local reasoning and situated agency might enable us to disaggregate the concept of the consumer further into its various changing parts. By highlighting diversity and contingency, they also might avoid the provincial and presentist image of consumers as resisting global capitalism. History suggests, rather, that organised groups who saw themselves as citizen-consumers in the past have also helped to shape the global capitalist order, as in the case of citizen-consumers rallying to support Free Trade before the First World War. Instead of posing a grand historical narrative – of Americanisation, Westernisation, McDonaldisation, the rise of one-dimensional man – attention to local reasoning and situated agency might lead us to enquire about the evolution of different species of material culture and economic rationality from different centres and their uneven flow and interaction across the globe.

While we would warn against making any substantive associations of the moral, political, or cultural mentality and practices of consumers – be it that of the consumer as dupe, as active and self-seeking, as progressive, or as apolitical – we might suggest that an analysis of consumption in terms of local reasoning and situated agency suggests a somewhat distinctive account of social practices and social coordination. Coordination can occur in civil society even in the absence of markets.[30] Situated agents intentionally and unintentionally create all kinds of formal and informal associations, and it is these associations that then coalesce into complex patterns of societal coordination and governance. Because this concept of an association refers to contingent, changing, and contestable practices that arise out of situated agency and local reasoning, it differs from the sociological concept of an institution as defined by fixed norms or rules, and from those sociological ideal-types, such as networks, which are alleged to have fixed characteristics that explain their other features across time and space.

This analytical point would not have surprised the many consumer groups in the 19th and 20th centuries, especially in radical, progressive, and feminist traditions, that saw consumption as a terrain in which people who were excluded or at the margins of society could cultivate their independence, humanity, and democratic skills and sensibilities. This was especially the self-image of the consumer cooperative movement. G. J. Holyoake, the influential 19th-century British cooperator, who spread the gospel of the 'Rochdale

Pioneers' across the world, made much of the emancipatory and pluralist qualities that set cooperative consumption apart from more totalising social and political projects:

> It is the common mark of the quack mind to pretend that one thing will do everything. The co-operators is not of those who believe ten times more than they can provide, and who can provide ten times more than anyone else can believe.... Those who propose to remake the world – as the "wilder sort" of social reformers do – must remove the human race, since the past is in the bones of all who live, and a nihilistic removal of everybody would render the reconstruction of society difficult. In these days of State Socialism it is not the interest of statesmen, or of any who influence public affairs, to discourage the increase of co-operators, who preach no doctrine of industrial despair – who do not hang on the skirts of the State – who envy no class – who counsel no war on property – who do not believe in murder as a mode of progress – as many do in well-to-do and educated circles, as well as among the ignorant and miserable. Co-operators are of a different order of thinkers. They believe that in a free country justice can be won by reason, if the agitators will make but half the sacrifice of time, comfort, money, liberty, and life, which have to be made by those who seek social change by civil war.[31]

If it is easy to be critical of the self-limiting political (and economic) vision propagated here, it would also be easy to underestimate the amount of self-cultivation and social capital that was generated by these consumer movements several million strong.

But what about consumers in far less liberal systems? Since so many of the anxieties and moral condemnations of 'consumerism' emerged out of a critical engagement with Nazi Germany and the impact of 'mass culture', a brief word should be said here. Whatever one's view of the merits of the concept of civil society, a civil society Nazi Germany clearly was not. But this should not mean that we automatically should throw out our earlier emphasis on the particular processes of coordination and creative knowledge that are channelled through consumption. Readers will be familiar with Adorno and Marcuse's writings on the crippling, enslaving, and dehumanising dynamics of modern 'mass' consumption that left people in the grip of fascist power. What may be less well known is the degree to which it was consumption especially which also provided Germans after 1933 with a space relatively separate and immune to the totalising ambition of the fascist regime. Commodity culture, advertising, product design and exhibits, PR, and advertisers kept alive and openly encouraged dreams of difference. Major companies, like Henkel, the household products firm, promoted images of a private sphere of comfort, convenience, even luxury – with shiny new kitchens, plastic bathtubs, and elegant living rooms – that are conventionally associated with exhibitions of the American way of life after the Second World War. Such images may well have reinforced a sense of a specifically German entitlement to material comfort that would be sustained during the war by the ruthless exploitation, enslavement, and extermination of inferior races. At the same time, however, they also kept alive ideas and practices of social life that to a degree offered a shelter from fascistic culture.[32] To provide a moral evaluation of such dimensions of consumption is beyond the scope of this chapter, but the complexities involved and the resilience of local reasoning (however distinct from a domain of formal political engagement) suggest that consumption, because of its local level of coordination, involves a circulation of rationalities that sets it apart from states and markets.

By moving beyond the two opposed languages of choice/consumerism and community/citizenship, this chapter provides an opportunity to rethink concepts and practices of democracy. Neoliberals equate freedom with participation in a market economy and even a consumerist society, and they think of democracy as a way of protecting such freedom, while also expressing concern at the ways in which majoritarianism can interfere with the market economy. Communitarians often accept such a view of freedom or rights while arguing that an excess of rights or autonomy results in dysfunctional communities – hence they call for homogenous, even rather closed communities that would place restrictions on personal choice in the name of a common citizenship. To retrieve languages of civic choices is, in contrast, to rehabilitate the possibility of practices of choice and consumption acting as bases for civic associations and community. Consumers can choose civic or communal ways of life. Citizens can engage one another, reflect on value systems, and modify their preferences through their choices.

Recognition of the possibilities of civic choices might encourage us to place greater emphasis on the ways in which people actively make their own freedom through their participation in a plurality of self-governing practices. For a start, concepts such as local reasoning suggest that citizens often have a knowledge of how they will respond to policies that is not available to experts. They help us to understand why policies designed by experts at a distance from those they will affect can fail or have unintended consequences due to their lack of fit with the lived practice of those very people. Public policies, it suggests, might be more effective in contexts of high levels of civic engagement and public participation. Concepts such as situated agency ascribe to citizens capacities for choice and innovation. If we value those capacities, we will have an ethical reason for seeking to promote self-governing practices. These concepts thus encourage us to retrieve a pluralist ambition to secure popular deliberation, voice, and influence through various associations in civil society: they encourage us to look to consumer groups, worker participation, and local bodies as sites and means for extending our democratic practices.

3

Consumption and Politics in Twentieth-Century China

Karl Gerth

The publicity [generated by the government-run Chinese Consumers Association] over more than a decade has helped bolster the sense of consumers' rights protection. Armed with laws, the consumer has started to become a self-reliant "god" in a real sense. In the course of learning and applying laws, they are upgrading their traditional ethical values. Mere tolerance is no longer a valued virtue. Victims' failure to safeguard their rights is now regarded as impotence and tolerance of illegal acts. They will stand up to protest and argue with the firms that have infringed upon their rights and lodge complaints or lawsuits to the administrative departments concerned, the Consumers Association and the court. As the sense of self-protection is being enhanced, more consumers have acted to battle the fake and shoddy product makers.

– Ding Shihe, Chinese Consumers Association

The consumer 'has started to become a self-reliant "god" ' in China? Why, then, is there such a large gap between consumer rights on paper and realities in China? This paper offers an historical explanation. Across the twentieth century and into the twenty-first, the Chinese state has had a long history of distrusting 'subjects,' 'citizens,' and now 'consumers' to make the right choices in the marketplace. This article explores the continued tension between citizenship and consumption in China. The first part lays out this argument: a deeply embedded and historically based relationship between citizenship and consumption continues to subordinate and constrain consumption in the name of 'national interests.' The second part examines the history of this relationship at its inception in the early twentieth century, and a final part suggests the continuation of this tension and its modification through state-sponsored consumerism in recent years.

The subordination of consumption and choice to 'national interest' discourse reflects similar limitations imposed on the concept of 'citizenship' in China. The term 'citizenship' in the Chinese context does not automatically refer to the assertion of the right to participate in the exercise of political power. Until recently, there was little of what T. H. Marshall calls 'political citizenship' of the sort developed in Western Europe in the nineteenth century.[1] In the post–Mao Zedong era (since 1976), the development of citizenship has involved, as political scientist Merle Goldman argues in a new book, moving 'politics from the exclusive domain of the party and the intellectual elite into the public realm by at times including other social groups in their political activities and calling for political reforms that would allow political engagement beyond elite circles.'[2] But political scientist Elizabeth Perry does not agree that this constitutes political citizenship, arguing that the protests and political engagement of ordinary citizens more often reflect 'rules consciousness' and not 'rights consciousness.' Rather than demand the right to protest and politic, individuals insist the state *uphold* rights it had already established. Perry suggests this undermines the development of political citizenship in China.[3] In contrast, Goldman insists the two began to blur in the 1990s. And she finds reasons to be hopeful in limited political reforms that *allow* civic participation: local elections since 1987, a relaxed media environment allowing exposés, and signs that the National People's Congress no longer automatically and unanimously rubber-stamps major policies. On one level, this is cosmetic political citizenship sanctioned by the Party. But, as Goldman argues, rights consciousness has spread to the general population, and individuals have begun to 'act as citizens.'[4]

In this context, scholarship on Chinese political citizenship concentrates on looking for the promise rather than the reality of independent opposition and the assertion of 'rights' against the state. Such scholarship often identifies, as a recent book by political scientist Suzanne Ogden phrased it, the 'inklings of democracy,' or the nascent manifestations of citizenship and political rights.[5] Indeed, such quests for the 'sprouts of citizenship,' to paraphrase an earlier search for the initial signs of capitalism, constituted a major trend in Chinese studies throughout the 1990s. Such studies sought to locate the origins of an emergent Chinese public sphere/civil society in the late nineteenth and early twentieth centuries.[6] Since the 1990s, China scholars have looked for similar potential oppositional centers throughout contemporary Chinese society, even in state-sponsored business organizations. Could one identify 'business interest' advocacy that is separate from 'national interests,' even when these interests are still largely couched in terms of national interests, the Chinese equivalent of claiming 'what's good for Shanghai Automotive, is good for China'? Bruce Dickson, for instance, finds that business elites have remained studiously apolitical but thinks they 'may set the stage for the emergence of a more explicit concept of citizenship.'[7] Indeed, he argues that such business groups are much more interested in enhancing their embedded status than creating autonomous organizations. The Chinese Communist Party (CCP)-state returns the favor by creating new organizations to embed their interests as well as recruit leading entrepreneurs into the CCP.

The general puzzle for both historians and political scientists remains the same whether one is investigating the early twentieth century or the present: why are 'citizens' so utterly subordinated to the nation-state? I wish to relate this question to the specific issue posed for in this volume, namely how has the politics of consumption constrained the emergence of notions of political citizenship?

The development of political citizenship in semi-colonial China

The concept of 'citizenship' was introduced to China via Japan at the end of the Qing dynasty (1664–1911). But the specific notion of 'rights' introduced at this time was not inherent, inalienable, or natural but rather bestowed by the state. Rights allowed citizens to contribute to the state rather than protecting them from it; rights promoted state interests rather than individual ones. The expansion of 'citizenship' that included the establishment and spread of local councils and provincial legislatures in the early twentieth century, then, was intended to stabilize the political order and, ultimately, strengthen and enrich China rather than recognize rights.[8] The rights of citizenship were granted to enhance state interests at a time when imperialist powers threatened an already weak Chinese state.

Moreover, if we divide 'citizenship' into three sequential and distinct categories of civil, political, and social forms, as proposed by Marshall, according to historian R. Bin Wong, China developed notions of citizenship in a different order, with social rights coming first and even earlier than Europe. According to Marshall, citizenship evolved from property rights, personal liberty, and justice to include the right to participate in the exercise of political power, and, finally, culminated in the welfare state's emphasis on economic and social welfare, including education, morality, and the material conditions of the poor. In China, the order was reversed.[9]

Historical circumstances reinforced the emphasis on state power at the expense of individual rights exercised through political citizenship. The two most important early-twentieth-century Chinese political philosophers, Kang Youwei and Liang Qichao, initially introduced terms *gongmin* ('public person') and *guomin* ('national citizen'), as 'citizen,' terms which imply popular participation.[10] Discursive support for political citizenship got another boost during the intellectually iconoclastic May Fourth era (*ca.* 1919) with the introduction of another term functionally similar to 'citizen,' *shimin* ('city people'). But political chaos and imperialism returned the emphasis to state building. After the establishment of the Communist Party and reorganization of the Nationalist Party, both in 1921, the primary intellectual agenda shifted from creating strong individual citizens to creating a powerful state with a subordinated citizenry. Moreover, the tradition of 'establishment intellectuals' in China, wherein the Chinese state 'consulted' the intellectual elite, reinforced this shift. Indeed, even in the post-Mao era, intellectuals remonstrated with the leadership rather than asserted their political rights. That is, intellectuals claimed to act 'on behalf of the people' rather than as people. Again, the concept of political citizenship was not advanced as a means of defining, developing, and protecting individual rights. Rather, the promotion of political citizenship was advanced as a means for nation-state building.

Moreover, leading Chinese intellectuals as well as politicians argued that an overemphasis on 'private' and 'clan' interests promoted 'selfishness' (*si*) (defined in Chinese as the opposite of 'public'). In a time of civil war and imperialism, Chinese needed to make sacrifices, not demand rights. Desperate times authorized desperate measures, including a willingness to cut out or exclude groups deemed counterproductive to the nation-state-building process. Such exclusions included racial and ethnic minorities (e.g., the Manchus) in the early Republic to economic classes under Mao (e.g., the 'comprador capitalist'). At various times in the twentieth century, the politically excluded also included those with the wrong political consciousness (e.g., 'Communists,' 'counter-revolutionaries,' and 'revisionists'), those with the wrong gender (women), those with the wrong hometown (migrant workers), and, as I argue in *China Made* (2004), those making the wrong decisions in the marketplace.

It is against this unpromising backdrop that we must examine the recent reappearance of the Chinese middle class, estimated to include 150–300 million of China's 1.35 billion citizens. Will the emergence of this class in China provide a potential source of active, political citizenry? Or, should we expect the continued dependence of such citizens on the state? The current trend, according to Merle Goldman, is the expansion of 'rights' discourse beyond the intellectuals and political elites who have monopolized such discussions since 1898. Goldman emphasizes the spread of 'rights consciousness' among elites. But we might also add 'rights creep,' the gradual, incremental addition of rights outside the traditional bounds of discourse altogether. Such rights may include those the state has bestowed on consumers, including the right to demand a refund for counterfeit or faulty products. How might consumer activism operate in China to expand rights? To take a specific example, how might deciding to shop at Wal-Mart rather than its Chinese competitor Wumart because of their respective store policies be a form of individual protest? Likewise, how might such shopping represent a rejection of nation-state demands to 'buy Chinese'?

If one loosely defines political citizenship in this way, then China is a fertile hunting ground for instances of rights assertion. The 87,000 protests in 2005 officially acknowledged by Beijing regularly included the manipulation of official 'rights' discourse to advocate individual and local interests against the state.[11] We see similar use of official discourse by individuals invoking 'consumer rights,' a term now frequently used in Chinese official media. In 2005, for instance, the 22-year-old government-run China Consumers Association (CCA) received 703,822 complaints about misleading advertising and poor after-sales service. On International Consumers' Day (March 15) of 2006, the CCA disseminated a list of ten consumer victories in court. But such high-profile cases were the exceptions. Despite national legislation protecting consumer rights, few people successfully use the legal system to assert their rights.[12]

The subordination of citizenship and consumption to the nation

The origins of the subordination of political and proto citizen-consumers to national imperatives lies in early-twentieth-century China, when an emerging urban consumer culture became a primary means to define and spread modern Chinese nationalism.[13] By 1900, China had begun to import and manufacture thousands of new consumer goods. These commodities changed the everyday life of millions of Chinese who used, discussed, and dreamed about them. At the same time, the influx of imports and the desires they created threatened many in China. Politicians worried about trade deficits and the new consumer lifestyles exemplified by opium dens and addicts. Intellectuals, who had begun to read works on Western political economy, feared the loss of sovereignty implicit in the growing foreign dominance of the commercial economy. And manufacturers, faced with inexpensive and superior imports, wondered how they would preserve or increase their market share.

The growing conceptualization of China as a 'nation' with its own 'national products' influenced the shape of this nascent consumer culture. The politics of consumption played a fundamental role in defining nationalism, and nationalism in constraining consumption. Nationalism molded a burgeoning consumer culture by applying the categories 'national' and 'foreign' to all commodities, creating, in effect, the notion of 'treasonous' and 'patriotic' products. This nationalized consumer culture became the site where the notions of 'nationality' and of China as a 'modern' nation-state were articulated, institutionalized, and practiced. The consumption of commodities defined by the concept of nationality not only helped create the very idea of 'modern China' but also became a primary means by which people in China began to conceptualize themselves as 'citizens' of a modern nation. From its origins, the concept of citizenship was directly tied to consumption.

China Made reveals the innumerable social manifestations of the links between politics and consumption. A broad array of political, economic, and social forces placed political as well as cultural constraints on consumption through a massive but diffuse social movement. The National Products Movement (hereafter 'the movement'), as it was known at the time, popularized the meaning of material culture around the duality of 'national products' (*guohuo*) and 'foreign products,' and it made the consumption of national products a fundamental part of Chinese citizenship. This movement included new sumptuary laws mandating the use of Chinese-made fabrics in clothing, frequent anti-imperialist boycotts, massive exhibitions, and myriad advertisements promoting the consumption of national products, a Women's National Products Year, and the mass circulation of biographies of model citizens: patriotic manufacturers. These aspects of the movement politicized consumption and drove modern Chinese nation-making.

The politics of consumption played a central role in persuading people in China to see themselves as 'citizens' of a modern nation-state in a world of similarly constituted nation-states. But discussion of such politics is surprisingly absent from contemporary scholarship on Chinese nationalism, citizenship, and consumption. Early scholarship on the emergence of modern nationalism in China attempted to locate China along a 'culturalism-to-nationalism' continuum stretching from the late nineteenth to the early twentieth centuries. In political scientist James Townsend's summary, 'the core proposition is that a set of ideas labeled "culturalism" dominated traditional China, was incompatible with modern nationalism and yielded only under the assault of imperialism and Western ideas to a new nationalist way of thinking.'[14] In recent years, historians have greatly expanded our knowledge of China's final dynasty and questioned the purported cultural unity of late imperial China by identifying regional and ethnic tensions. Nevertheless, scholarship examining the emergence of modern nationalism continues to take two general forms: top-down and bottom-up. The first approach explores the role of intellectual, military, and political leaders in redefining the Chinese empire as a modern nation populated by citizens. The second investigates the development of nationalism and citizenship within specific contexts, such as the expansion of local customs and religious practices to broader arenas, or sporadic anti-imperialist acts such as the killing of foreign missionaries or the picketing of foreign companies.

Studying nation-making through the politics of consumption allows us to connect all levels of Chinese society. This approach extends the top-down approach to reveal the broader institutional and discursive environments in which notions of nationhood were conceived, diffused, and enforced. At the same time, examining nationalism through the politics of consumption expands the bottom-up approach by integrating different levels of Chinese society and connecting diverse phenomena over time. This extension of the analysis of Chinese nation-making should make it hard to imagine histories of Sino-foreign relations, business enterprises, the lives of leading figures, popular protest, the women's movement, urban culture, or even the Communist Revolution of 1949, which do not consider the linking of consumption and citizenship through nationalism in early-twentieth-century China.

The elaboration of the movement

Scholars unfamiliar with modern Chinese history often wonder why 'the Chinese government' did not simply and straightforwardly bind the politics of nationalism and consumption by banning or restricting imports through high tariffs. The answer is simple. Because of imperialism, the Chinese state, when such an entity even existed, lacked the power to do so. Successive defeats by the imperialist powers after the Opium War (1840–1842) compounded deep institutional problems within the Chinese state and culminated in the collapse of China's last dynasty in 1911–1912. Imperialist countries imposed a series of 'unequal treaties' that 'opened' China to trade by, among other methods, denying China the ability to restrict imports by raising tariffs. When China recovered tariff autonomy in the late 1920s, it used internationally accepted means of forcing its citizens to 'buy Chinese' by immediately imposing tariffs to restrict market access. By one estimate, the tariff rate of 1934 was seven times the pre-1929 rate.[15] However, in this formative period for Chinese 'citizens' and 'consumers,' roughly 1900–1937, China saw itself as inundated with imports but powerless to use tariffs for a quick solution. Instead, interested parties tried to create other ways of restricting foreign access and forcing citizens to 'buy Chinese.' The movement was the expression of these diverse efforts.

There was never one centrally controlled national products movement (think of the US civil rights movement, not one strand or organization within it such as the National Association for the Advancement of Colored People). Silk manufacturers, student protestors, women's organizations, business enterprises, government officials, and ordinary citizens alike invoked the term 'National Products Movement.' As the movement grew, its name, its slogans, and the categories of nationalistic consumption it created became ubiquitous in cities and even appeared in the countryside. Its manifestations included the Clothing Law of 1912, the *National Product Monthly* and many other magazines, the government-sponsored 'National Products' campaign of the late 1920s, official 'National Products Years' in the 1930s (Women's in 1934, Children's in 1935, and Citizens' in 1936), weekly supplements published in a major national newspaper (*Shenbao*) in the mid-1930s, thousands of advertisements, regular national-product fashion shows, and specially organized venues – visited by millions – for displaying and selling national products, including museums, fixed and traveling exhibitions, and a chain of retail stores.

The movement, then, was not a bounded entity but an evolving, growing, and interactive set of institutions, discourses, and organizations which sought new ways to incorporate reluctant producers, merchants, and, above all, emergent citizen-consumers. The movement was initiated by a few groups, expanded by others into new domains, and appropriated by still others, for multiple purposes, many of them directly at odds with the interests of movement supporters. Participants ranged from men leading recognized movement organizations to women organizing movement events as a way to take part in politics to entrepreneurs jumping on the movement bandwagon to sell products to gangsters manipulating movement discourse as a means of extortion to consumers consciously or unconsciously acting on the nationalistic categories of consumption.

Institutional elaboration

The movement involved much more than new term coinages and name-calling. At its core, it also attempted to create, introduce, and reinforce new patterns of group behavior and new systems of social regulation and order and to integrate them into a nascent nationalistic consumer culture. The development of national product certification standards can serve as a model for understanding this institutional elaboration of the movement as a whole. In the early stages, there was no clear-cut way of defining and identifying national products. Various systems of certification emerged in non-government organizations as makeshift centrifuges for separating foreign contaminants from the Chinese market. Then, growing links between organizations popularized the desire for a single standard of certification. Regular anti-imperialist boycotts intensified the need for explicit standards that identified precisely which products Chinese should and should not boycott. Finally, in 1928, a new national government formalized national certification standards. It made these standards law, and institutionalized incentives for their application.

Clearly, national product standards codified the pre-eminence of product-nationality, but Chinese did not automatically come to view products in this way. The more elaborate the movement, the greater the efforts of recalcitrant individuals to circumvent it and hence the greater the need for further controls to persuade them to adhere to the movement's goals. Physical and visual spaces – what I call 'nationalistic commodity spectacles' – functioned as forums to concentrate attention and condition individuals to recognize and valorize certified products. The movement, then, included a specific form of socialized or culturally constructed vision, a *nationalistic visuality* centered on training the eye to identify visual clues and to distinguish between the foreign and the domestic across social life. This attempt to construct a nationalistic visuality was part of all aspects of the movement. The National Products Exhibition of 1928, to take one example, essentially achieved the movement's goal in miniature by creating a completely nationalized visual and physical space, intended for the nation as a whole. Everything – from the advertisements on the walls of the exhibition hall to the dress of attendees, to every product on display, to the towels in the men's room – was a certified national product. Within this miniature nation of national products, citizen-consumers learned that they themselves could lead a life that was materially pure Chinese. Indeed, within this nationalistic commodity spectacle, it was impossible to visualize or live any other life.

'Chinese people ought to consume Chinese products'

Consumerism has become a key concept in analyzing the modern history of North America and Western Europe. Many academic disciplines have begun to posit that individuals increasingly experience life as 'consumers' living in 'consumer societies.' Individuals are said to construct their identities increasingly through, as I have defined consumer culture, the consumption of branded, mass-produced commodities and the orientation of their social life and discourse around such commodities. In American history, the ideology of this culture, consumerism, has been called the 'real winner' of the twentieth century and 'the "ism" that won.'[16] Likewise, historians of Western Europe have identified a 'consumer revolution' that accompanied or even predated the better-studied Industrial Revolution.[17] Historians continue to push the origins of this revolution back by centuries and into historical subfields as diverse as gender and labor history.

Although these concepts are less commonly applied to other areas of the world, it is a mistake to assume, as these studies often do, that consumerism is a uniquely 'Western' phenomenon. Consumerism was critical to the creation of modern China. More important, the development of consumerism was not uniform around the globe. Studies of the history and economics of consumerism routinely emphasize the role of the market in enabling the exercise of personal choice;[18] indeed, as sociologist Zygmunt Bauman observes, the very notion of individual freedom itself has been conceptualized in terms of consumer choice.[19] In contrast, consumerism in China was not only, or even primarily, about individual freedom, self-expression, and pleasure, and it would be a mistake for students of consumerism to reach the same conclusions for China. Rather than solely providing agency- or freedom-generating mechanisms, the nationalization of consumerism in China also imposed serious constraints on individuals. The purpose of the movement was to stress the national implications of the behavior of the individual consumer. A consumer was either patriotic or treasonous. According to the movement's rhetoric (exemplified in the heading of this section, 'Chinese people ought to consume Chinese products,' a common slogan), Chinese, newly defined as 'citizens' or 'national people,' were to envisage themselves as members of the new political collectivity known as the Chinese 'nation' by consuming 'national products.'[20] Through this simple equation of citizenship, nationality, and consumption, the movement denied the consumer a place outside the nation as economy and nation became coterminous. The movement did not recognize an abstract world of goods; rather, it divided the world into nations of products.

Freedom in the marketplace may be more the exception than the rule in the histories of consumerism around the world. China is not the only country that attempted to nationalize its consumption practices and constrain personal choice. The *swadeshi* (belonging to one's own country) and noncooperation movements in India (1904–1908 and 1920–1922 respectively) are the best-known and best-studied equivalents of China's National Products Movement. Likewise, Americanists have been aware of links between consumption and nationalism since late colonial times.[21] These are not isolated cases. Japan, Ireland, Korea, Britain, France, Germany, Nigeria, and Spain, among other countries, also experienced similar 'national product movements' with varying intensity in nation-making projects from late colonial times to the present.[22] Indeed, advocates of the movement in China regularly sought to inspire consumers with reports on the activities of similar movements in other countries.[23] The movement in China, then, should be seen as one among many rather than a unique phenomenon. That is not to suggest these movements unfolded in a uniform way. What makes the Chinese case particularly interesting for comparative purposes is that the country was not formally colonized yet lacked many aspects of sovereignty, including the ability to set tariffs. It was, to use the common Chinese term for its situation, 'semi-colonial.' And, for this reason, the movement was not, nor could have been, solely state-directed.

Despite the emergence of such movements throughout the globe, historians have neither devoted much attention to them nor suggested that they are key aspects of nation-making. When mentioned at all, the nationalization of consumer culture is treated as a natural by-product of the creation of nation-states. In fact, the causes and consequences of nationalizing commodities played a crucial role in creating nations. I argue here that a Chinese nation did not precede the notion of 'Chinese products.' The two constructs evolved together. Nation-making included learning, or being coerced, to shape preferences around something called the Chinese nation and away from items deemed foreign – a problematic process reinforced by institutional elaborations.

Most discussions of consumerism have not placed it at the center of nationalism. None of the studies of India, the most promising parallel to China, provides comprehensive accounts of a national products movement; these studies generally subordinate aspects of the national products movement to either business strategy (e.g., attempts by Bengali textile producers to preserve their market share) or Mohandas Gandhi's (1869–1948) attempt to promote spiritual revival through self-reliance.[24] Indeed, the National Products Movement agenda provides a sharp contrast to Gandhi's emphasis on simple living and tradition.[25] Likewise, survey introductions to nationalism rarely discuss attempts to nationalize consumer culture.[26] Finally, studies of economic nationalism focus on the political discourse of economic and political leaders rather than on a widespread and multidimensional social movement.[27]

Studies that do integrate consumerism and nationalism emphasize voluntary participation in consumption (e.g., watching movies, reading newspapers, going bowling); because such consumption is 'shared,' it helps create the basis for a shared national identity.[28] In contrast, consumption in China was often coerced. The movement contributed to nation-making not only by spreading a new consumer culture of mass-produced tastes and habits (that is, the basis of shared, nationwide consumption) but also by attempting to restrict consumption exclusively to national products, often through violence. 'National products,' moreover, were themselves closely scrutinized for national content in terms of the four categories of raw materials, labor, management, and capital. Thus, my emphasis differs significantly from the histories of the late-nineteenth- and early-twentieth-century United States, which, when examining the role of consumption in creating a shared national identity, stress only that the consumption of a particular article or activity took place domestically.[29] For the Chinese movement, it would not have been enough for citizens simply to read the same nationally circulated newspaper and imagine the same national events. Rather, regardless of the event being reported or editorialized, citizens were expected to read papers printed on the products of Chinese paper mills, produced by Chinese workers and managers, and owned by Chinese capitalists. Enforcing these principles led to the proliferation of specific institutions and laws. The modern Chinese nation was not simply 'imagined' – it was made in China.

Problems of pre-eminence

Citizens acting in the name of the nation clearly saw themselves as involved in an aggressive campaign, to use their own terms, of 'cleansing China's national humiliations' (*xue guochi*). Part of this campaign was the forcible removal of foreign elements from Chinese production and markets, thereby producing 'authentic,' 'pure,' and 'complete' Chinese products. This was an impossible ideal, especially at this point of Chinese economic and political development, and it was certainly never fully realized before the re-emergence of a strong centralized state with the Communist Revolution in 1949.

Still, the central problem for the movement was how to make product-nationality the pre-eminent or most important meaning of a commodity – that is, to 'nationalize consumer culture' – even in this problematic context. Price and quality certainly challenged the supremacy of product-nationality. It is safe to assume that consumers wanted to buy the least-expensive and best-made goods, which were often mass-produced imports. Brand loyalty, including loyalty to foreign brands, also hindered the ability of the movement to assert the pre-eminence of product-nationality. Indeed, in 1937, Carl Crow, who established one of the first advertising agencies in China, claimed Chinese consumers scrutinized brands and packaging to avoid ever-present counterfeit goods: '[Once they] have become accustomed to a certain brand, no matter whether it be cigarettes, soap or tooth paste, they are the world's most loyal consumers, and will support a brand with a degree of unanimity and faithfulness which should bring tears of joy to the eyes of the manufacturer.'[30]

Considerations of style were also of clear importance to many urban consumers in China in the early twentieth century. In fact, foreign fashions, introduced by Japanese, British, American, French, and other imperialist powers, exerted a heavy influence. To a great degree, imports of any kind were by definition fashionable. Foreign residents of the treaty ports, Chinese students returning from abroad, missionaries in inland areas, and a plethora of new foreign and Chinese media exposed many in China to images that challenged the pre-eminence of nationality within the marketplace. As a result, the social requirement to appear cosmopolitan frequently over-whelmed the injunction to 'Buy Chinese.' Then, as now, the power of 'Paris,' and, more generally, 'the West,' was often unrivaled, certainly by any domestic equivalents.

The question for the movement was how to push product-nationality to the forefront, given all these competitors – how to make it the foremost consideration of consumers in China. As I have suggested, the campaign began with appeals to civic duty and patriotism. But because the concepts of citizenship and patriotism were new and meaningless to many millions, such appeals were largely unsuccessful. The movement soon turned to more persuasive tactics ranging from legal institutions to brute force. Building national consciousness in China was a long and complicated process. The movement played a key role in this process, but it was neither a uniform movement at all times and in all places nor an uninterrupted success story. A triumph in Shanghai might not be matched in Nanjing, let alone further away in the communications grid; gains were often followed by setbacks.

Nationalizing consumer culture does *not* refer to the removal of products or product elements simply because of the non-Chinese origin of their *invention*. As one collection of essays on the history of imports in Latin America confirms, the notion of a national product is in fact an 'almost infinitely plastic concept.'[31] Both 'Chinese' and 'foreign' were flexible constructs. The definition of foreign could vary over time in order to stigmatize specific commodities, companies, and consumers. For stylistic simplicity, I use the terms 'imports' and 'foreign products' synonymously. However, within the movement, the term 'foreign products' came to include certain commodities made in China. Similarly, in the controversy over 'authentic styles' for Chinese men and women, movement advocates opposed certain clothing fashions not because the styles originated outside China but because they were made without (or with too few of) the four critical ingredients of a national product: raw material, labor, management, and capital. Indeed, traditional Chinese clothing was susceptible to the same scrutiny and action, whereas goods of Western invention might be worn without censure, provided such commodities met the movement's production standards. The movement eventually enshrined these standards in a seven-tier classification scheme of product purity based on the percentage of domestic content in each of the four categories.

This attempt to draw sharp distinctions between foreign and domestic products is not unique to China and is common today. 'National cultural content' regulations are routinely used throughout the world to preserve national identities (often, to resist 'Americanization'). France, for instance, requires theaters to reserve 20 weeks of screen time per year for domestic feature films. Similarly, Australia demands that domestic programming occupy 55% of the television schedule. And in Canada, 35% of the daytime play list of radio stations must be devoted to Canadian content. In the Canadian case, music with 'Canadian content' is defined not with respect to form, instrumentation, or lyrical content but according to its conditions of production, a direct parallel to definitions of national products in China considered here. 'Canadian' songs are composed, written, and played by Canadians; presumably the subject matter or message of the song is unrestricted.[32] Similarly, within the National Products Movement, national product–brand tuxedos and electric fans qualified as perfectly 'Chinese.'

This recognition of the complexity of commodities is not new. As Karl Marx famously observed, analyzing them reveals that they are actually 'a very queer thing, abounding in metaphysical subtleties and theological niceties.'[33] Of course, Marx and, later, Chinese Marxists 'defetishized' commodities and criticized capitalism and imperialism by arguing that commodities presented social relations between people as relations between things, thereby facilitating the alienation of workers and products.[34] For Marxists, labor is the preeminent meaning of commodities. Chinese Marxists, in fact, had more in common with movement business people than might at first be imagined. Both focused on production. But movement supporters emphasized that the provenance of production, not the individual labor involved in production, was of paramount importance as a unifying principle of a people ('Consumers of the Chinese nation unite!'). In essence, Chinese Marxists aided the movement in the 1920s and 1930s by promoting the elimination of what they considered the concrete manifestation of imperialism in China: foreign commodities. The business and government leaders involved in the movement did not return the favor; they asserted that 'labor' and 'capital' should 'cooperate' in the interests of developing the national economy. Strikes were 'unpatriotic.'

There are clearly countless possible meanings that can be assigned to commodities. Today various social movements have sought to elevate other concerns to a position of pre-eminence in the marketplace.[35] For example, the environmental movement promotes the notion of ecological impact as the chief meaning of commodities. Environmentalists stigmatize manufacturers (and consumers) that undermine their agenda. Similarly, the civil rights movement in the United States adopted slogans such as 'Don't buy where you can't work' to promote racial equality through consumer boycotts. When Americans became concerned that there was a 'glass ceiling' for women at major companies, John Kenneth Galbraith created a fictional character who promoted the idea of disclosing the 'female executive content' on all product labels.[36]

In contrast to these and all other conceivable criteria, proponents of the National Products Movement claimed to uncover a different but truly pre-eminent meaning of commodities: nationality. Its advocates attempted to convince consumers that products – like Chinese consumers themselves (indeed, like consumers of any country) – had essential or inalienable national identities as citizens. The movement insisted that wealthy and powerful nations in the industrial West as well as Japan had already established the supremacy of product-nationality. In classic hegemonic fashion, the movement, like the social movements just cited, advanced a universalistic claim. Ironically, the movement's claim functioned to particularize the world.

As the movement expanded, the notion that there were such things as national products to which citizen-consumers automatically owed their allegiance gained currency. Increasingly, the lines became drawn, and a nascent state apparatus backed by revolutionary elements in the society became willing and able to enforce nationalistic consumption. Thus, the movement was not important only, or even primarily, because of its influence on immediately expressed market preferences. When given the option, plenty of consumers still chose inexpensive imports over patriotic 'national products.' Rather, it was significant because it made such alternatives increasingly unavailable. The ultimate irony, perhaps, is that the largest economic interests supporting the movement, those Chinese capitalists who were involved in the production and circulation of domestically produced commodities, may have inadvertently provided the noose the Communists used to hang them after 1949. The logic of a movement which insisted that products were 'national' was easily used to undermine the notion that profits derived from selling such goods ought to be 'private.'

Conclusion: The successful union of consumption and citizenship?

Was the National Products Movement a success? Did the movement reach its goal of integrating citizens and nation through consumption? The answers to these questions depend on the criteria for success. It would certainly be easy to interpret the movement as a dramatic failure. Indeed, one might easily conclude by acknowledging the impossibility of nationalizing consumer culture in modern China. Given the tremendous obstacles the movement confronted, the view that it was a failure would have been understandable. China's lack of statecraft tools such as tariff autonomy and, indeed, genuine sovereignty allowed imports to pour into the country. Likewise, the powerful associations between imports and fashion/modernity heightened demand, as did price and the mechanized uniformity and quality of imports. Most important, a weak sense of national and civic identity among the vast majority of Chinese who evaluated their interests also in terms of themselves, their families, lineages, communities, and regions made sacrificing on behalf of 'the nation' difficult, even unthinkable. Not surprisingly, the movement never convinced or forced consumers to avoid imports completely and buy only certified national products. Nor did the movement persuade consumers that they ought to consume something called 'national products.' In short, the movement did not instill product-nationality as the pre-eminent attribute of a commodity. Appeals for Chinese compatriots to consume Chinese products often went unanswered. Import statistics substantiate this fact. Indeed, the movement's own incessant pleas for treasonous consumers, merchants, officials, and others to heed the call to buy national products confirm that the movement was an ongoing war, to use its own metaphor, rather than a single battle.

On other, subtler cultural, institutional, and discursive grounds, however, the movement was much more successful. The movement insinuated nationalism into countless aspects of China's nascent consumer culture, and this combination of nationalism and consumerism became a basis for what it meant to be a citizen in 'modern China.' This is visible throughout China: from the growing hostility toward and negative perception of imports in the nineteenth century through the establishment of a nationalistic male appearance and visuality in the late Qing era to the repeated anti-imperialist boycotts and the development of an exhibitionary complex of nationalistic commodity spectacles in the Republic to the proliferation of gendered representations of unpatriotic consumption and patriotic producers. This nationalized consumer culture influenced Chinese life from top to bottom, from elite discussions of political economy to individual students' decisions of what to wear to school. The movement did have an immediate impact on fashion, business, appearance, and language. Its legacies include the representations of unpatriotic consumption and patriotic production that persist in present-day China (witness the recent euphoric coverage of Chinese-manufacturer Lenovo's purchase of IBM's Thinkpad brand). This pervasive cultural influence is the movement's chief success. The general principle, if not the individual practice, of nationalistic consumption is deeply rooted. The breadth, depth, and creativity of the movement described here make it difficult to deny a central role to this movement in the making of the modern Chinese nation and its idea of citizenship.

Again, the legacies of the movement are visible across the twentieth century, particularly after the Communist Revolution in 1949. The effects of decades of Communist historiography, which emphasized the singularly exploitative nature of the imperialist presence in China, are easy to identify. Personal histories from the Cultural Revolution (1966–1976) all demonstrate the Chinese Communist government's overt hostility to foreign products and practices. This same sort of nationalism and anti-imperialism permeates textbooks, museums, and popular consciousness down to the present. To the Communists, their victory over the Nationalists in 1949 was always a dual liberation: both from the political oppression of class domination at home and from the economic control of imperialist powers.

The history of the movement captures China's long-standing ambivalence toward foreign involvement in the Chinese economy. True, direct state-sponsored attacks on the evils of foreign involvement in Chinese life have become less frequent since Deng Xiaoping's decision in the late 1970s to 'open China to the outside world' and permit the use of private foreign capital to develop the economy. But the deep suspicion of foreign capital is still there. China remains concerned with 'self-reliance,' even as the definition of the term changes.[37] Moreover, this lingering concern regularly manifests itself outside government activity. Runaway best-sellers such as *China Can Also Say No*, for instance, passionately plead for renewed anti-American boycotts and urge readers not to fly on Boeing airplanes.[38] Demonstrations in the mid-1980s railed against Japanese 'neo-economic imperialism' and the 'second occupation' of China. Likewise, the 'war of the chickens' – between Kentucky Fried Chicken and domestic fast-food competitors – called on the 'Chinese people to eat Chinese food.' These contemporary 'national product' campaigns reflect the deep ambivalence over the role of foreigners in the Chinese economy even as China's 'new middle class' flocks to these restaurants.[39] Domestic manufacturers continue to use nationalistic appeals to win customer and state approval.[40]

Where did this continual appropriation and expansion of the movement lead? The ultimate proof that Chinese capitalists did not control the movement lies outside the scope of the present inquiry. Yet it seems possible to suggest that the movement helped legitimize the abolition of private enterprise in China – in other words, that the Communists used the logic of the movement to justify the destruction of capitalism in China. If products were national, why should profits be private? If all citizens within the nation as whole should consume Chinese products, why should the wealth derived from patriotic purchases go to particular citizens of that nation? Perhaps the Chinese Communist Party was one more interest group legitimizing the link between nationalism and consumption for its own purposes.

The movement never ended. Elements of the National Products Movement agenda – judging national wealth and power through production and assessing patriotism through consumption – continue to this day. Indeed, its themes continue to shape interactions between Chinese, their material culture, and their sense of nation and citizenship. The relevance of nationalistic consumption did not die with Mao Zedong in 1976, although the irony of China voluntarily ceding tariff autonomy by joining the World Trade Organization (WTO) suggests so. Nevertheless, it is doubtful that a treaty alone can undo the deep connection between nationalism, citizenship, and consumption. Rather than eliminating the issue of nationalistic consumption, China's entry into the WTO has reinvigorated it. China may open itself to international trade in the short term, but what will happen if China stops running massive trade surpluses? Or what will happen as multinational companies continue to buy Chinese brands and companies?

New interest groups will embrace the notion of nationalistic consumption for their own reasons. As tariffs decline and less-expensive imports again threaten Chinese enterprises, the plight of millions of workers at state-owned enterprises undoubtedly will be invoked to attack imports and foreign capital. Indeed, there are already outspoken Chinese critics of the nation's growing international capitalist relations.[41] Nor is this criticism directed solely at traditional imported commodities. Cultural goods have come under attack as undermining domestic industries. Dai Jinhua, a well-known Beijing University professor and cultural critic, for instance, bemoans the 'invasion of Hollywood blockbusters,' which 'have dealt a destructive blow to the home film industry.'[42] Likewise, a new generation of students continues to invoke the language of nationalistic consumption, as did those protesting the US bombing of the Chinese embassy in Belgrade in 1999, with poems that include lines such as 'Resist America Beginning with Cola, Attack McDonald's, Storm K.F.C.'[43] Plans for a boycott directed against American companies active in China soon fizzled out.[44] However, the attempt itself re-legitimized the subordination of consumption and citizenship to 'national needs.'

4
Sartorial Manoeuvres in the Dusk: Blue Jeans in Socialist Hungary

Ferenc Hammer

Introduction

This study is an initial discussion of my empirical research results focusing on representations (personal histories and media pieces), regulatory practices and consumption strategies regarding blue jeans in Hungary between the 1960s and the mid-1980s.[1] Jeans offer a surprisingly useful juncture for an array of social enquiries regarding past and present issues of domination, agency, community, memory and the politics of difference. I outline in this paper how ideas and practices associated with wearing, or not wearing, jeans represented and in a way 'performed' the change of relationship between state and society in socialist Hungary in the three decades preceeding 1989. I have chosen histories of this particular piece of clothing for the following reasons.

First, memory and nostalgia are crucial aspects of this research. In fact, what sparked the whole enterprise was my noticing that almost every friend or acquaintance over forty whom I asked about their first pair of jeans told me a detailed, often rather emotionally fuelled story. My investigation of these personal stories has revealed a unique landscape of desires. These memories very often elude the conceptual grid of the usual ways of remembering life under socialism. Therefore, they highlight hermeneutically – hence politically – profound aspects of the communist past.

Secondly, the spread of jeans-wearing in Hungary was related to changing written and unwritten dress codes. People's decisions on the wearing of jeans (or not) can, therefore, be seen to reflect key aspects of social change, and particularly those affecting young people. The hierarchical rules of jeans-wearing, and the ways these were contested, reveal a finely tuned exercise of power, or subtle challenge to it. As I will show, the convenient abstraction of 'state vs. society' is in reality an often paradoxical network of relations – somewhat akin to a Moebius strip – between youngsters, parents, school authorities and everyday practices of cultural governance in schools, cultural institutions, youth clubs, and arts and media pieces about life in Hungary in the 1960–1980s. I will show that the norms that drove family or school jeans-wearing policies and the drive to wear jeans always unified seemingly distinct considerations of morality, aesthetics and politics that enabled the actors (whether teenagers in the 1960s or János Kádár himself) to utilize jeans for their own interests.[2] Though wearing jeans can be understood – perhaps all too easily – as an act of resistance or as an example of image-seeking consumer behaviour, my discussion of jeans-wearing under socialism reveals a set of histories that highlight certain neglected aspects of power affecting everyday life in the Eastern bloc.

Thirdly, we should note that the wearing of jeans becomes a mass phenomenon within the span of a single generation, a remarkably salient factor in material culture that may deserve enquiry in itself. As elsewhere in the world, jeans represented a distinctive form of clothing in Hungary. They signalled something Western, probably American, of altogether greater significance in socialist cultural politics than polka dots on scarfs or the origin of raisins in the grocery. But perhaps more importantly, meanings conveyed by blue jeans and the ways of wearing them, in the West and somewhat later in the East as well, have in turn transformed the significance associated with the clothing. By the 1980s, jeans had been worn in the United States by death row inmates as well as Lagerfeld boutique strollers and even by the president himself, thus losing most of their immanent, lexical meaning. The choice of the style in which they were worn also meant that jeans gradually ceased to be the subject of a binary regulation (in/out, yes/no) and became instead an array of symbolic tools of agency. These functioned similarly to auxiliary verbs in the English language, enabling the 'wearer-speaker' to express decision or doubt, consent or rebellion, submission or courage, ability to act or helplessness, flux or static status and so on. This property of blue jeans turned out to be chiefly important for people in the political masquerade of softening the authoritarian regime of János Kádár. For the socialist state, particularily for the police, the look of its citizens (their outfit and the nature of written texts they presented on their body and in their environment) had become an important way of regulating citizen behaviour. Jeans had become a perfect medium for both state and its citizens to convey messages without saying anything, and to say something between the lines, the most popular poetic form in public life of the era. Jeans manaufacturing, in cooperation with Levi Strauss Co. in the 1970s, was utilized by the political leadership to express political/cultural pragmatism and to highlight quality and progress in the Hungarian economy.

Fourthly, a study of jeans-wearing offers a unique perspective on consumption because, during the era in question, consuming Western commodities was, quite paradoxically, a truly informal grass-roots activity. Knowledge, attitudes and skills of consumption were largely produced through interpersonal relations prior to the emergence of large-scale advertising of Western commodities in the 1980s. Furthermore, the longing for jeans was principally directed by brands (i.e., by a logic of uniformity), but authentication of the 'raw' jeans (through sometimes crude technologies and essential re-tailoring) resulted in a truly individualized garment, experienced by owners as a second skin (most youngsters had one pair of jeans at best in the period). Informal knowledge distinguished between brands, the real and the fake, or specified the proper way of handling and wearing them. Privately produced and exchanged knowledge about jeans can be regarded as a textbook example of how informal public spheres operate when they are controlled by authoritarian measures: they are vulnerable to manipulation and misinformation, but they perform their central task of cultivating discrimination between the real and the false.

The context: The politics of consumption after 1956

In the aftermath of the 1956 October revolution, the Party was fierce in its retaliation against activists, but held back from Stalinist-style interference in people's everyday life. At the same time the regime took measures to improve the standard of living and expand consumption. A year after the first amnesty for political prisoners, the first large self-service food store was opened in Budapest in 1960. The 1960s not only brought an end to food shortages, but introduced paid maternity leave, and new housing and agricultural policies that significantly improved the life of millions. The increase in real wages was paralleled by gradual improvements in the retail industry. More Hungarians started to travel abroad (very often with their recently purchased car or motorcycle), and the monthly *Ifjúsági Magazin* (Youth Magazine), founded in 1965, contained not only politically loaded stories about democracy in schools, but also fashion advice and the music and lyrics of *Satisfaction* or *Michelle*.[3] A decade after the 1956 revolution, one needed a television set and a sofa for the two major excitements of the year: the football victory (3:1) over Brazil at the world championship in England, and the first Hungarian popular music contest.

The term 'negative consensus' captures quite aptly the emerging *modus operandi* in the relationship between state and society in the 1960–1970s. In this deal, the state provided (modestly growing) material advancements and (modestly) liberalized public life in return for silence on 1956 and other taboo issues, such as the one-party system, the alliance with the Soviet Union and the question of Hungarians in the neighbouring countries.[4] The consensus was 'negative', however, because, although it implied self-constraint on both sides, it never brought trust, and thus drove both state and society into a culture of pretence and mutual deceit. While people showed a certain eagerness to forget how, exactly, the Iron Curtain happened to appear on the western border of the country, in return, the Iron Curtain – the symbol of 'political realities' – started to appear in everyday calculations and decisions, offering a convenient argument for lack of initiative, cowardice and failure.

The painful memories of the oppressed revolution, and the ensuing fears, could be eased somewhat by the emerging culture of forgetting and cushioned by the pleasures of modest material advancement.

Compliance with the state implied rules that were predominantly controlled and rewarded (positively or negatively) through the workplace or school. Lower or higher levels of cooperation with the state were met by differentiated promotion and career opportunities, and affected earning levels. Non-compliance with political rules could automatically exclude the person from end-of-year premiums, or from receiving state-subsidized loans to purchase a house, a refrigerator, a television, or from obtaining a passport or telephone line (all of which required a recommendation from the working place). Dissidents could jeopardize their children's chances of college admission.

Such forms of power were complemented by an important generation change. The American baby boomers' Hungarian contemporaries (and their younger siblings) had either vague childhood memories of the 1956 performance of Soviet heavy artillery in Budapest, or none at all. For the generations born in the 1950–1970s, the truly gruesome Stalinist years (1949–1953) were either school-book history, or figured only in unhappy family memories. For these, brought up during the Kádár consolidation, 'goulash communism' was much less an achievement than a timeless condition, a field that needed fresh scrutiny to understand and evaluate. For these generations, waiting 5 or 6 years for a new Czechoslovak, East German or Soviet car had gradually lost its appeal. They had also become more critical of the hypocrisies and compromises of the post-1956 consolidation. During the 1960–1970s, this new-found political disquiet discovered in jeans the perfect means of expression for its quest for a more authentic life.

The Sinister Predecessor: The *Jampec*

'*Jampec*' (pronounced yam-petz), the Budapest imitation of the US zoot suiter, was under severe attack from Hungary's Communist government. The government flayed the *jampec* as a sinister penetration of US 'barbaric culture' into Hungarian social life.

Managers of state-owned clothing shops displayed mannikins dressed in the *jampec* style, along with the warning that 'everybody who imitates this American fashion madness belongs to the capitalist U.S. in spirit'. One shop window (see Plate 4.1) showed a gorilla next to a *jampec* and a telegram from the Budapest zoo's monkey house protesting against the insult of comparing a *jampec* to one of their kind.

The Communist Party organ Szabad Nep called on the government to crack down on *jampec*-dressed youngsters. Szabad Nep cried, 'They portray the dismal picture of imitating the American gangster's misanthropic

International

JAMPEC & FRIEND
Moral decay: capitalism and sambas.

Plate 4.1   Jampec and friend, October 23, 1950
Source: 'Barbaric Culture,' *Time Magazine.*[5]

spirit, moral decay and spiritual degeneration . . . Can we treat with indifference the fact that our youth are taught to dance sambas to the tune of the Hungarian czardas?' (*Time Magazine*, 1950).[6]

The main impact of the communist takeover in the late 1940s was the nationalization of nearly everything: businesses, factories, banks, shops, cafes and services. Except for a privileged few, those who had retained a car after the destruction of Second World War had to offer it up for communal use for the state. Libraries as well as toy stores had to re-profile their selection according to the needs of the progressive working class, a measure that made Freud's work or Monopoly games underground materials for a decade or so. Clubs and voluntary organizations were mostly dissolved or forced in an ideological direction. During the chilliest days of the Cold War in the 1950s, virtually no aspects of everyday life escaped socially divisive forms of political signification. Workers might belong to the class-conscious 'progressive majority' or the retrograde social democratic 'worker aristocrats'. A white-collar worker could belong to the 'progressive intelligentsia' or be a reactionary. The youth was mostly regarded by the propaganda as innocent and progressive, except for those under clerical influence, and the West-aping *jampec*. Clothing was not exempt from these crude binary classifications, certain types of garment being regarded as the apparel of the enemy within. In the political cartoons of the communist press, one could see a priest's black robe or a tuxedo, usually depicting the Pope and Churchill plotting against the people's democracies.

The *jampec* was probably one of the most reckless subcultures in Hungary's social history.[7] (The word, from Yiddish, was already used in the 1930s to describe a man dressed or behaving in a foolish way.) These young men, mostly of working-class origin and having acquired certain survival skills as children during Second World War, were perhaps the most visible of the social groups that regarded the communist regime as a temporary bad joke in the 1950s. Similarly to the zoot suiters, and later the mods in the United Kingdom, a *jampec* could be recognized by his shiny leather shoes with their thick rubber soles (subsequently appropriated by the skinheads). Together with drainpipe trousers, he wore a checked-pattern jacket and a colourful tie. Other traits included rocker-style hairdo, a particular slang, contempt for politics, a longing for jazz music and skill in fist fighting. The *jampec* acquired a mythic aura by virtue of their stigmatization by the Communist state as youthful enemies of the people's democracy.[8] This meant that if, in the 1950s, a young boy decided to walk on the wild side the *jampec* repertoire was ready to hand.

Though not yet a jeans-wearer, the figure of the *jampec* is of prime importance to this study. The repertoire of reactions to *jampec* values, attitudes, appearance, clothing, behavior and presumed intentions provides a snapshot of the disciplinary social geography, envisioning and regulation of citizens by the communist state in its early years. Also, as we shall see, the state's changing attitude to the 'proper citizen' can be traced in tandem with the career of jeans in the 1960–1980s. The Hungarian Stalinist regime was far from regarding the *jampec* as the most dangerous enemy of the workers' state. The *jampec* was a minor mischief compared to such dedicated and 'truly dangerous' opponents as the clergy, the former ruling classes or other treacherous agents of imperialism. But what makes the figure of the *jampec* unique is the fact that his perceived harmfulness for the people's democracy was 'decoded' mainly from his everyday customs, consumption preferences and physical appearance, especially the outfit. The political treatment of a social group on the basis of its clothing (especially the charge of West-aping) was a novel element in Hungary's social history, setting a pattern for the period, a few years later, when the first pairs of jeans appeared on the streets of Budapest.

First encounters

We enter the clothing store. They show us a great selection of fabric or cloth that makes choice really not easy: which are the cloths or shoes which are nice and useful too? And fashion brings a viewpoint too that we also have to consider.

Our age has brought more freedom in choosing the outfit. The times are over when 'the cloth made the men', when social status or class position determined what has to be worn by people. A basic task of our society is to bring more beauty, quality and value to our life. Everyone in the workers' society has got an opportunity to enjoy fruits of the work. And it is expressed through the way we dress. (...) We have to oppose the skewed claim that wearing a nice and fashionable dress is a petit bourgeois habit and therefore it is 'not appropriate' to do so. No way! Everyone should dress nicely according to his/her financial opportunities. (...)

We have to highlight a few striking mistakes. Sometimes it occurs that one can see women wearing pants at a theater or in a club. Or when men, taking off their suit jacket, expose their braces while dancing. The exhibitionist young people's West-aping, *jampec* dressing is similarly tasteless.
Burget–Kovácsvölgyi: *How to behave? (On Dressing)*[9]

As this dressing advice from 1962 may suggest, there had been a considerable shift since the class warfare–based sartorial regulatory regime of the early 1950s. János Kádár's two-front consolidation battle is neatly captured in this quote. The authors warn dogmatic communist believers against their 'skewed claims', and the reader is given to believe that the West-aping *jampec* is more a tasteless than a dangerous actor. The new sartorial norm in the workers' society had become 'nice and fashionable dress'.

The first pairs of jeans appeared in Hungary by chance or mistake in the second part of the 1950s. As the 'my first pair of jeans' respondents tell me, the first (usually used) pieces were sent to Hungary in charity cloth bales, parcels from American relatives, or brought to Hungary by young people who had witnessed the emerging jeans fashion in a Western country. Wearing the first pair of jeans in the late 1950s in families, schools and public spaces was sometimes successful and, as the story below suggests, sometimes close to disastrous. Teachers, parents and even, at times, peers initially equated jeans with a particular outfit, the *cejgnadrág*: a workers' or peasants' working pant made with thick (usually grey or blue) cotton fabric. One respondent recalled that after bringing jeans from Italy, where he saw them as cool, he was so ridiculed by his peers that he wore them for outdoor excursions only, until at an excursion, some years later, a friend was shocked to recognize that, amazingly, he had jeans.[10] When they first appeared, indeed, jeans had no common name. Somewhere, it was called *kovbojnadrág* (cowboy pant).

> After 1956, many people sent things to Hungary, in support. For us children, it was new and interesting. Biscuits of milk powder taste! Chewing gum ('don't swallow, just chew it')! Instant cocoa powder! (For about three years, I could drink cocoa for breakfast, seriously!) School exercise books with colorful covers! Milk powder! Russian canned milk!! It was all awfully good. And the clothes, of course. These things appeared through different channels. The cowboy pants, for example, came through the Lutheran Church. I attended bible classes at the local church, and when they received parcels from western connections, they distributed them among the people who attended the church.
>
> [The cowboy pants] were amazing gear! Of course, I could never go to school in them, but apart from that, they could not have been taken from me – quite understandably, I think. It didn't include any sense of superiority or anything, it was just 'American (*amcsi*) gear'. (Maybe it wasn't American, I don't know.) At that time, the word 'American' (*amcsi*) was absolutely positive.[11]

In another family, jeans had caused excitement for a different reason:

> I got my first jeans when I was in kindergarten. They weren't called either 'farmer pants' [*farmernadrág*, the most common name for jeans in Hungarian] or 'blue jeans'; in our family, they were called the 'many-pocketed' (*sokzsebes*). Everyone in the family, including my parents, were amazed by the enormous number of pockets on them (5), because most pants had 3 or, with the clock pocket, 4. Jeans were not a status symbol; jeans were simply unknown at that time.[12]

As these three stories of early owners suggest, jeans were *terra incognita* in the late 1950s. Apart from the curious similarity to working cloth, it had no wider significance in clothing discourse, and because people seemed to abstain from wearing jeans in public places, the authorities did not bother with regulation. This was to change in the course of a few years.

Regulating jeans: The logic and politics of cultural governance under socialism

A key element in Hungary's cultural politics in the last three decades of socialism was the fact that the Party had always regarded culture as a field that could impact on the acceptance of its rule. The Party had never treated people's habits or way of life as something 'given' or irrelevant in terms of the exercise of power. When the authorities decided to withdraw regulation from a certain field (e.g., the registration of bicycles), the leadership calculated that the material benefits associated with this relaxation would be accompanied by popular reactions acknowledging the Party's pragmatic and enlightened attitude.[13] Since the communist regime so extensively regulated everyday life – the economy, business, culture and the media – observers in the 1960s–1970s could sense, paradoxically, that living under communism was akin to the common nightmare in which one feels one has been walking for hours only to realize that one has not moved an inch. Miklós Haraszti, an ardent dissident critic of the regime, wrote in 1985 about an anonymous writer: 'What he's writing today, could not have been published yesterday by any means; maybe it can be published today, but certainly tomorrow.'[14] This continuous feeling of liberalization could conceal the fact that there were certain things (the items on the 'demand side' of the negative consensus) that the Party controlled as forcefully as ever. Perhaps I do not need to devote too much time to how and why this 'relative freedom' was truly disruptive for the whole society. The culture of goulash communism had encouraged a belief that reading between the lines was a higher art than straightforward talk, and promoted a culture of self-deceit, hypocrisy and double-talk.

Under György Aczél, Kádár's chief advisor on cultural affairs, an informal categorization system was developed in the mid-1960s. Whatever the forms of expression in public life, whether books, theatre, pop groups, long hair, mini skirts, punk, sociology, jokes about János Kádár, psychotherapy, Coca Cola, body building, avant-garde art or pornography, all were judged within cultural governance as either officially supported, banned and prosecuted, or unwillingly tolerated. Promoted culture included Soviet cinema, classical music, folklore, Plato and football. Such items as James Bond, Polish Solidarity pins, pornography, Hungarian immigrant publishing, Boney M's *Rasputin*, to mention a few, were banned and prosecuted.[15] Cultural expressions between these two spheres constituted a dynamic grey area: the unwillingly tolerated cultural sphere that included avant-garde art, heavy metal rock, Boney M disco, social research on poverty or topless beaches. The rules of this classification were never explicit and were very often incoherent. The system varied both temporally and geographically. It could easily happen that a banned play from a country town would be staged half a year later at a small theatre in Budapest (or the other way round). Similarly, as the 'my first jeans' respondents tell me, in some secondary schools jeans were already allowed in the late 1960s, while in others they were being banned. This highly confusing (therefore very effective) system of promotion, prohibition and toleration was supported by two further interconnected principles. First, in the over-regulated polity there were many unwritten rules that were never made explicit (e.g., one would hardly find a Cultural Ministry memo about the accepted length of boys' hair or girls' skirts in school). Secondly, each unit leader created an organization in the image of his/her own personality. This was true of janitors, football coaches, company directors, school principals, military chiefs, and of János Kádár himself.

An understanding of the logic of cultural governance under socialism is indispensable to an appreciation of the nature and significance of the changing regimes of jeans regulation in Hungary. Nor, without it, can one appreciate the true significance of youngsters' longing for blue jeans in socialist Hungary. Living in the 1960s–1980s, people expected to spend their whole life under communist rule (unless they opted for exit to the West). Therefore, since the country was far from being a Pol Pot–like terrorist regime, certain sets of chances or choices were available. The consolidated regime of János Kádár offered people a sense that – despite the sobering moments experienced while driving alongside a mile-long Soviet military base – there were opportunities (if restricted) for a better life. I want to stress here the anticipated immortality of communism in people's everyday life-plans. When the state allowed travel to the West in the 1960s, why should anyone complain that it was available only every third year, rather than revel in a trip to Rome to see Michelangelo's work, sip real orange juice and buy Levi's? When a father bought a cool red corduroy Lee jacket for his daughter, which fitted perfectly, and she was painfully beautiful in that, why talk about the years of waiting? When there were more and more youth clubs open to boys with long hair, would it not be nit-picking to claim that a youth club has no business with the length of its male visitors' hair? When a teenage boy notices that as he put on his new Turkish copycat Wrangler suddenly lots of girls want to dance with him, would it not be hypocritical to expect him meditate on why his jeans cost nearly the equivalent of his mother's monthly salary? The key thing was that jeans enabled the wearer to transcend boundaries between conventional fields of action. Jeans received from a politically privileged relative became a source of aesthetic pleasure. A pair of Levi's acquired from a dangerous and remote black market could become the source of the owner's sex appeal. Sitting like a free-floating hippie in a denim suit in an armchair in a village disco could operate as a source of privilege. In these stories, privilege is transformed into aesthetic pleasure, aesthetics into sensual appeal, sex appeal into authority, freedom into exclusivity, lack of freedom into opportunity and so on. But all of these magical transformations were possible only because of the political restrictions on the acquisition of jeans imposed by the Kádár regime. Youthful passion and political restraint, here, proved to be mutually reinforcing. It testifies to the success of the Kádár regime that it was able in this way to channel, and thus control, its clients' whimsical and contradictory passions and interests. The story of jeans under socialism is evidence for the argument that hegemonic cultural domination took its clearest form in some of the consolidated, semi-authoritarian East Central European regimes, such as János Kádár's Hungarian People's Republic.

The first conflicts: *Not in my house!*

The second half of the 1960s saw a rather spectacular change in Hungarian youth culture. Within a couple of years, a set of previously unknown phenomena appeared in a single 'package'. Following the Beatles mania (heard through the jammed airwaves of Radio Free Europe and Radio Luxemburg), dozens of 'beat groups' appeared around 1965, at first playing English songs, and later developing their own repertoire. This music scene could be compared to the subsequent DIY punk culture, with the notable difference that in the 1960s boys often fabricated even their electric guitars from the lid of a wooden toilet seat, a stick and a couple of piano strings. Boys started to grow their hair a bit longer; girls cut their skirt a bit shorter. Students living in Budapest dormitories returned to their home town with the records of the new bands; passionate fan groups emerged around the country. Still there, though, was the yearning for a pair of jeans.

The authorities reacted differently, now, to the sweeping change in youth culture. Parents were very often confused. One problem – reflected in contemporary letters to the press – was that they often simply did not understand the lyrics of the new Hungarian bands. Then, children were asking their parents for the equivalent of a month's salary for a pair of trousers that looked like a mason's work outfit. Parents, of course, could not keep pace with these changes: either they were loathe to do so, or they sympathised with the ruling power's hostility to the *jampec*, or (having learnt the lesson of the 1950s) they wanted to protect their children from cultural-political retaliation and restriced career opportunities. But the money factor turned out to be the real sticking point. Hungarian society was just emerging from an impoverished and shortage-hit decade, in which saving had been the key to survival: for many families it was unimaginable to spend 800 forints for a garment when a loaf of bread cost 3 forints.

These concerns were probably most acute in the 1960s – due to their novelty – but, as is revealed by my repondents' stories, they continued to surface in debates over jeans-wearing in the following decade as well:

> My first jeans were women's jeans . . . . A sculptor student of my father's got them from the west, and they were too small for her, but were just my size.

It could have been in 1965, so I was 13. They teased me in school over the female cut, but envied me too, because most kids hadn't got jeans at that time. A couple of years later, in the summer of 1968, the incident took place that was depicted more or less accurately by Márton in his novel [Hungarian writer Márton Gerlóczy] . . . . My uncle – with a military record and military sensibility – ordered his son and me to take off our jeans (embroidered with flowers, hippie-style), cut them to pieces with scissors, throw them into the garden toilet . . . and to shit on them, one after the other. For a long time, I couldn't forgive my uncle (let him rest in peace) for having to execute this order. The militaristic petit-bourgeois generation, trodden down by dictatorships, feeling a sense of danger, tried to humiliate the young rebels. It was a Pyrrhic victory, though. My uncle appears as Winnetou in the novel; my cousin is Jagger, and I'm Gyugyu.[16]

Another story, dating from 15 years after this garden drama, also has its surprising elements:

In the Spring of 1983, in the eigth grade, I wanted to get a pair of Levi's with a red tag, but they were hopelessly expensive (980 Forints) for a family of two engineer parents and three children. In my class in a [Budapest] downtown school, about every fourth student had a pair of jeans. Then I downsized my demands: they could be Trapper jeans (450 Forints).[17] Two or three classmates of mine were ridiculed over these jeans, but my father declared that we had no money even for Trapper. On the Sunday of that week, I joined my father at church for the Easter mass. I was sitting next to him, and saw him fold a 500 Forints banknote and throw it into the donation box. There were no words for my outrage but I didn't tell him.

My initial anger lasted only a couple of days, but later I felt morally obliged by that church scene to play a trick in order to get the jeans. The next week, we got a list from the school about things we had to take to the Summer Pioneers' camp.[18] It was a typed list of things such as the pioneer uniform, a battery lamp, drinking flask, etc. There was an office with a typewriter in the school. I asked permission to use it for typing the program for the school May Day celebration. I typed the program, then neatly re-typed the Pioneers' camp list with only one modification. I replaced the item 'trousers' (*nadrág*) with 'jeans' (*farmernadrág*).

My mother knew nothing about my jeans-lust, and I submitted the forged list to her. Two days later, she simply gave me the money, and I bought my first jeans, seven short years before the regime change.

These two examples suggest that parents and children were not particularly choosy about their weapons in the struggles around jeans. It is amusing that while a key motive for acquiring a pair of jeans was to become 'different', the parents' social network, money and personal sacrifice were often utilized in the process of acquisition. More minor debates concerned the type of family, school and social occasions that could accommodate jeans-wearing, or endless conflicts with mothers who could not resist ironing creases (*pinces*) into jeans, which drove most respondents to desperation. While early official criticisms pointed to Western ideological infiltration in jeans-wearing – following the *jampec*-bashing logic – jeans horrified older generations for an entirely different reason: because they bore a visible inscription.[19] As is evident in the following story, the normative discourse on jeans combined elements of aesthetics and social moralizing:

> Once I was on a train with my father. We were sitting at the window on opposite sides, both of us reading. We didn't talk. Of course, I had my jeans on. At the next station, two middle-aged women got on the train, and sat next to me and to my father. They were staring at me quite strangely, but made no comment. It was a non-smoking car, and I went out to have a cigarette, but again I said nothing to my father. I had a couple of puffs when my father came out in shock, and told me that I must not say a word to him when I got back after my cigarette. When we got off later, I asked him what happened. He said that after I went out to smoke, the two women had said: 'Did you see how that kid looked? How can one wear such incredibly awful things? But the kid is not to blame, but his parents; they should be taught a lesson', and so on . . . . . So that's why I wasn't allowed to say a word to my father for the rest of the trip to Budapest.

This story eloquently captures the conflicts and interests around jeans. Parents tried to reconcile the ideological expectations of school and media with their children's longing for difference, while also negotiating the social mores and norms of the day.

Jeans and the officialdom: Hesitant approaching

> A few remaining downtown private tailors whose businesses had not been nationalized made custom-made western-style pants. But when Kecskés tailor in Váci Street displayed in his tiny shop window a sample pair of jeans that he had made, a diligent journalist was eager to reveal the case in the Party paper. The jeans disappeared for a few weeks from the shop window and then reappeared. Since all the arrestable "counter-revolutionaries" had been arrested already (. . .), without many targets, the power placed the question of the "bourgeois" pants on its agenda. The pant-problem vanished for good in the following few years, when communist cadre's children started to cruise downtown in denim pants with copper rivets.

Rudolf Ungváry: 1959[20]

When jeans started to appear in the early 1960s – not as a charity bale item but as a fine fashion product – for the official reaction there was the obvious analogy of the Coca Cola–doped *jampec*. But in a few years, especially because the children of the elite were over-represented among the first jeans-wearers (as in the Soviet Union),[21] a visible shift took place. Instead of crude judgements about the likely nature of the jeans-wearer, a more qualified response began to develop corresponding, it seems, to the adoption of a new policy on youth culture in the mid-1960s.

It was not that the authorities decided to withdraw totally from sartorial regulation, but that the demarcation line was different, though patrolled no less vigorously. In the first part of the 1960s, *jampec* culture overlapped with jeans-wearing to an extent, both stylewise (there are occasional reports about jeans-wearing *jampecs*) and in official reactions. Both the *jampec* and jeans-wearers were regarded as slightly dangerous and grossly distasteful. From about 1965, a radically new set-up started to emerge: the *jampec* culture was on the wane, and jeans had been moving towards the mainstream, when a new – again sartorially defined – enemy appeared on the scene, the hippies.

The 1960s brought the first truly extended and developed youth politics that was more than merely a set of bans, and which took into consideration certain perceived needs and wants on the part of the youth. After Kádár's dictum that *those not against us are with us*, the Party had decided to include mass entertainment into the repertoire of communist youth politics.

Partly as the result of the rapid spread of TV sets, and the 1964 opening of the Western border to (westward) tourism, society had become much more informed about what was happening in the West than in the isolated 1950s. The West-aping *jampec* was no longer an enemy, especially because as a result of the growth of information from the West there were now more 'West-aping' youths than ever: British and Italian music (generally English language), French cinema and Western outfits (black turtlenecks, olive or blue raincoats) swept through Hungary.[22] The Party's oligarchic reaction to the perceived popularity of Western culture was this: if you cannot beat it, you must incorporate it. The Hungarian Television hosted in 1966 its first, and from the beginning wildly popular, pop music contest, creating new youth idols. A year later, Hungarian Radio started a Sunday weekly music magazine called *Csak fiataloknak!* [Only for the young!], with the sole task of presenting the latest hits from England and Italy. (The explicit goal of this latter programme was to divert the young from the music on Radio Free Europe).

The Budapest Committee of the Communist Youth Organization opened a live music venue (Buda Youth Club) in Budapest overlooking the Danube with a capacity of 2500 (Balázs, 1994). When opened in 1961, the intention was to entertain the youth with popular culture (light jazz, folk dance, concerts), and their strict dress code (suit with white shirt for men and skirt for women) was overseen by the director at the entrance to the club. Jeans were gradually permitted from the late 1960s. The *Ifjúsági Magazin* [Youth

Magazine], published from 1965 by the Communist Youth Organization, had centrefold posters of The Animals and The Beatles, as well as carefully crafted debates about youth problems. In the articles and readers' letters, jeans no longer possessed inherently dangerous traits. The stress was much more on the personality and actions of the jeans-wearer ('let's not judge from appearance') and on the suitability of jeans for the occasion. For example, the fashion section from a 1967 issue contains a photo (Plate 4.2) with a mild pegagogical caption: *Our photograper took a picture of these two elegantly dressed girls and the boy in jeans at the hall of the National Theatre. An evening suit would have been more in style, wouldn't it?*[23]

This was also the period, possibly around 1962, when the most common word for jeans (*farmer*, or *farmernadrág*, i.e. farmer-trousers) was invented.[24] A respondent argues that this word came from the media, and his clue was to connect the jeans mania to a progressive American experience. This connotation with Steinbeck and the American progressive Left provided the necessary ideological pedigree. Rather paradoxically, while the Party-promoted youth media was carving out a recognition for jeans in the avant-garde of the official public sphere, most schools and youth clubs in the late 1960s (including the most popular Buda Youth Club) did not allow jeans on their premises. Respondents recall, too, that boys in jeans (especially those with longer hair) were frequently stopped in the street by policemen in this period, and sometimes taken to a hairdresser.

As we see, cultural struggles about youth culture, 'beat music', jeans and long hair were taking place simultaneously on numerous fronts. In this context, János Kádár's comment in his address to the seventh KISZ (Organization of Young Communists) Congress in 1967 made a big difference:

There are, for instance, certain Western fashions that have, to a certain degree, spread here as well; one of these is cynicism and indifference to questions of public life. In the West this is accompanied by the wearing of wild-west pants, long hair, and neglecting to shave . . . . I do not want to talk about wild-west pants, beards, or hairstyles . . . . What's important here is that the Party, the Youth League, is not a fashion designer or a hairstyling salon, and does not need to deal with such things.[25]

As suggested in the section on the logic and politics of cultural governance, this soft dictatorship works by ceding a relatively important role to local leaders in the administration of mundane matters in their constituencies. As director, László Rajnák's personal taste determinded which bands were to play at the Buda Youth Club and which style of outfit would be welcome (including the musicians' outfits).[26] János Kádár's few words on long hair and jeans had an impact.[27] His words, noted widely in the press and on the streets as a sign of pragmatism and open-mindedness, were accompanied by a growing toleration of jeans in public places.

A NEMZETI SZÍNHÁZ ELŐCSARNOKÁBAN KAPTA LENCSEVÉGRE FOTÓSUNK
A KÉT ELEGÁNSAN ÖLTÖZÖTT KISLÁNYT A „FARMERES" FIÚVAL ALKALMI
ÖLTÖNY STÍLSZERŰBB LETT VOLNA. IGAZ!

Plate 4.2   Jeans in the National Theatre, 1967
Source: Ifjúsági Magazin [Youth Magazine].

The long farewell: The appropriation of jeans by the mainstream

One of the most popular Hungarian movies in 1975 was János Zsombolyai's
The Kangaroo, based on Bulcsú Bertha's short novel of the same name. From
the perspective of the present analysis, it is an act of farewell to the magic of
blue jeans: many of the characters wear denim without attaching any significance to it. In one important scene, a globe-trotting truck driver (just back

from Nice), dressed in a fashionable denim suit, presents the protagonist Kanya with a leather jacket that he had ordered. Though it is not evident from the 'my first jeans' accounts, official Hungarian popular culture seems to have eliminated jeans from the inventory of magical clothes by the mid-1970s.

The meanings carried by jeans and, more importantly, the social and cultural changes in Hungarian socialism signified by changes in jeans-wearing practices can be traced not only to the most dramatic and conflict-ridden period (roughly 1960–1975), characterized by the popular craze to possess something that was both unavailable in stores and stamped by official disapproval. The process of taming or incorporating jeans, together with their massive spread, took place both through changing popular representations of blue jeans in films, commercials, fashion columns, adverts, novels and record sleeves, and through the swift increase in the accessibility of jeans at state retailers. This process eloquently exemplifies the chief paradox in the culture of socialist Hungary in the 1970–1980s: the contradiction between the obvious liberalization of culture and the fact that the changing of the cultural borderlines did not mean any less rigour and seriousness in the official patrolling of borderlines (set by official norms and regulatory practices) than in the early 1960s. Under the changing-but-not-changing cultural regulation, while jeans entered the mainstream, other marked outfits emerged, such as the black leather jacket, the punk outfit or the tightly tailored 'ragged-jeans'.

The last enemy

Some people say nothing's happening in Hungary. People are happy to be left alone with politics; in their spare time they build their own houses, breed poultry and devote their time to DIY hobbies. The intelligentsia has locked itself to the garden of culture, and left politics, too, for politicians. The churches collaborate with the state. The old-fashioned reactionaries and western-minded democrats have died out (. . .) The power sometimes exposes its iron fist but when seeing that nobody's making trouble, puts it back to its pocket hurriedly. Perhaps the fist smashes on a few leatherpants or drunkard troublemakers but the public in these cases applauds and calls for even harsher retaliations.[28]

These sentences have acquired a certain historical glamour by now. This quote is from the opening editorial paragraph of the first issue of *Beszélő*, the most influential samizdat publication in Hungary. The editor presents a simple, sensitive and powerful image of the social climate in Hungary following the introduction of martial law in Poland. I find it highly significant that this key publication, still in the early 1980s, chose to describe a despised group by a sartorial reference, but this no longer referred to jeans-wearers but to 'leatherpants'. This was probably because many of those siding with the establishment were by now wearing jeans. The leather outfit (especially trousers) worn by punks and heavy metal fans were the 'shock-garment' by the 1980s.

As indicated in the introduction, this account represents the first reading of my research results. A couple of things already seem obvious. The thickly woven threads of varied passions and interests in the jeans histories cannot be accommodated within some convenient grand theory of consumption. Despite its successful incorporation into the mainstream, jeans-wearing still marked a space of autonomy. Also, contrary to the glibber connotations of individuality and freedom, jeans-wearing often meant exclusivity or privilege. Jeans were, no doubt, often a passport to different social worlds, but many could still read where that passport-holder was coming from. In my view, the jeans story not only offers a perspective that enhances our understanding of the Cold War period, but highlights a feature of consumption – as an informal grass-roots activity – that contributes to a better understanding of consumption in mainstream capitalism.

Part 2
Talk and Action

5

Consuming Without Paying: Stealing or Campaigning? The Civic Implications of Civil Disobedience Around Access to Water

Bronwen Morgan

Introduction

Yoking together citizenship and consumption readily brings to mind practices and norms of 'ethical consumption'. In turn, 'ethical consumption' conjures the following typical example in many readers' minds: a consumer who buys fair trade coffee refuses to consume one kind of good and simultaneously chooses to support a substitute good that promotes fairer production methods. What if the same consumer refused to promote what she or he believed to be unfair production methods by withholding payment for, but continuing to consume, a good that had no substitute and was essential for survival? Consider two narratives that expand just such a scenario.

In Durban, South Africa in 2000, the municipal water company disconnected Christina Manqele from her water supply for failure to pay for consumption above the free basic limit provided to all citizens. The context was one where thousands of people in South African townships had not paid their water bills, in some cases for many years on end, in a complex context of poverty, the lingering effects of apartheid and anger against the new democratic government. Christina was a 35-year-old washerwoman living below the poverty line and a single mother with seven children. At some point following the disconnection, she was reconnected illegally to the water supply by what people in South African townships call 'moonlight plumbers'. Later, her case was brought to court by public interest lawyers, who argued that the disconnection breached her right to access sufficient water, a constitutional entitlement fleshed out by the Water Services Act 1997. Extensive evidence was brought by the water company about the fact that she had tampered with the network, which was defined as criminal activity by the legislative framework. Against this, her own lawyers brought evidence showing that the network was leaking very badly, causing water bills to be significantly out of proportion with the actual consumption levels of citizens. Christina Manqele lost the case because of a technical decision that more detailed government regulation was necessary before the court could enforce the statute. There was no reference in the final judgement to any of the evidence about her conduct or about the state of the network, but witnesses in the courtroom on the day of the trial argued that the judge's attitude was sharply altered by the evidence of her dealings with moonlight plumbers.[1]

In Auckland, New Zealand, a group of citizens came together to form the Auckland Water Pressure Group (AWPG) in 1996. With a fluctuating membership of as many as 2000 people, mainly from lower-working-class families, their primary aim is to lobby for the dismantling of a corporate (though still publicly owned) legal structure for the largest of the six municipal water companies in the capital city: Metrowater. Their actions also target shifts from property rate–based flat tariffs to volumetric user-pay methods of charging, and the disconnection policies of the various water companies. Sister groups in other districts of Auckland formed in the wake of the AWPG, and alliances developed with existing environmental community groups, all focused on protesting similar structural changes of varying magnitude that were proposed in relation to three of the remaining four companies. Soon after forming, a subset of up to 500 members of the AWPG refused to pay some or all of their bills. When disconnected, they reconnected themselves illegally to the system and poured concrete over their water metres to prevent further disconnection. In some cases where Metrowater responded by digging up the pipes linking their houses to the mainline road pipes, they parked a fire truck over the road housing the pipes. In time, Metrowater brought a series of legal actions against the payment boycotters in the Disputes Tribunal, a forum for small claims resolution. The boycotters defended themselves against these claims by a variety of legal strategies, all of which were sufficiently plausible to win them time, but which ultimately failed. In that time elapsed, though, political and legislative changes were secured through routes other than the courts. Today, though the number of boycotters has thinned over the years, the struggle continues.[2]

These two situations involve a number of obvious similarities, but the consumers in question are of course situated in radically different material and political-legal contexts. They are drawn from a research project which shows ordinary citizens and civil society groups in at least six different countries, both developed and developing, systematically mobilising in protest against the restructuring of water service delivery and often – though not always – engaging in civil disobedience. This paper mines the two narratives briefly articulated above for insights on the civic potential of civil disobedience in the context of political consumerism. Given evidence from the larger research project of collaboration across borders between activists, there is also purchase for a brief consideration at the end as to whether the civic implications hold for transnational identities and collectivities.

I take as a starting point the importance of 'ordinary consumption' and my argument can be read as a series of claims in dialogue with both Matthew Hilton's and Michele Micheletti's chapters in this volume. Hilton correctly emphasises the way in which the habitual and seemingly routine is a crucial constituent of agency for both consumption and citizenship.[3] But where the agency implicit in practices of consumption runs *counter* to that implicit in practices of citizenship, unusual and spectacular behaviour in one domain can be an important spur to the transformation of the other. Indeed, it is important in precisely the domain that Micheletti rightly stresses: the communicative dimensions of consumer acts and the ways in which they can politicise market processes. Here, too, however, illegal acts pose particular challenges for communicative opinion formation, specifically in terms of whether they can successfully 'instill the practice of consumption with the values and responsibility of citizenship and sustainability'.[4] I will argue that they can, but only via a more circuitous path than more law-abiding ethical consumption practices. And law and legal practices are crucial turnings in that circuitous path.

Boycotts, bills and choice

The argument I am making depends on unravelling the way in which civil disobedience in relation to consumption of a basic necessity is related to choice. As the opening paragraph emphasised, consumers of water services provided by monopoly infrastructure industries cannot (usually) choose an alternative product ('buycotting', as discussed in detail by Micheletti in Chapter 8), nor can they exit altogether as a more comprehensive boycott. All they can do is boycott payment and continue to consume: 'disloyal exit', perhaps one might say. Can we then reconcile the demands implicit in the payment boycott with the emphasis on choice that typically underpins notions of ethical consumption?

The specific resonance of 'disloyal exit' imports notions of community and trust whose role will become clearer if we unpick the assumptions that bind together choice and ethics in conceptions of political consumerism of the more law-abiding kind. Here, one might say there is a pervasive social contract which imbricates norms of consumerism and aspirations to social citizenship, especially at the level of everyday practice. Citizens have a right to buy products that reflect their ethical values, provided they fulfil the responsibility to pay for them. Provided both sides of the bargain are kept, there is continuity between consumer rights, social citizenship and civil responsibility. The mutual trust that is a necessary constitutive part of any functioning market depends on the 'everyday' expectation, held by both buyer and seller, that payment will follow provision. The routinisation of 'responsible consumerism' makes this so obvious as to take it for granted: it becomes in effect a kind of cultural contract which underpins the more explicit compromises secured by the social contract.

If the cultural contract is made visible in addition to the social contract, then what becomes clearer are the social relations embedded in exchange. The irony of law-abiding ethical consumption is that it is an act of choice that makes an explicit reference to the social relations of production, but only by avoiding contentious social relations of exchange. The fair trade coffee buyer simply exits the offending brand, chooses a more palatable brand, and fulfils their civic duty to pay the seller of the second kind.

When protestors refuse to pay for water, however, they are in part driven to this by the absence of choice in the structural context of monopoly provision. But it is also a question of the social relations of exchange. As Ben Page eloquently argues,[5] by taking these into account we can make much more sense of the choices of people who live below the poverty line in developing countries, refuse to pay a large water company providing services under government contract, but pay instead some ten times more per litre to individual vendors. 'Willingness to pay', argues Page, is not just a case of having the money and valuing the good, but also of trusting the person you are paying to the extent that you are willing to bind yourself with them in a pact of social relations. When water is provided on commercial terms, and particularly by a company that is foreign (however defined at different scales), these taken-for-granted trust relations are brought to the fore.

Civil disobedience from this angle challenges the link between consumption and production on much more structural terms than law-abiding ethical consumption: it demands a voice in delimiting the actual boundaries of the political community in which production and consumption take place, rather than expressing a choice about specific forms of consumption or production. This does not mean that it is decoupled from responsibility or duty. But it invokes a conception of agency allied to a different type of responsibility from that invoked by ethical consumption *per se*. The vision of responsibility and agency invoked by consumer choice is nicely captured by the illustration overleaf (Plate 5.1) from UNESCO materials for primary school children:

More political conceptions of choice can be illustrated by two examples, one each from the fieldwork in South Africa and New Zealand. South African citizens who were engaging in mass civil disobedience allied this strategy to a range of political mobilization activities, one of which involved marching *en masse* to the municipal water office waving 10 rand (66p) notes and chanting a willingness to pay 10 rand/month and no more for their water. In so doing they expressed a particular vision of 'responsible consumer behaviour' that was explicitly part of a practice of collective representation, one linked to the history of anti-apartheid activism. This action turns attention away from the mutual expectations of the service delivery environment and towards issues of political representation. Some of those who fought alongside the

Plate 5.1 UNESCO material for primary school children, 2003
Source. © UNESCO[6]

protestors against water cut-offs during apartheid now sit in municipal government offices. The macroeconomic structural context in which those political representatives find themselves exacting payment through disconnection and repression is beyond the scope of this article, but also clearly beyond the scope of the seller–buyer relationship – and the 10-rand march directs its expression of choice to that larger political context.

In New Zealand, the direction of the energies massed for civil disobedience towards choice of political representatives was literally the route taken by protestors. The Water Pressure Group used the publicity garnered from the events described above to back up their lobbying of certain key members of parliament. By the late 1990s a new small party (the Alliance), backed by the activists at local level, had won seats at the national level and held the balance of power in coalition with the Green Party. When the government moved to reform the Local Government Act, this coalition was able to secure a crucial amendment that limited the involvement of the private sector in water service delivery.[7] Moreover, in the committee hearings on the bill, the Department of Health took the opening created by the Water Pressure Group to move an amendment prohibiting disconnection of water. This gave the activists fresh leverage to access information under the Official Information Act to create pressure for implementation of this new state of affairs. In the process of gathering information from the six different municipal councils in the Auckland region, they were able to illustrate important disparities between the policies of public and private providers in relation to disconnection, providing fodder for their broader campaign of electing political representatives committed to a policy of reinvigorating public sector supply of water.

Propriety, practice and norms: From consumer to citizen

The tension between political and consumer conceptions of choice articulated above flows from the fact that agency is necessarily partly constituted by collective endorsement of the appropriate scope of 'proper' behaviour. Refusing to pay bills, especially but perhaps not only when one can afford to pay them, is clearly a breach of expectations in everyday consumer practice. Such heretical practices, however, are clearly linked for the activists who practice them, to experiences of collective identity that enact competing norms of citizenship. Here, for example, is the comment of the lawyer who acted on Christina Manqele's behalf:

> They came and said no, it is criminal, she hasn't paid her account for so many years, we've given notices upon notices. I mean, apart from not being financially able, most poor people are not the most literate of people. So that standard clause that can say if you don't pay your account within, whatever, 10 days, we are going to disconnect, you're not going to pay attention to it when the roof is falling down, there's no food on the table – you've got other priorities. . . . there is a very rigid contractual interpretation to the entire thing, that in order for you as a citizen of this country to get services, you have contracted to pay for the amenities that have been provided, and should you not pay, you cannot be allowed the opportunity of continuing to use those services, because you're creating a precedent for the rest of this country, and the more people are paying, then services will benefit.
>
> (Shanta Reddy, solicitor)

The normative rejection of the 'rigid contractual interpretation' is taken up in the practices of civil disobedience, which simultaneously create agency and generate alternative norms of what is 'proper':

> I like the reconnections precisely because it's that taking back of control, and it's illegal as well which I think is important. People don't end their politics at the Constitution, because the Constitution is biased against poor people, so the very principle of being illegal against the State is very important in terms of being capable of taking powerful action.
>
> (Jo Guy, community activist)

This agency creates new forms of community that cross racial and ethnic lines:

I'm now able to see all that's happening, not just in Chatsworth...The same thing is happening in Wentworth, the same thing is happening in Umlazi, the same thing is happening in Inanda, and in all these areas there are African people, coloured people, white people, Indian people...It's happening everywhere. It is really a class issue...we've grown and absorbed so much, we've learned so much in the struggle, that we shun [those who cast it as a racial issue] off immediately and say to them, would you stop coming and telling us this because we are living here together, my next door neighbour is an African person, and we live together in this community together, and we're united across poverty and you should stop coming and telling us that this is what's happening because we don't want to segregate ourselves from these other people.

(Brandon Pillay, community activist)

Similarly in New Zealand, the actions of the water protestors created collective mobilization from the ground up that went beyond water issues to other policies of housing and land use:

So within a year of quite large protests and so on – and I mean it was going on, on multi-levels, we were in the Western Leader, even the Herald at that time, because it was all sort of new you see. So the Herald covered us, we got interviewed on the national radio... government ministers were being interviewed and we were replying to them, and all this sort of stuff and talk back and all that and we were getting – people were getting involved who weren't necessary left-wingers or socialists, they were just like 'this is wrong'... – we weren't organising then the traditional left-wing Marxist, Leninist type...you know, follow us.... We can't do it for them, not on the basis that we were coming from. To create a structure and a platform in the community to fight this defensive fight back, sometimes struggle. And that's the basis that we started off on and became very successful and of course from there we've branched out into other community assets as well.

(Meredydd Barr, community activist)

As with the South African protestors, the communities created forged mutual respect across colour lines:

It was amazing you know, but it was great because we finally made that great sort of contact with the Maori radical groups and you know I've got their respect as it were, because I mean it's always a thing I find in all these grass roots struggles is actually you have to earn your respect to be able to speak and be listened to... You know, it's all very well turning up like flies around the honey pot, you know outside factories and all this shit, but what we've managed to do at least is earn enough respect with the community where we're taken seriously and listened to and the perception is that these people are good guys sort of thing and people listen. And we managed to create all sort of links therefore within elements of Maori life, especially in the more radical sort of types.

(Meredydd Barr, community activist)

And these effects are literally connected to the visceral experience of collective protest:

> We've been able to build that and maintain those contacts ever since . . . we do get in conflict with a lot – not conflict, but you know there are a lot of people who discuss this at an intellectual level and they all turn up to the meeting and go 'yes that's fucking terrible' and off they go, but we are at the sort of cliff, right at the coalface more or less and we just have, you know it's hard yakka.

(Meredydd Barr, community activist)

From the above, we can clearly see that civil disobedience helps constitute both a sense of community and a sense of that community's normative commitments. But does this blend of practice and meaning diffuse outwards and influence those outside the circle of protestors? Here, law acts as a crucial hinge. Courts and tribunals can act as a forum for amplifying and, importantly, legitimising the (often negative) media publicity that activists are accorded for their protests. This happened in both South Africa and New Zealand, and in both, with an interesting dual focus – partly on the legality of the policy framework of water service delivery and partly on civil and political rights more generally. The difference emerges through examples.

In New Zealand, the activists allied with the Water Pressure Group brought a series of different legal actions in pursuit of their primary goal of preventing or reversing the application of commercial principles to water service delivery. Some challenged the policy framework of water service delivery directly. For example, one case argued that the old common law 'doctrine of prime necessity' applied to water, in particular the principle that monopoly suppliers of essential services must charge no more than a reasonable price. The High Court declared that although this principle existed, it was displaced by the Commerce Act. They ruled that water services came within the scope of the Commerce Act even though the legislation was entirely general.[8]

Other cases in this category used legal arguments based on the status of water as a commercial service to fight against commercialisation itself. Payment boycotters lodged a 'letter of dispute' defending their non-payment as a response to misleading information in the water bill that allegedly breached the Consumer Guarantees Act.[9] The very same letter also claims that the water prices breach human rights standards of disproportionate charging.[10] After 3 years, however, the dispute letter was declared invalid by the District Court.

A second category of cases concerned the civil and political rights of protestors. In one, local government officials ordered protestors to remove banners they had draped across their houses, on which they accused named politicians of betraying the public interest by creating a corporate structure for Metrowater. The activists argued that the removal order breached their right to free speech under the New Zealand Bill of Rights Act 1990. Although they lost the case, the substantial political ramifications[11] led to a legislative amendment to clarify that the Human Rights Act does apply to local government.

Another case illustrates with some irony the different qualities of political and consumer choice. The protestors asked the court to nullify a local election on the basis that electors had been induced to vote by a misrepresentation.[12] Candidates who had been elected on an anti-privatisation platform had later revealed their support for public–private partnerships in water services. The notion that they had misrepresented their position depending on equating 'privatization' and 'public–private partnerships' (essentially long-term contracts of 20 or 30 years that delegate the technical and financial management of water service delivery to the private sector). After taking expert evidence from an economist, the judge rejected this equation, in revealing terms:

> Some might say that it is of the very nature of politics that candidates will promote their policies in a way [that] takes advantage of knowing that different interpretations might be put on the meaning of his or her words, unrestrained by any political equivalent of the 'misleading or deceptive conduct' provisions of the Fair Trading Act relating to commerce.
>
> (para 47)

Clearly, and quite literally, political choice is distinct from (and apparently less binding) than consumer choice!

Although not one of the above actions was successful in legal terms, the activists combined the legal actions with direct and often illegal action to great effect. In many ways, the actions were all the more successful *because* of their frank disregard for the coherency and consistency of their strategies *in legal terms*. Most of their potentially successful legal arguments would at best have tempered the commercial provision of water at the edges. What they cared about was the ability to mobilise politicians to vote, asserting repeatedly, 'it's not the court of law that counts but the court of public opinion'.[13] The cases legitimised, at least in part, the political cost of being perceived as unruly and irresponsible consumers. One of the protestors (who has no legal qualifications) was even asked to give a training session to the police on proportionate responses to social protest. Moreover, at least for 3 years Metrowater recognised the 'letter of dispute' as a legitimate basis for not disconnecting customers who refused payment. And the election case fostered a public debate about popular versus technical meanings of the word 'privatisation' that created the political space for key politicians, who were being continually lobbied by the protestors, to insist on amending the Local Government Act 2003 to place significant restrictions on public–private partnerships in water.[14]

In New Zealand, then, the combination of illegal protest and the use of courts enlarged the space for political participation of ordinary citizens in policy making. In South Africa, similar dynamics can be observed but with a more tempered impact, and more self-conscious ambiguity about the legitimating impact of law. As in New Zealand, some uses of the law focused directly on water policy; others on civil and political rights. The opening paragraphs have already related the failure of early litigation about access to water. Later constitutional litigation won consumers the right to be warned in advance about disconnection – but no limitation on disconnection itself.[15] Leaving aside the question of whether the practical result was a disappointment or not, the activists were ambiguous about its legitimating effects. On the one hand, the court provides a public forum for communicating the competing norms that challenge the taken-for-granted practices of responsible consumerism, reconstructing criminal delinquency as responsible parenting:

> [Moonlight plumbers] are going around reconnecting everyone's water and electricity and all this, and she obviously is not going to say this in court, and she couldn't, you know, I mean let's be straight to the point – she has to live, she needs the water, the children who depend on her, she has a responsibility to ensure that they survive, so she has to see to it that the water's reconnected. And that is the model argument and the constitutional argument.
>
> (Shanta Reddy, solicitor)

To the moral valency of responsible parenting, other commentators added more macro-structural forms of legitimation to the effects of litigation:

> There is this huge ideological project – the local press and the vast majority of academics are all saying 'there is one way of doing things, it's the way that competitive nations do things. We've all got to pull together, these [water activists] are messing it up for us, they're holding us back.' Now getting a court case can really help with the ideological stuff – it helps show these people are not criminal, they are not lazy, [their actions] are actually in line with the values of the new society that was founded.
>
> (Richard Pithouse, academic and organiser, Durban)

On the other hand, this kind of law has important disadvantages that *undermine* political agency:

People would love to have someone come in on a white horse and save them – people desire that – but that's something that's been deliberately decided against . . . in that way [the Durban legal activists] have been very reluctant to use legal skills to replace the politics, because it's disempowering – law takes a long time, that kind of [big test-case] law, and people tend to rely on this elite lawyer and if they don't deliver there's nothing to fall back on.

(Richard Pithouse, academic and organiser, Durban)

But if there are mixed feelings about using legal tools to address water policy directly, there is less ambiguity about a different role for law in relation to civil and political rights. The context here is more polarized and more brutal than the free speech and election cases of New Zealand:

It's . . . brutal in Cape Town – I've seen with my own eyes in Khayalitsa a woman with 200R (£13) debt [for water] having her goods removed – she had no electrical goods so they took her bed and clothes – it's completely blindly, fanatically, fundamentalist ideology – you send armoured vehicles and men with guns, that costs money, much more money, all the young men come out of their houses, there's a stand-off, people can end up in prison – I sound melodramatic but it's insane, the policy is insane.

(Richard Pithouse, academic and organiser, Durban)

Following these events, the Anti-Privatization Forum in Cape Town called for assistance in setting up a legal defence fund that would provide cover for water warriors and all activists and community members engaged in active, grass-roots struggle against privatization and neo-liberal policies (e.g., evictions, forced removals, cut-offs, education and environmental struggles). Law here is a buffer, a tool for clearing a political space:

The [Durban-based activist lawyers] have taken great care to use the law in ways that keep the space open for politics, in the way that the Zapatistas talk about using their guns to keep the space open for civil society, for politics.

(Richard Pithouse, academic and organiser, Durban)

Shifting dichotomies: Consumer/citizen and legal/illegal

I have focused on the practices of protestors, and not on the discursive terms by which they would categorise their activities, nor whether they identify individually or collectively as 'consumers' or 'citizens' as such. Instead, what I hope to have pointed towards, in traversing the observations made so far, is a threefold insight. First, the process by which an identity status such as 'consumer' or 'citizen' comes to make sense as an interpretive category usually involves its gradual emergence out of a web of everyday practices that frequently imbricate or blur the two kinds of status together. Second, despite this actually moving threshold between consumer and citizen, social norms nonetheless impose judgements of propriety on certain forms of conduct that reflect relatively stark concepts of 'insider' and 'outsider'. Third, these practices of exclusion shift depending on the larger ideological context in which they operate. More concretely, as Trentmann and Taylor's important historical work has shown,[16] political activism around water in nineteenth-century London was a critical constituent of the very emergence of the category of consumer, imbricating it with citizenly choice and practice from its very inception. We can take this further, and argue that civil disobedience as a *limit* case of political activism invokes not only the category of citizen, but also that of two other congruent identities – the criminal and the subject of human rights. A highly schematic representation of this drawing on an equally schematic triptych of contemporary political ideologies might thus look as follows:

Framing	Individual————————> Collective		
Liberalism	Consumer		Citizen
Economic rationalism	Consumer-citizen		Criminal
Utopian cosmopolitanism	Consumer	Subject of human rights-citizen	

This suggests that the boundary between citizen and consumer is an interactive, and fluid, product of the process of drawing two other boundaries: consumer/criminal, and consumer/subject of human rights. Civil disobedience in relation to the consumption of water brings into sharp focus the salience of these other two identities in constructing the limits of propriety in the zone of everyday ordinary consumption practices. It also shows how prior political commitments will frame practices in differing ways: Christina Manqele is either committing a crime or claiming her fundamental human rights, depending on the frame in which her actions are perceived.

Moreover, as we have seen, specific legal actions can play a part in shifting the frame. The larger research project from which this chapter draws, which conducted case studies in six different countries, has shown that protest and direct action are allied to law through contentious dispute resolution in the majority of the case studies: South Africa, Argentina, France and New Zealand.[17] Detailed analysis of the effects of this indicates that this particular synergy can sometimes redefine the basic rules of the game[18] and at least can foster significant political agency.[19] This chapter has now embedded those observations in an argument about the relationship between choice, illegality and consumption of basic goods that suggests that in these circumstances, civil disobedience can be viewed as a component of political consumerism that 'instils the practice of consumption with the values and responsibility of citizenship and sustainability'.[20] This adds an interesting twist to what some scholars are calling the 'ethical problematization' of choice of everyday consumption.[21] They argue that 'people are increasingly subjected to all sorts of demands that they should treat ordinary practices like the weekly shop, their journey to work, or their choice of holiday destination, as bearing a number of moral burdens', and challenge the ways in which these moralities are increasingly imposed from the top down by government and even by influential non-state organisations. The insertion of imbricated practices of civil disobedience and legal strategies of legitimation into debates about political consumerism suggests that practices of ordinary consumption can be moralised in ways that both challenge existing structures of authority and governance, and also draw powerfully on the collective agency of ordinary people.

An insurgent global citizenry?

The relationship between securing some effective result through civil disobedience (whether with or without law's help) and the formation of collective agency and perhaps identities is a complex one. This chapter will not explore in detail whether both are necessary to sustain the claim that civil disobedience is an important component of political consumerism. But it is a question raised by the larger research project from which this is drawn, and specifically the way in which that project details the extent to which the 'frame' of water service delivery increasingly crosses national boundaries.[22] When that occurs, the limits of law come into sharper focus. If protestors use civil disobedience to pressure local political elites, such pressures will have far less effect if the provider of water services is a powerful international corporation which can itself (and does) invoke international legal processes to pressure the state. I have explored elsewhere the implications of governance contexts that allow some but not all actors to switch between national and international levels.[23] In this context, the availability of such strategies raises the question of whether the political implications for consumer agency that civil disobedience catalyses can be sustained at the level of transnational relations between civil society groups that share beliefs and strategies?

Here we return, as foreshadowed, to the importance of banality. I have argued elsewhere[24] that the tension between struggle and routine threatens to undermine the process of building sustained links between civil disobedience and the more banal, everyday activities required to reconstruct water service delivery in a more humane or sustainable form, the goal for which the protestors fight. If civil disobedience can foster a sense of shared identities across national borders, that is more likely to sustain the necessary banalities that must follow. There is some evidence in support of this. In South Africa and New Zealand, activist groups have provided mutual support (occasionally financial but more often in the form of political advocacy support) in assisting those who are disconnected from their water supplies as a result of payment boycotts. The New Zealand activists hosed down the Bolivian embassy with a fire engine owned by one of the activist groups to express solidarity with Bolivian activists in Cochabamba. Bolivian and Canadian water activists have met face to face to share strategies and tactics, and North American press coverage of the Bolivian conflict that reached the Bolivian activists provided a sense of international solidarity that encouraged them to persist with the mass blockades they had imposed on their town, as did news conveyed in a local left-wing Bolivian newspaper about a prior similar struggle over water privatisation in Tucuman, Argentina.[25] Activists speak with passion about the energy and sense of purpose that they acquire from these experiences and links:

> Yes, yes, yes, well I mean, we've been at the forefront, New Zealanders and the South Africans, from what I can see in terms of civil disobedience campaigns. So whether that connection is part of our background, and it's like solidarity in action, I mean, it's wonderful, and I've had more supportive emails from South Africa than I've had from unions and people in New Zealand. The bond is very strong, especially when you meet the people.
> (Penny Bright, New Zealand activist)

They also emphasise the way in which transnational connections can replace national connections alienated by the methods of civil disobedience and unruly dissent:

> Look, remember also that earlier it was like a desert here because people had been smashed but everyone still believed in the government, [the current South African government] was able to have its agents everywhere, people have been confused so, you know, people like myself, we got inspired, you know, we could keep our work going on and workshops ... it's a support structure, personally, yes, yes, and also, comrades around you, you know, people meet other people, so if you break ties with [the government] then you meet new friends, new comrades. That keeps us going.
> (Trevor Ngwane, Anti-Privatization Forum, South Africa)

Yet these energies are often transient and sporadic. And, as this chapter has argued, it is crucial that such energies can become embedded in more routine, enduring forms of social relations of exchange, if the civic implications of civil disobedience are to be fully realised. There are two possible routes, profoundly different from each other, suggested by the different threads of this essay. Particularly when read with other essays in this volume, one route would point to the tacit creativity of repeated, banal, everyday practices. Arguably only the banal everyday can establish routines, implicit understandings and tacit assumptions: Dan Jacobson's 'shared, unspoken assumptions; oblique allusions and quasi-familial understandings; mutually recognized expectations and discreet, insistent curiosities; obligations informally accepted and returned; rights to both intimacy and aloofness acknowledged; practices and forms of speech cunningly coded to include some and exclude others'.[26] Such is the true weft of a cosmopolitan community that has collective political agency, the thread that weaves together the dispersed and disaggregated activities characteristic of individualized consumers. In the absence of such practices, the civic potential of consumer agency is diluted. But can such practices, *when willed and self-conscious*, effectively catalyse the sense of integrated identity crucial for cosmopolitan democracy? Might not such a willing, particularly under the instrumental pull of pragmatic policy goals, fracture the aesthetic and cultural dimensions that make collective identities meaningful and socially viable?

This question is important, but the alternative route towards focusing the energies of civil disobedience into enduring social relations of exchange would answer 'no' to this question, in part by turning towards a literature less present in this volume. This paper has brought in debates about consumption and choice and a series of observations about the mobilisation of law by individual citizen-consumers in a context where law is also being breached. The apparent paradoxes in this are the subject of an extensive literature on rights consciousness and the mobilisation of law,[27] which argues that litigation, as well as the invocation of rights in contexts where law does not (at least presently) confer any legal entitlements, can be a powerful catalyst for the building of collective identity. Importantly, the precise ways in which this catalysis works are not dependent on the instrumental outcome of litigation itself, and while it may be sparked by intentional willing on the part of activists and citizens, it is less allied to programmatic forms of coming together and more to the forms of social learning that accrue through the episodic practices of coming together to protest, mobilise and sue. This literature has not yet extensively explored transnational sites of rights-claiming practices, nor has it engaged directly with literature on consumerism and consumption. But it suggests that law may be one of the most fertile sites for exploring the fluid and hybrid practices that construct identities such as those of consumer and citizen. Law is a structural form of exercising power and authority in ways that significantly shape and constitute macro-social processes. But law is also inherently dispute-centred, mobilised by individuals often in unplanned, cumulative aggregate actions , enacting microcosms of ways in which the 'everyday life' of macro-structural processes play out. Questions about how rights consciousness and a turn to legal strategies interact with the constitution of collective identities that fracture neat boundaries between consumer and citizen are rich with potential. They would flesh out both the content of the social relations of exchange and the processes by which those relations emerge and endure, relations which are crucial not only to understanding the civic implications of civil disobedience, but to the relationship between citizenship and consumption more broadly.

Conclusion

This chapter has argued that agency is necessarily partly constituted by collective endorsement of the 'proper' and that practices of civil disobedience construct, perpetuate and breach norms of 'proper' behaviour. The content of norms of civic propriety, however, has a different valence for consumption practices than it does for citizens, with the consequence that political agency and consumer agency are often in tension with each other. When norms of 'proper' consumer behaviour are breached by civil disobedience, the practices involved (not necessarily the motivations or goals) simultaneously constitute competing norms of 'proper' citizenship. Whether those norms gain acceptance beyond the community of protestors, however, is unpredictable. Such diffusion is assisted by judicial and legal strategies that can sometimes legitimise civil disobedience and reconfigure what is connoted by 'proper'. When this occurs, civil disobedience can be viewed as a component of political consumerism that 'instils the practice of consumption with the values and responsibility of citizenship and sustainability'. But this may depend upon the mutual influence of successful policy change and the building of collective 'outsider' identities. If this is lacking, as it is more likely to be in a transnational context, political consumerism may suffer. To build collective identities that will be significant for future trajectories of political accountability in the context of cosmopolitan democracy, civil disobedience must be able to generate routines, implicit understandings and tacit assumptions amongst its adherents. Whether it can is still is an open question, one which could be beneficially addressed by bringing socio-legal literature on rights consciousness into dialogue with literature on political consumerism.

6
The Banality of Consumption

Matthew Hilton

Consumption is banal, but this is not necessarily a bad thing. This is not a statement in keeping with the usual associations of 'banality', a word often employed in reference to consumption. 'Banal' may once have been a neutral term, referring simply to the trivial and the everyday as derived from its original reference to the commonplace or its openness to use by all (as in banal-oven), but by the twentieth century, in the English language at least, it had become firmly associated with the negative effects of modern life. 'To banalise' has come to mean the reduction of a higher value to a common trait, often through the medium of consumer society, and, indeed, modern character has often been trivialised and rendered indiscriminate, as in the 'banalised masses' of Saul Bellow's *Herzog*. Accordingly, for many commentators, mass consumption has been inextricably bound up with a notion of the banal, and thus today banality cannot escape these negative or pejorative connotations.

The aim of this chapter is to explore the concept of banality in relationship to consumption and to suggest means by which it can be perceived as a positive term, and one which even serves to offer a more humanist understanding of consumer behaviour and the act of consumption. In addition, it will be suggested, attention to the banality of consumption will further explore the links between the everyday and the political, between consumption and citizenship. By accepting that much of consumption is indeed banal, it opens up the possibility for exploring how ordinary, everyday, mundane and seemingly trivial acts impact upon political beliefs and actions which must be considered if consumption is to be rooted in a modern form of citizenship.

The editors of this volume have made a useful distinction between a 'public domain of citizenship' and a 'private domain of the supposedly self-interested consumer'. Correctly, they point out that this is a problematic division, not only because it ignores the wider social and even collective considerations brought to the act of consumption in the past, but also because it is predicated upon a contemporary political rhetoric which has sought to reform the public sector according to the logic of the private market. Thus in separating the public from the private, citizenship from consumption, a model of the consumer is created which in its individualism and instrument-alism matches the principles of economic theory, but which pays little atten-tion to the wider concerns of the average citizen-consumer. Ultimately, there is the suggestion that the notion of the citizen is to be adapted in reference to a predetermined notion of the consumer as shopper. What is not suggested is that the notion of the consumer as practised in real life might already include several aspects and dimensions usually associated with citizenship.

If academics are to join this debate about citizenship and consumption then the flow of ideas between consumer and citizen must travel in both directions. Yet it is not obvious that such a dialogue could take place, not-withstanding the tremendous growth in research – especially in historical studies – or the links between consumption and citizenship. Criticism remains overshadowed by the legacy of the luxury debates of an earlier century, and mass consumption itself is still associated with the banal. For all the investigations into the economic, social and cultural aspects of con-sumer behaviour over the past 20 years, it remains to be seen whether scholars have really incorporated the trivial and the everyday into their analyses. It is as though for all the celebration of the diversity of the consumer, the sense of consumption as referring to eating up, wasting away, still lingers, and it is only through his or her own productive efforts in writing and creating studies of consumption that the scholar alleviates his or her own guilt in dealing with the banality of the non-productive realm. To put it another way, there may well have been a re-appropriation of the terms 'consumption' and 'the con-sumer' in consumer studies, but has there been one of 'consumerism' too? Consumerism – the general culture of commerce argued to dominate the modern condition – remains a negative force, no matter what the agency or activism of any particular consumer in any particular field or sphere might be.

In order to address these academic attitudes to consumption and the banal, before moving on to discuss the implications for politics and consumption, this paper will build on the analytical distinction between the public and the private, accepting that it does not necessarily respond to the reality of con-sumer practices. The first section of this essay will therefore discuss banality and the culture of consumption, arguing that the focus of investigation has often been on the luxurious, the extraordinary or, in monetary terms, the high-ticket item. A recent development in the literature, however, has been to turn to the ordinary and the trivial in recognition that the vast majority of consumption decisions are not made to communicate self-identity or to consciously proclaim membership or affinity with a group or subculture.

This is a development which will guide the second section, dealing with the politics of consumption. As in the investigations into consumer culture, attention has largely been focused on the spectacular and the dramatic rather than the ordinary, but a case study on the most pre-eminent form of con-sumer politics over the last 50 years – organisations of consumers concerned with comparative testing and legislative protection – will demonstrate that just as in the turn to the ordinary in consumer culture, there is a more banal form of consumer politics available for analysis. These everyday politicisations of consumer concerns perhaps better explain our relationship to goods and, consequently, the relationship to citizenship. It would be a mistake, therefore, either to argue pessimistically that consumption reduces citizenship to the logic of market relations or, more optimistically, that it can spectacularly revive contemporary debates about being a citizen. The reality is far more mundane than that, and this paper cautions against making too much of a link between consumption and citizenship.

This paper, then, seeks to reject the pejorative associations of banality and, in reference to consumption, render it seemingly synonymous with what a growing number of scholars have referred to as the 'ordinary'. Yet it concludes by offering 'banality' as an especially useful concept. Not only does it serve as a provocation to all those who have used banality in relation to consumption, but also it offers an analytical bridge between the focus on the ordinary practices of consumption and the more mundane forms of political action consumers have often undertaken. Banality serves as a potentially humanist interpretation of consumer behaviour, especially if it draws on the meaning offered by Hannah Arendt in her study of the nature of evil. Accordingly, the conclusion will return to the definition of banality in order to invoke an understanding of consumption which is admittedly commonplace but never just ordinary.

The culture of consumption

It is in the works of the Frankfurt School where one might expect above all to find the use of the term 'banality', particularly in reference to consumption. Yet here, as in other areas of consumer studies, the term is rarely used and never as a developed analytical concept. In Horkheimer and Adorno's *Dialectic of Enlightenment*, the classic text on consumer society, the word 'banal' appears only once, being employed to describe the average narrative of a commercially produced movie.[1] In his later return to *The culture industry*, Adorno does use the term in a manner one might expect from the Frankfurt School, but the term is not used analytically in any of the other writings of its associated figures.[2] Plenty of synonyms do appear – 'impotence', 'pliability', 'uniform', 'rubbish', 'alienated', 'false', illusory and so on – both in Horkheimer and in Adorno, as well as Herbert Marcuse's *One-Dimensional Man*, and it is the rise of the trivial and diverting influence of mass consumption which puts the final nail in the coffin of Habermas' public sphere.[3] Thus if the word itself was not used, the condemnation of the banality (or something like it) of mass society had become a central trope of early consumer cultural criticism.[4]

Indeed, in the founding pillars of post-structuralist thought the shadow of the Frankfurt School loomed large. Guy Debord complained of modernity's process of *banalisation* such that banality had become the defining image of the age: tourism, or 'human circulation as consumption', is 'fundamentally nothing more than the leisure of going to see what has become banal'.[5] Jean Baudrillard refrained from using the term in his earliest writings on consumer society, but banality and banalisation begin to appear in a number of his texts throughout the 1970s and 1980s.[6] At all times, his use of the word is linked to the perceived negative dimensions of modern media, particularly in the reduction of everything to the image. Yet he takes banality much further than Horkheimer or Adorno, and sees in contemporary culture a process of banalisation which breaks down any meaningful distinction between high art and low.[7] Later still, such a culture has permeated other Western states too. Writing of the French population's enthusiasm for TV reality shows in 2001, Baudrillard further commented that the mundane aspects of people's televised lives that viewers found so fascinating represented a 'spectacle of banality . . . today's true pornography and obscenity'.[8]

Baudrillard's invocation of the banal smacks too much of an older elitist disdain for popular culture. Meaghan Morris certainly believed so, asking, in 1988, why 'such a classicly dismissive term as "banality" [should] re-appear, yet again, as a point of departure for discussing popular culture'?[9] Equally, Dick Hebdige questioned Baudrillard's assertion of the 'desertification' of the real and the banalisation of art, culture and theory. Accusing Baudrillard of nihilism and gloomy decadence, he argued that Baudrillard's fatalistic – if inescapable – notion of banalisation acted as a pessimistic counterpoint to the project of cultural studies. A more optimistic engagement with popular culture and consumption would embrace the banal, seeing in it the under-pinnings for wider beliefs and even hope for the future.[10] Yet the very stuff of Hebdige's popular culture was never banal. They were spectacular. And it is to the spectacular that so much of his version of cultural studies he helped pioneer is directed.[11] For the focus on the cultures of consumption has not been on bread and cheese, but on motor scooters and televisions, department stores and advertising hoardings, movies and clothing, all objects which are either extremely visual – and hence useful at communicating styles, identities and dispositions – or which add to the general proliferation of images and brands said to dominate contemporary life. Baudrillard's critique of Marxist use-values and his development of the concept of sign-value attests to that proliferation of the image which many commentators have pointed to.[12] Thus the banality of popular culture can never be truly banal. In the society of consumption, so many goods have become important communicators of the owner's identity, self-perception and status in the modern city that there has been no space for an analysis of the ordinary.

So what are the sign-values of the most mundane of everyday items pur-chased on a weekly supermarket trip? The focus on either the spectacular luxury item or the products which seem to embody the spectacular nature of mass consumption misses the ordinary and posits in the consumer a constant ability to appropriate, resist or reject the meanings contained within the sign. As Morris puts it, she gets 'the feeling that somewhere in some English publisher's vault there is a master-disk from which thousands of versions of the same article about pleasure, resistance, and the politics of consumption are being run off under different names with minor variations'.[13] It is as though the true nature of the investigation has not been to understand the banality of everyday consumer experiences but to make that consumer serve a higher ideological end: either to reflect on the banality of mass consumption generally (i.e., the Frankfurt School) or – and in reaction – to celebrate the profundity of agency in the midst of such seeming banality.

Caught between the fantastic and the trivial, there has been little room for the analytically neutral or the practically ordinary in consumption. Yet there is a critical space for a notion of the banal which lies between the unconscious dupe and the self-conscious *bricoleur*. In David Harvey's analysis of local space vs. the cosmopolis, he develops an understanding of the banal that goes some way to assisting an analysis of everyday consumption. He draws upon Satish Deshpande's exploration of 'hindutva' in India, which maintains as one of its elements a resistance to homogenising Nehruvian developmentalism through an emphasis on local culture. Deshpande therefore refers to the 'sedimented banalities of neighbourliness – the long-term, "live-in" intimacy of residential relationships among persons and families and between them and their local environment'.[14] Harvey takes these local banalities as fundamental to the human condition, which become the basis for so much knowledge about the world. Yet both Deshpande and Harvey see in these localised banalities a consequence of globalisation, such that the banal stands in contrast to the universal. Harvey even takes the political analysis further, dialectically observing in local geographical banality resistance to the 'bland homogeneities of globalisation' and calling upon Deshpande's 'sedimented banalities of neighbourliness' 'to do duty in political lines of fire'.[15]

The truth of these banalities lies less in their ability to develop political knowledge which serves the wider ideological end of opposing globalisation and more in their essential mundanity. For within the banality of everyday life – be it through consumption or neighbourly interaction – lie a variety of coping mechanisms and practices which give rise to many different forms of knowledge. Some, indeed, may give rise to wider political projects, but others too simply politicise the everyday in more banal ways, ranging from grumbling to complaining to identifying a specific problem and seeking to rectify it in practical ways suspended – if only at least temporarily – from any wider ideological vision. This is not to deny that the banal practices of everyday life cannot develop into a wider political identity – there are plenty of studies which demonstrate that 'consumption and civility do not stand in opposition'[16] – but it is to point to the inevitable diversity of forms of knowledge arising from the intrinsically diverse practices of consumption.

These ordinary elements of consumption have in some of the most recent literature come to be an academic concern. In his study of consumer society in eighteenth-century France, Daniel Roche has produced *A History of Everyday Things*. French reads *Histoire des choses banales*, though banality in the French context is less pejorative than in English and for much of the book *des choses banales* is replaced with *la vie quotidienne*. The translator is therefore correct not to use banal in the English version, and *banalise* is interpreted as 'treats as commonplace'. Yet in one instance, Roche deliberately invokes the negative connotations of banality and its association with the Marxist concept of alienation in studies of mass consumption, to suggest that his work explicitly chooses to avoid such condescension and to treat the banal seriously.[17] Likewise, in sociology, Alan Warde and Jukka Gronow have drawn attention to the ordinary in consumption. They agree that the focus of their discipline has been on the visible, the spectacular and extraordinary, resulting in a neglect of the more habitual, repetitive and social. Their interest is therefore in the 'unconscious, non-reflexively applied routines' or acts which often take place without any reference to a source of authority and without any political intent.[18] Warde and Gronow prefer a notion of the consumer as somebody who constantly seeks to express their individuality but does so often out of habit and while conforming to a standard of normalcy.

There is here a deliberate nod to Pierre Bourdieu, a theorist of consumption whom Warde and Gronow believe offers perhaps the most purposeful insights into 'ordinary consumption'. Bourdieu's emphasis on status and 'distinction' help explain the motivations of many consumers, while 'habitus' provides the backdrop which makes so many acts of consumption almost predictable.[19] Yet habitus is not determining; rather, it provides the set of dispositions which enable individuals to act in certain ways, thereby rooting individual agency and rationality within a social system.[20] Within the framework offered by Bourdieu, much of consumption is indeed ordinary and banal, though those with a better 'feel for the game' can obtain greater social and cultural capital within the habitus.[21] Warde further argues, however, that what Bourdieu's concept of habitus does not do is pay attention to the ways in which people behave differently with regard to different objects. Bourdieu might provide a degree of stability in our expectations of consumer behaviour, but he does not deal so much with the contestation over conventions or the development of new interactions with goods. For Warde, the notion of 'practice' provides a 'powerful counterpoint to expressivist accounts of consumption' and reminds us that use-values remain important considerations beyond the communicative dimensions of Baudrillard's sign-values.[22] And, building on his other work, Warde claims, 'such a view is consistent with an approach to consumption which stresses the routine, ordinary, collective, conventional nature of much consumption'.[23]

Recent developments in the literature therefore admit of the banality of consumption in a non-pejorative sense. The culture of consumption does not have to be the cure or the symptom of modernity. It can be both, but more often it lies in between. In this banal hinterland, there is the potential for a more humanistic approach since the consumer does not always have to be a protagonist in the analysts' ideological battles. The consumer is understood in all of his or her manifestations, and the diversity of their interactions with goods is acknowledged. The banal culture of consumption, if less easily graspable, is a reflection of the limitless engagements consumers can have with the world of goods. But it is between the conscious and the unconscious that consumers usually interact with the material world around them, often through habit and routine and just as often developing new engagements with goods which always have the potential to develop new forms of knowledge about the world.

The politics of consumption

If it is the spectacular rather than the banal which has triggered much research into the culture of consumption, then so too is it the case in the public arena of political engagement and citizenship. Indeed, one might suggest more broadly that in the new forms of civic engagement which have proliferated over the last half century, rarely is it that consumer politics has become the object of study. While some attention has been given to movements of consumers in their various guises, considerable effort has been made to investigate the movements of women, peace campaigners, students, civil rights advocates, ecologists, and supporters of radical lifestyles and countercultural experiment.[24] The proliferation of non-government organisations (NGOs) and the growth in single-issue pressure politics outside the mainstream institutions of political discourse has given rise to debates about contemporary citizenship and how the agendas and interests of various stakeholders can influence policy. If it is accepted that the image predominates in a media-driven world, then too often it is the organisation which can play the media game that achieves success; hence the high profile obtained by such NGOs as Greenpeace and Amnesty International. The banality of consumer complaints and consumer protection cannot compete with the spectacular nature of these make-or-break causes and, in any case, consumption itself is often seen as the problem not the solution. Moreover, former protestors have turned analysts and it is no surprise that the attention of a politically broad-ranging scholarly community raised on the critique of a Marcuse or a Christopher Lasch text has diverted its attention to other areas of concern in the debate over the meaning of citizenship. Instead, politically, consumption has been reviled. Notwithstanding the discussions over the culture of consumption outlined above, the more pernicious notion of consumerism is held to have triumphed over other forms of structuring society. If consumption was related to citizenship in politically significant ways in the past, this is now held not to be the case. As Lizabeth Cohen writes of the United States, the republic has become 'consumerised' over the last 20 years, society being overridden with the logic of the market and citizenship being reduced to the dictates of the acquisitive individualist shopper.[25] Consumer agency might be celebrated in the past but all the negative associations of banality are brought to bear on discussions of present-day consumer*ism*.

Banality has been avoided in the accounts of consumer politics through the cherry-picking tendencies of a scholarly community's normative bias. While there has been little written on food and drugs legislation, trade descriptions acts and so on – the almost literal meat and vegetables of consumer-citizen concerns – there has been much on the spectacular interventions of consumers in other realms. Spectacular here means the bringing of wider ideologies, beliefs and interests to the act of consumption, enrolling the consumer into a political enterprise which has as its primary beneficiaries those groups other than consumers. Relevant, therefore, are the various boycotts that have attracted much concern, from the boycotts of entire countries such as South Africa (and the businesses that traded with it) to multinational firms such as Nestlé which have engaged in unethical business practices in the marketing of, particularly, breastmilk substitutes.[26] Ethical consumerism as a whole is beginning to capture the interests of many sociologists, while the fair trade movement is achieving a momentum both academically and in the marketplace.[27] In the chocolates, orange juice, coffee, tea and bananas of this movement, and in their promotion by such socially conservative groups as the Mothers' Union, there is in this form of politics the very stuff of banality. Yet it is spectacularly not banal, since there is an almost utopian edge to the commitment of many ethical consumers who see an opportunity to reform the entire marketplace.[28] And they are even more spectacular because they put the burden of the whole world in the shopping bags of the consumer, to borrow Daniel Miller's earlier and unfortunate exhortation to housewives to form the vanguard of a new politics based upon consumption.[29]

Most prominent of all have been the consumer – or, rather, anti-consumer – concerns of the imprecisely but popularly termed 'anti-globalisation movement'. Naomi Klein's exposition on the branded nature of much of contemporary life has spearheaded a reaction against the multinational firm, the market and consumer society. Most commonly cited have been the French farmer José Bové's protests against Macdonalds and the attempts by the Canadian-based Adbusters organisation to 'culture-jam' the propagandistic visual culture of capitalism, though a whole range of campaigning journalists have stamped their feet at the inequities of modern consumerism.[30] But banality here lies not so much in the society being rejected but in the imagination of the efforts to offer a new emancipatory politics. All too many of these works flounder in the cul-de-sacs reached after an expenses-paid trip to track down the Zapatistas of Mexico and their enigmatic leader, Subcommandante Marcos, while Kalle Lasn's Adbusters now resembles more an institution for marketing students to spend a pleasant, if not 'cool', gap year than a radical anti-capitalist organisation.[31] The intellectual failure of many of these efforts seems to be symbolised most of all in the voluntary simplicity movement, an apparently radical gesture by wealthy middle-income liberals to supposedly express their contempt for the banality of their acquisitive society by refusing to continue buying into it.[32] But, significantly, the shift to refuse to buy only ever seems to come after lots of stuff has been acquired in the first place.

Historians have been attracted to many of the same concerns and have unearthed a whole variety of forms of consumer action which bring to bear wider political issues to the act of purchasing. In the United States, consumption was the focus for the fight for independence, while it remained a key political weapon for abolitionists, labour activists and modern nationalists in the Buy American campaigns.[33] In the early twentieth century, consumption was a central tactic of Chinese and Korean nationalists in their struggle against the Japanese, while the *swadeshi* movement politicised homespun cloth for generations of Indian nationalists inspired, in particular, by Mahatma Gandhi.[34] Consumer protest has been expertly uncovered in the revolutionary spirit at the end of the First World War and in the various consumer groups mobilised in anti-sweating campaigns.[35] The list is seemingly endless, and suggests a perpetual politicisation of consumption from the eighteenth century (if not earlier) to the present. Yet in all these forms of consumer protest, the banality of consumption is actually avoided, since each movement sought to raise the act of shopping to a higher ethical, political or ideological end.

In contrast, the truly banal forms of consumer politics have received relatively little attention, especially if weight is given to their historical importance. The co-operative movement is, in many ways, intrinsically banal. The dividend-on-purchases offered a system of consumer ownership which many of its advocates thought had the potential to replace the existing capitalist system. For a generation of labour activists and labour historians, though, the co-op 'divi' offered little in the way of consumer politics and was, instead, regarded by the massive majority of co-operators as a method of either saving or serving their own individual or familial economic interests. Yet, it is in the detail of how money is spent that politics emerges, and a revisionist scholarship has begun to see in the weekly purchases made at the co-operative a mundane form of political activism which nevertheless had important repercussions in defining and promoting the Co-operative Commonwealth. Peter Gurney in particular has used Bourdieu's concept of 'practical knowledge' to argue that ordinary working-class co-operators, lacking economic and cultural capital, made use of the 'divi' not only for material concerns, but also to communicate a sympathy with the ideological bases of the co-op.[36] Even within the banality of co-operative shopping there existed a politics to these actions. As with the focus on the ordinary in the cultures of consumption literature, the consumer, in Gurney's analysis, becomes neither the

politically unconscious pursuer of individual monetary reward through quarterly divided payments, nor the spectacular advocate of the ideology of co-
operation. The positive banality of consumption exists between these two
extremes, suggesting a notion of consumer politics that cannot be captured
through an analysis of sign-values or the uttered and written statements of
activist consumers deliberately aware of the implications for citizenship.

In the latter half of the twentieth century, comparative testing organisations have come to replace the co-operative movement as the principal advocates of consumer rights, protection and politics. But as with co-operation,
modern forms of consumer activism have been overlooked, and relatively
little is understood about these literally millions of consumers who have
come together in consumer protection organisations. Beginning in the
United States in 1929 with the foundation of Consumers' Research (and the
subsequent formation of Consumers Union in 1936) and expanding into
Western Europe in the transition to affluence after the Second World War,
organised 'consumerism' (as opposed to the more pejorative culture of 'consumerism') has concerned itself with the everyday objects of our consuming
lives. The larger, more financially stable and more prominent organisations,
such as Consumers Union, the UK Consumers' Association and the Dutch
Consumentenbond, have been primarily concerned with the production of
tables which compare the relative merits of different branded goods and
services. Testing and asserting a 'best buy' are perhaps areas which touch on
the most banal aspects of mass consumption and, following the negative sense
of the term, have led some scholars to conclude that organised consumerism
has merely reinforced the acquisitive, individualist tendencies of contemporary culture.[37] Certainly, the image of the rational middle-class shopper, as
frequently male as female, poring over a report on a washing machine in
Which? or *Consumer Reports* invokes in some an image of small-minded
penny-pinching that could never hope to claim to be, politically, anything
other than trivial, banal and self-interested.

Yet this has been only one aspect of the modern consumer movement and,
originating at a time when the physical reliability of products was far more
questionable, it is likely that such rigorous attention to detail has done much
to produce a fairer and safer marketplace.[38] But comparative testing has also
given birth to an international movement. The American and European
consumer groups came together, in 1960, to form the International
Organisation of Consumers Unions (IOCU). Originally intended as a clearing
house for the transfer of information about testing practices and results
between the different national associations, IOCU soon redefined itself as
an international advocate of consumer rights. It immediately took as its
operating philosophy the four consumer rights outlined by John
F. Kennedy in March 1962 – the right to safety; the right to be informed;
the right to choose; and the right to be heard – and it used these to spread the
message of consumerism across the world. During the 1960s, consumer

organising emerged in most developed nations and incorporated the state-sponsored consumer agencies of Scandinavia and even the more co-operative ventures such as those proliferated in Japan.

In the 1970s, however, international consumerism took on a very different perspective. Gradually, consumer organisations were set up in developing world countries. Beginning in India in 1956, consumer organisations proliferated across Southeast Asia in the 1970s, to be followed by similar developments in Latin America a few years later. In the 1990s, consumerism spread into the former Soviet bloc and into Africa, such that today there are around 250 affiliates to IOCU from 115 different countries. Moreover, IOCU – or Consumers International as it is now known – has established regional offices for Asia, Latin America and Africa, providing it with a global reach and communications system far more extensive than those enjoyed by many more prominent and well-known NGOs. Significantly, through the 1970s and 1980s, the centre of gravity of the consumer movement relocated from the developed to the developing world. A particularly active first regional office was created in Penang, Malaysia, in 1974, which, under the directorship of Anwar Fazal (a founder of the well-known Consumers Association of Penang), redirected the attention of the consumer movement to the problems faced by the majority of the world's consumers – the ability to live in a healthy environment and the access of poor consumers to basic goods and necessities such as water, healthcare, shelter and food.

To this extent, by the 1980s, IOCU could claim to enjoy something of a leadership within global civil society as it spearheaded many of the campaigns supported by social and economic activists the world over. It fought for and obtained a set of United Nations Guidelines on Consumer Protection in 1985. It had set up various networks to co-ordinate campaigns on targeted issues. The International Baby Food Action Network (IBFAN) was established in 1979 to campaign against what it perceived to be the inappropriate marketing of breast-milk substitutes. Health Action International (HAI) was formed in 1981 at a meeting of the World Health Assembly to press for a code of conduct on the sale of pharmaceuticals and especially their 'dumping' in the developing world. Pesticide Action Network (PAN) was created in 1982 to deal with not only the ingestion of pesticides by consumers that Rachel Carson first brought to the world's attention, but also their use by many poor farmers and agricultural workers. Other networks were also developed against the promotion of cigarettes and tobacco products, and IOCU lobbied the UN to establish, in 1982, a Consolidated List of Banned Products while, more generally, it fought, though ultimately without success, for a UN Code of Conduct on Transnational Corporations.[39]

In these examples, the politics of consumption promoted by IOCU does lend itself to a more spectacular, rather than a banal, reading. And, certainly, the consumer movement in its various domestic settings has witnessed its share of spectacular moments. In 1972, several consumer activists were imprisoned by the Greek military rulers, while in 1987, the Malaysian consumer activist Meena Rahman was imprisoned and detained without trial for her work with the Consumers' Association of Penang and its sister organisation *Sahabat Alam Malaysia* (Friends of the Earth Malaysia) in protesting the dumping of nuclear waste and the destruction of the rainforest in Borneo. Within Western states, certain consumer activists have enjoyed a public profile more typically enjoyed by other civil society leaders and activists, the most famous by a long margin being, of course, Ralph Nader.

Yet for all these notable achievements – and defeats – the bulk of the work of the consumer movement has come from protecting consumers from aspects of the market to which domestic organisations were often first alerted through their comparative testing activities. In the United Kingdom, the consumer movement grew incrementally as it began to address issues not only related to specific products but with the structures of the market that provided those products. The Consumers' Association (CA) quickly began to address a range of questions related to advertising, trade descriptions, commercial fraud, competition policy, consumer credit, food quality, packaging and so on. In addition, the founders and organising Council of the CA were closely, if not entirely, from the social democratic wing of the Labour Party, who saw in consumerism the potential for providing a middle-way between the organised interests of business and trade unions. Some viewed consumerism as a new social movement and actively encouraged the proliferation of local consumer groups in the 1960s, while others went on to work for the National Consumer Council (NCC), a government-funded body set up in 1975 which explicitly linked consumer politics to issues of citizenship rather than self-interest. The NCC's initial objective was to fight for the 'poor and disadvantaged' consumer, a goal which, if not so much the primary focus during the wider market reforms of the 1980s and 1990s, has at least in recent years come to the fore again. But in all of these aspects of consumer politics, few raised concerns that would have been likely to have, for instance, inspired the citizen activists of the '68 generation. Yet, for all that, one *Times* commentator was able to claim that by 1980 the CA had 'filled more pages of the statute book than any other pressure group this century'.[40] Credit and commerce are the banal everyday stuff of political lobbying. They attract little need for ideological expression and promote instead more pragmatic, vaguely social democratic ends which, nevertheless, remain important interventions in a slow process of reform.

Similarly, in the United States, the revival of the consumer movement in the late 1960s owed less to ideology or to the dramatic subversion of the meaning of goods, but to the practical issues of auto-safety. Ralph Nader's *Unsafe at Any Speed* offered a consumerist critique of the motor industry which triggered a series of public interest legislative measures which had been matched only in the Progressive Era and during the New Deal.[41] Legislation regulating the car industry was followed by measures to promote the wholesomeness of meat and consumer product safety generally, while regulatory agencies such as the Federal Trade Commission and the Federal Energy Administration were strengthened and new agencies such as the Environmental Protection Agency, the Occupational Safety and Health Administrations and the National Highway Traffic Safety Administration were launched.[42] Nader's tactics might well have been spectacular, but the subject matter of the regulatory public interest movement of the 1970s was fundamentally banal. In broaching these subjects, he further avoided an explicitly ideological stance, reflecting a widely held feeling among consumers that politics ought to act upon the everyday concerns that consumers face in their ordinary spending routines.

Even in those contexts where the poverty and exploitation of consumers has resulted in more overtly political agendas, the consumer movement has still been largely concerned with everyday affairs. In Malaysia, for instance, bodies such as the Consumers' Association of Penang (CAP) have achieved a national reputation for protecting ordinary people in their struggles with the processes of development, and several of its activists have gone on to enjoy a reputation on the global stage, not least through the number of times CAP staff have won the Right Livelihood Award (the 'alternative' Nobel prize).[43] Yet CAP and other state-based consumer groups have mainly focussed on dealing with consumer complaints, offering advice on obtaining redress within the market and taking up the causes of consumers affected by a particular market abuse. For example, consumer activists have mobilised on such banal objects as prawn-paste, a staple of Malaysian cooking, which was found at one point to be adulterated with the toxin Rhodomine-B. As in the American and British contexts, such basic injustices could then inspire more general calls for reform of the marketplace, often to the immediate benefit of consumers but without the grander vision being imposed by the ideology of the activist or the interpretative framework of the scholar.

These domestic concerns have continued to steer the direction of the international consumer movement such that today it campaigns on a broad range of everyday concerns. Its programmes are based around established agendas of the movement, such as educating consumers to be more self-aware and improving the technical standards set out to regulate the manufacture of goods and the provision of services. Its core areas of focus remain food safety and food security, as well as health, the provision of basic services by utility companies, trade, the environment and corporate social responsibility. It continues to seek legislative measures for consumers and it promotes the implementation of consumer protection measures for consumers around the world based on the best practices of schemes set out in countries with established consumer protection regimes. Consumers International remains a robust organisation, in terms of its own structure, finance and membership, but its continued attention to the banal, as well as its refusal to develop a theory or all-encompassing vision of the world's social and economic problems, means it remains hidden behind the far more prominent activities of other NGOs.

Again, then, and just as with the cultures of consumption, there is in the modern consumer movement an engagement with wider political concerns that is neither passive (in the sense that the consumer movement has inadvertently pushed its members into a heightened acquisitive culture) nor wholly self-aware (in the sense that activists have set out a coherent ideology or consumer-political manifesto). Instead, the banality of its focus has been reflected in the banality of its actions. The consumer movement has deliberately sought to transcend the party political divide to focus on issues which might appear trivial to other social activists but which have nevertheless had important consequences for being a consumer in the market and a citizen in the public sector.

This is not, however, to proclaim some normative judgement about the type of politics being practised by the consumer movement or to suggest the superiority of the focus on the banal as a model for good citizenship. But it is to suggest that there is in the consumer movement a banality of consumer politics which highlights an interaction with the world of goods which has implications for the practice of citizenship. It forms one part of a broader spectrum of interactions between consumption and citizenship which can, at either end, be truly spectacular and banal (in the negative sense of the term). But the positive aspect of a banal politics has to be emphasised. It suggests an interaction with consumption that leads to specific political interventions in which consumers do care about the wider social aspects of their consumption if not to the extent that they want to set out a sweeping model for all of their interactions with citizenship and politics. Consumers can therefore be regarded as banal because they are neither the passive dupes of the marketplace nor the vanguard of a new citizen-based activism. Sometimes they do want to overturn the structures which enable fundamental abuses to take place, but sometimes they want to forget about the wider implications of their purchasing decisions. Neither too much nor too little can be expected of them – and it is the agenda of the organised consumer movement which reflects this.

Conclusion

All of this suggests the efficacy of a revised concept of banality. The banality of consumption must be embraced as a non-pejorative concept in order to better understand the full diversity and complexity of human interactions with consumption and the subsequent development of concerns more appropriately recognised as falling within the sphere of citizenship. In Hannah Arendt's notion of 'the banality of evil' there is, perhaps, the roots of a more humanist understanding of consumption. At first, such an analogy might seem inappropriate, given the relative immediacy and import of consumption concerns with those of Arendt – the trial of the Nazi's chief architect of the 'final solution', Adolf Eichmann. Furthermore, in the reactions to Arendt's work, the use of the word banality remains negative. Arendt's identification of Eichmann's unthinking, non-malevolent and indiscriminate willingness to follow orders and pursue them so efficiently has led many to believe that the invocation of banality somehow lessened Eichmann's guilt. He is portrayed as a cog in a bureaucratic machine which paid no attention to the human consequences of its actions and therefore he was as much a product of the machine as he could be considered its motor. In assessing Eichmann's guilt, these factors, it has been held, ought not to be taken into account, since it seemingly dehumanises an atrociously anti-human act: 'the lesson of the fearsome, word-and-thought-defying *banality of evil'.*[44]

But the point about Arendt's notion of banality is that this does not excuse Eichmann of his guilt. After identifying the essential banality of his actions she goes on to pronounce his death sentence in her own words. She accepts – far more than the actual judges at the trial – the horrible normalcy and ordinariness of the man and that, even, many others would have done the same thing in his place. But she also points out that for all the apparently unconscious actions, there was always the opportunity not to carry them out. Thus, Eichmann cannot avoid responsibility, and the humanity of 6 million outweighs any more humanistic understanding of his actions: Arendt is clear that he 'must hang'. What Arendt manages to convey in her account of Eichmann is just how ordinary his extraordinary actions were, just how routine were his acts of grotesquery, and just how interrelated were the concepts of the ordinary and the extraordinary at one and the same time. The notion of evil that emerges is something that is not always deliberate and calculated. But neither is it something that is entirely bureaucratic. Indeed, her analysis of Eichmann suggests that evil is perpetrated without conscience, not because the perpetrator chooses, or simply is unconscious of it. Rather, they are conscious of their evil, but it is a semi-conscious state which resides alongside other considerations. Evil is thus as much about forgetting the consequences of one's actions as it is about remembering them.

Banality as understood here therefore resides between the ordinary and the extraordinary, between the trivial and the spectacular. Notwithstanding the dubious moral implications of drawing upon the banality of evil to explain the banality of consumption, there is clearly a notion of banality here that enables consumption to be seen as ordinary, trivial and mundane, but which is no less important for that. The engagement with consumption is not something that is done entirely passively (as in the banality of mass consumption favoured by the Frankfurt School), but neither is it done entirely consciously (as in the deliberate playing with images of the cultural studies project). Instead, agency (in the cultural or the political sphere) is always there and consumers always have in the back of their minds the bigger picture of consumer society, but sometimes this picture is lost and sometimes consumers are just focussing on themselves. But even when consumers are being at their most passive, most herd-like or most self-interested, they always know they have the option not to be so, and that they can choose to choose differently. Consumer agency, like evil, is banal in the sense that it is everyday, it is common, but this does not mean it is either passive or spectacular.

In terms of the implications for scholarship, this means we should expect neither too much nor too little of consumption. The focus on the ordinary in the cultures of consumption literature provides a model for the everyday nature of consumer action in the political sphere. Consumption cannot be said to de-politicise citizenship, since everyday interactions with the world of goods bring together the various networks of practices which constitute the consumer world-view. It is only to be expected that political agendas will therefore emerge out of the act of consumption. But, equally, consumption cannot be said to offer an entirely new form of political engagement, and it would be mistaken to expect the housewife or some other such consumer to become the 'vanguard' of any new liberatory politics. The politics of consumption will always remain banal since it will involve a straightforward defence of the consumer interest in any particular sphere, but not according to any consumer manifesto or consumer ideology. As in the modern consumer movement, this will sometimes lead to an incremental growth in both the membership and the sphere of interest of consumer politics, but equally it will place limits on the development of 'consumerism' as a political philosophy comparable to any other 'ism'.

And in terms of the implications for citizenship we must also expect neither too little nor too much from the banality of consumption. In the literature and public debates on consumption, it often seems that political rhetoric seeks to make the private concerns of consumption the basis for public policy, while scholars have tried to politicise the domestic, bringing all the political and citizenship concerns of the public sphere into the private acts of consumption. The actual nature of the interaction is likely to fall between these two extremes. As in the case of the modern consumer movement, consumption is brought to bear on wider questions of citizenship, as the defence of the consumer has become a central component of the 'public interest'. And aspects of citizenship – such as access, rights and duties – have been used to redefine consumption as something more than an individual, self-interested act. But there are limits to this engagement. The consumer movement has brought the everyday concerns of consumers into the public sphere, but the banal nature of consumer politics and consumer political engagement has prevented consumerism developing a wider world-view on the relationship between consumption and citizenship. This has resulted in some perhaps naïve interventions into global politics, as in IOCU's retreat from high-profile campaigning in the 1990s and its conciliatory moves to work with the new World Trade Organisation, a tactic which proved to bring very little actual discussion of consumer rights in subsequent trade negotiations. But the consumer movement was aware that in the sheer diversity of concerns of consumers the world over, the attempt to formalise either a consumer political creed or a precise relationship with consumption and citizenship would have resulted in a rigid definition which might preclude the incremental nature of its very expansion over previous decades. In this sense, consumer politics offer a banal and positive engagement with wider questions of citizenship, but there are limits to this and one should not expect the consumer to stand as a replacement for the citizen in the public sphere.

Therefore, consumption is indeed banal and this is not necessarily a bad thing. Banality improves our understanding of the profundity of the trivial in, first, the cultures and, secondly, the politics of consumption. It better helps us to understand that consumer behaviour constitutes an interaction with the world that falls between the conscious and the unconscious, an engagement that is more often ordinary than spectacular but which is no less important for that. In terms of the interaction between consumption and citizenship, banality is also relevant. The banal politics of consumption raises everyday issues to the political level and addresses the concerns of the citizen in an unspectacular manner. Yet, for all this, the banality of consumption also restricts the range of citizenship issues which it can address and also means that these intermediate interventions are not always the most appropriate. Sometimes the spectacular, and not the ordinary, is needed in the addressing of citizenship issues. The banality of consumption cannot always provide these spectacular interventions and consumption cannot therefore be the only basis for citizenship: citizenship remains much wider than that.

7

'Public Connection' and the Uncertain Norms of Media Consumption

Nick Couldry, Sonia Livingstone and Tim Markham

This book aims to disrupt the apparent divide between consumption and citizenship. In this chapter we seek to advance that general move by examining the role of one term that lies hidden but crucial on *both* sides of the citizenship/consumption divide: media. The result will be, we hope, to open up an area of normative and empirical uncertainty about an often, but not always, 'banal' area of consumption – media consumption – and to consider its contribution to the maintenance of democratic legitimacy. This points to some interesting implications for just what is at stake in the consumption/ citizenship divide, itself much more than a matter of academic precision.

Media as consumption and/or citizenship?

It is difficult at the outset to see where exactly media fits into the discussion. Starting with consumption, Colin Campbell argued a decade ago that the sociology of consumption should not extend to the 'use of intangible goods and services'.[1] He meant media,[2] though this could of course cover many non-media items such as professional and knowledge-based services, but the reason for this exclusion was somewhat unclear. At the same time, however, the very diversification of media and communications goods – particularly in terms of personalized and mobile media – meant that many came to acknowledge media on the map of 'ordinary consumption': see, for example, Longhurst, Bagnall and Savage[3] on radio and du Gay *et al.*[4] on the personal stereo.[5] Perhaps this was simply a matter of official definitions of 'consumption' struggling to catch up with actual research (media consumption has of course since the 1940s attracted a huge diversity of social science research), but we suspect there is more involved than questions of definition. For there *is* something *relatively* distinctive about *much* media consumption – namely its intrinsic informational or narrative content. Of course, wearing a particular item of clothing or drinking a particular brand of coffee can be a sign of something else, or be associated with certain types of attitudinal statement (or at least suggest a willingness to be associated with those statements by

104

others). But many acts of media consumption are linked to information and narrative in a different way: watching TV news *is* the act of consuming a particular narrative, a narrative that aims to communicate certain claims about the world directly through that act of consumption.

The distinctiveness of media consumption is important, and this is not overridden by either the uncertainties of information transmission/audience interpretation or the semiotic richness of material objects, important though those are. Roger Silverstone has captured the heart of this distinctiveness through his notion of double articulation.[6] Media, Silverstone argues, always have a double aspect: media as material objects (the television or walkman), that is, technological objects consumed in particular spatio-temporal settings; and media as texts (the news bulletin, the soap opera), that is, symbolic messages located within particular socio-cultural discourses and interpreted by audiences. Most (but not all) practices of media consumption are therefore *defined* in part by the direct exposure to informational claims or narrative intents that they involve. Presumably this is why, for all the banality of many practices of media consumption and their settings, 'media' have been so readily co-opted to the other term of the binary, 'citizenship'.

However, media's relationship to citizenship itself needs further examination. From Hegel's famous comparison of reading a daily newspaper at the breakfast table to a ritual performed to the nation, media have been claimed to belong to that special class of habits inseparable from having a stake in a wider polity. John Dewey argued that communication is already, from the outset, implicated in the question of how polities can be built and sustained. 'Communication', as Dewey put it, is 'the way in which people come to possess things in common.'[7] That argument is important, and has been often drawn upon to ground specific research into media's public role.[8] But media consumption remains also an aspect of 'the material culture of politics'.[9] If, however, we assume this is all media are, we also miss part of the complexity by co-opting media automatically to the other side of the consumption/citizenship binary. Media are *not only* relevant to citizenship. Media are part of everyday pleasure, entertainment and the practical information flows on which the conduct of our lives depend. Indeed it has been strongly argued that an over-politicized reading of media consumption forgets media's contribution to everyday unpolitical life.[10] In addition, recalling Silverstone's notion of double articulation, media use involves in part the consumption of goods (from DVDs, to newspaper subscriptions, to satellite dishes), which it makes no sense at all (contra Campbell) to exclude from the notion of consumption. Like other goods too, they are also the product of a market, subject to the same logic of innovation, diffusion and competition.[11]

To sum up the argument so far, media as goods and technology are properly part of consumption, and do not *per se* raise questions of citizenship, although the lack of certain media goods may cut across the preconditions of effective citizenship (the digital divide debate, its precedents in the universal service obligation and its recent developments).[12] However, media – as content – do inherently raise questions of citizenship and have, in this regard, been widely addressed by media and communication scholarship. But it would be misleading to say that media contents *only* raise issues of that type since they are just as likely to raise *non-political* questions concerning identity, pleasure and belonging in the way that other forms of consumption do.[13] Indeed, media, and popular culture in general, raise some difficult questions that are precisely at the *boundaries* of citizen practice (for example, the recent debates around celebrity culture),[14] questions about the nature and substance of citizen practice which our research outlined in this chapter has aimed to investigate.

The 'Public Connection' project

The ambiguities about the practice to which acts of media consumption belong are now increasingly difficult to resolve, not just for the reasons just given but for other broader reasons which link to a crisis in the sphere of citizenship itself. Our starting point in this chapter is that it is far from obvious whether the everyday practice of consuming media (something all of us do) is, or even should be, orientated towards a sphere beyond the private, what we might call a 'public world'. We will explain our own normative position on the term 'public' later, but it is above all the empirical resonances of this question with which we have been concerned in our recent project 'Media Consumption and the Future of Public Connection'.[15]

In 'mature' democracies we cannot avoid questions about what our media consumption 'amounts to', what are its purposes and guiding values, and to what extent it sustains a clear relationship between individuals and a wider polity on some scale or the other. This is not just an academic uncertainty, we believe, but a practical quandary that matters for citizens in their daily lives. It is a quandary that Alain Touraine captured vividly, if rhetorically, when he wrote,

> Part of us is immersed in world culture, but, because there is no longer a public space where social norms could be formed and applied, another part of us retreats into hedonism or looks for a sense of belonging that is more immediate...both individuals and groups are therefore less and less defined by the social relations which until now defined the field of sociology, whose goal was to explain behaviour in terms of the social relations in which actors were involved.[16]

Leaving aside the wider issue of sociology's future which Touraine raises, a pragmatic question for every citizen in intensely mediated societies is this: what is the wider space to which I belong? In what way, if at all, does the media I consume sustain that belonging?

Put another way, our project has aimed to investigate what are the traces in citizens' everyday experience and reflections of the following two assumptions which, we would argue, constitute the bottom line of most political science, political theory and media sociology:[17]

1. In a 'mature' democracy such as Britain, most people share an orientation to a public world where matters of common concern are, or at least should be, addressed (we call this orientation 'public connection').
2. This public connection is partly, even principally, sustained by a convergence in what media people consume, in other words, by shared or overlapping media consumption (so 'public connection' is mediated).

These assumptions are detachable from each other. Some believe the first without the second because they argue public connection is unlikely to be served by people's use of media (Robert Putnam's well-known *Bowling Alone* thesis takes that position in relation to television).[18] Generally, however, it seems to us that many writers assume both, even if only tacitly. Our concern has been this: can we find evidence for those assumptions (and for 'mediated public connection') in UK citizens' own practice and their reflections upon it?

The first assumption is important because it underlies most models of democracy: informed consent to political authority requires that people's attention to the public world can be assumed, or at least that one can assume an *orientation* to the public world which from time to time results in actual attention. When in this project we talk of '*public*' connection, we mean 'things or issues which are regarded as being of shared concern, rather than of purely private concern', matters that in principle citizens need to discuss in a world of limited shared resources.[19] We have been careful not to assume that a decline in attention to 'politics' in the traditional sense means lack of attention to 'politics' in general, let alone apathy. People's understanding of what constitutes politics may be changing[20] at the same time as the *media* landscape is growing ever more complex. Leaving aside possible changes in the definition of 'politics' and the 'public world', our working assumption, then, is that the public/private boundary nonetheless remains meaningful in everyday life. But our understanding of the public/private boundary has not been prescriptive. The point of our research has been to ask people these questions: what makes up *their* public world? How are *they* connected to that world? And how are media involved, or not, in sustaining that connection to a public world (as they understand it)?

These are the questions we aimed to explore: first by asking a small group of 37 people across England to produce a diary for 3 months during 2004 that reflected on those questions; second by interviewing those diarists, both before and after their diary production, individually and in some cases also in focus groups; and finally by broadening out the themes from this necessarily small group to a nationwide survey (targeted at a sample of 1000 respondents) conducted in June 2005. The survey provided data on media consumption, attitudes to media and politics, and public actions, and also the contexts in which all of these occur.[21]

Our primary emphasis has been on obtaining multi-perspective data on citizens' reflexive sense of themselves as publicly connected, or otherwise, including some data produced without us as direct interlocutors (diaries). We have tried to register citizens' own stories of connection or disconnection, both explicit and implicit, while also through our survey contextualizing those very particular stories among broader nationwide patterns. In this paper, we explore the implications particularly of our qualitative data for understanding how, and under what conditions, a form of banal consumption (media use) might contribute, or not, to the preconditions of effective citizenship.

Mediated public connection as a 'dispersed practice'

We have introduced the term 'public connection' to capture a thread that may run through much of what we do in daily life: an orientation towards a public world beyond matters of purely private concern. We talk of 'mediated public connection' where that orientation is sustained principally by our practice of consuming media. 'Mediated public connection' (and 'public connection') is a 'practice' in the specific sense clarified recently in social theory; that is,

> a routine type of behaviour which consists of several elements, inter-connected to one another: forms of bodily activities, forms of mental activities, 'things' and their use, a background knowledge in the form of understanding, know-how, states of emotion and motivational knowledge.[22]

While a practice is made up of many heterogeneous elements, it is their routine interconnections, or articulations, *as* a practice that helps to structure social life itself.[23]

Practices may be ordered, according to Theodor Schatzki, in various ways and to different degrees.[24] Schatzki distinguishes usefully between '*dispersed* practices' (such as the general practice of 'describing', which is linked by shared understandings alone) and '*integrative* practices' (cooking or going swimming, which are held together also by 'explicit rules' and 'ends, projects and beliefs'). Given that media – and our media uses and their contexts – are so various (as are forms of public involvement), we would expect the object of our enquiry – mediated public connection – to be more like a dispersed practice than an integrative practice. Certainly it has no explicit rules although it may involve ends, projects and beliefs, that is motivating values. The concept of practice (particularly that of dispersed practices)[25] is impor-tant for mapping areas of life only partly codified in language, yet crucially connected as practice.[26]

We wanted to track evidence of an orientation towards a public world sustained through media consumption across the huge range of diarists' language, covering both accounts of daily practice and direct or indirect evidence of that practice. Here there is a similarity with Peter Dahlgren's recent reworking of Almond and Verba's original[27] notion of 'civic culture' in terms of a six-moment circuit of civic engagement:[28] values, affinity, knowledge, practices, identities and discussion. In a move that echoes T. H. Marshall's insistence on the multidimensional nature of citizenship, and its complex historical embeddedness, Dahlgren challenges the oversimplifications not only of Almond and Verba but also of the Habermasian public sphere ideal, which implies that formal public deliberation in itself is enough to ground effective democracy.[29] Civic culture for Dahlgren is neither a single attitude, nor even a set of attitudes, nor a unified cultural condition, but rather a six-point circuit or process in which causal influences may flow in more than one direction. 'Mediated public connection', although not specifically included in Dahlgren's circuit, is clearly relevant to it and itself is a complex practice, involving at least two dynamic components: media consumption and public orientation.

Because of this complexity we would not expect to find a single 'ideal type' of mediated public connection, and tracking the varieties of mediated public connection was a key part of our research. In fact there are more than two elements that potentially are articulated in the dispersed practice of 'mediated public connection': first, 'public orientation' breaks down into at least two types, an orientation to traditional politics and an orientation to a broader world of public issues; second, there are, as will be discussed shortly, negative and positive factors which may sustain or undermine either media consumption or public orientation; third, there are feedback loops which may sustain the links between media consumption and public orientation; and fourth, there are public actions (for example presiding as a magistrate, attending a school governors' meeting, going on a protest) which may in turn provide a context for further public connection.

Keeping up to date with news

How can we start to understand the processes which sustain or destabilize people's practice of orientating themselves towards a public world through media?

First, we found that the 'media consumption' component of mediated public connection is less likely to be destabilized than the 'public orientation' component. This is because the sources of media are varied and available across many linked formats, so people are normally able to establish over time what they consider to be a sufficient media flow; cases where levels of media access are disrupted suddenly (as when a school sixth-form diarist moved to university) are rare. But there are rather more factors which may affect 'public orientation':

whether *negatively* (factors such as specific political disillusionment, general alienation or lack of efficacy, or indeed a view of what matters in the public world which runs counter to dominant views, for example a principal emphasis on the arts or creativity) or *positively* (factors such as a family history of political practice, work-related opportunities to display knowledge about public issues, work that is directly affected by public issues, as well as particular grievances which provide an individual incentive to public action).

Second, feedback loops which stabilize *the link between* the two basic components of mediated public connection can be of different sorts: some social and processual (talking at work, or with friends, about what you have seen in media), some individual and value-based (having a sense that you should keep up with the news, indeed that you are the sort of person who does that). Clearly some overlap between the two types of feedback loop is possible. Here we want to concentrate on the way *values* can stabilize the practice of mediated public connection. Values may under certain circumstances serve as a 'bridge' between private and public worlds,[30] reinforcing links between habits of media consumption (essentially a matter of private choice) and a broader orientation to a world beyond the individual. Many diarists, both men and women, recognized a duty to keep up with the news; for example,

> Yeah, I've always felt that anyway that you need to know what's going on all over the world. If you can't, even though you can't always make a difference, but you try and do something and if you can't, just realise how lucky you are.
>
> (Kylie, 24, unemployed single mother, Inner City, South London)

The value of keeping up with news may be expressed, in negative form, through shock at *others* who lack that value:

> what I find quite astonishing really is that most people I know really just don't care about what's going on. They're focused on their own thing and as long as they know that David Beckham's had a new hair cut and that they can go and get it done at the salon just like this . . . they just carry on with stuff.
>
> (Josh, 23, architecture student, Northern suburb)

Importantly we found this value across classes, genders, age groups and types of media user.

This evidence of a duty to keep up with the news needs to be contextualized in two ways: first, in relation to possible shifts in media use following the normalization among some parts of the population of the Internet;[31] and second, in relation to how the 'public world' which diarists are concerned to track is understood.

On the first point, our diarist sample mirrored national trends in terms of *access* to different media: 57% of our diarists had some form of access to the Internet (in line with the national figure of 60% in October 2004).[32] Of these diarists, six had broadband access at home (16% of all diarists); this is also comparable with the then UK average for home broadband which in 2004 rose from 12% to 24% of all households.[33] The salience of the Internet for our diarists' news consumption, however, was much less than one might expect. Of 21 active Internet user diarists, 13 used it principally for *personal* information and only 8 (22% of overall sample) used it at all as a news source or site of debate; there was only one diarist (Josh, quoted above) for whom the Internet was the *principal* news source.[34] For our diarist sample the traditional media – television, radio and the press – were overwhelmingly the key means of sustaining mediated public connection. We are not of course pretending that this mix is immune from change and it may well be that the growth in home broadband will generate major changes in media habits. What remains unclear, however, is whether such possibly imminent changes will involve new and stable habits of *news consumption*, a point to which we return.

On the second point, we have tried to recognize throughout the *contestability* of the term 'public', which underlies people's sense of what counts as news. We mean more here than the important contrast between the public world as basically traditional politics and a more issue-based view of the public world (although our diarist sample provided more than one version of this contrast). Alternatively, someone might have a clear sense of engagement with a public world through media, but be oriented to something quite different from dominant definitions of 'public concern' (whether traditional politics or broader public issues). We were keen to register such alternative visions of the public world. One place to look, many would argue, is people with a strong engagement with celebrity culture and general media entertainment. We found plenty of evidence of such engagement with media as a 'collective' domain, but strikingly little evidence (even in diarists' own accounts) of how such engagement might be linked to public issues, even as broadly defined.

One apparent exception was our diarist Ross, a 25-year-old design student. His 12-week diary consistently covered only one subject, sport. Strikingly his diary account of sport shared language with dominant versions of the public world, for example the importance of arguing from facts and a sense of what is, and is not, an appropriate subject for that world:

This week the footballing world is again concentrating on matters that shouldn't be the main focus of sport ... I am slightly biased here because I support Arsenal but when you look at the facts I feel that I am being objective in my claims.

(Ross, 25, design student, Urban south)

This alternative definition of the public world must be respected but what is striking, again, is not its potential connection to other types of public issues but the lack of connection.

Satisfied distance

What of diarists who *lacked* the value of keeping up to date with a public world, the value of public connection? The evidence for this was generally only implicit, and against the background of the acknowledged dominant value:

> I read through the paper earlier and I read *the headlines* and I read *the first few bits* but and I know I should do, I always get told I should have more of an interest but I feel the people have such opinions of it and like I say, most stories are the government and things but it's something that's out of our hands. . . . I do tend to *go past* a lot of the stories.
>
>   (Andrea, 25, nurse, Midlands rural – added emphasis)

While Andrea did have some regularity to her news consumption habits, those habits were in part dependent on others (her male partner who brought home the daily newspaper from work; her parents who read the local paper and passed on information). Andrea justified her ability to maintain a distance from a public world in terms which suggest a group identification (of 'us' against a distant and unrepresentative 'them' in Westminster). This emerged generally and then when she commented on not getting involved in public action through her nursing union:

> Yeah, I think it [politics] just seems like it's a little bit of another world. You know, they're supposed to be making decisions on behalf of all of us but it doesn't generally seem that way. . . . it seems like we're a long way away from it . . .
>
> No don't get involved in things like that but if I did, I don't feel it would make any difference. Cause you know, there's a wider issue there you know, with money and the government and you know, all relating back to political issues.
>
>   (Andrea)

Paradoxically, she implies, it is the *presence* of a wider issue that encourages her to withdraw from action. This quasi-collective rationalization of distance from a public world clearly has complex roots in class, gender and the metropolitan domination of British politics.

It is quite distinct from the individualistic rationalization of public disconnection found in another diarist of similar age, Beccy. Beccy was 27, worked in marketing and lived in a comfortable northern suburb. She was also one of our most reflexive diarists and explored this issue on a number of occasions. She acknowledged that her attention to news was sporadic, but it was her self-defence that was most interesting:

> I think there's a hell of a lot of choice out there and I think … it's up to me to go and find out and be informed. … I think everybody would have their own line. My cynical friend would say that you know everybody should be obligated to know about politics and everybody should use their vote responsibly because he's really into that … Whereas me … I don't know where my line would be because I know I look at a lot celebrity news but that's not important and I wouldn't say people were obliged to know about that at all. But certain things in my head I think I should be obliged to know about I'm not.
>
> (Beccy)

Consumerist individualism, even if tinged with guilt, works here as an alternative 'value' that rationalizes the *separation* of media consumption from public orientation (note that she associated her friend's 'cynicism' with refusing that separation), while acknowledging in a vestigial way the dominant value of 'keeping up with the news' ('certain things in my head I think I should be obliged to know …'). Whether diarists' sense of the social expectation[35] associated with this dominant value led them to under-report this individualism to us is uncertain.

Also important here are the diarists we have called 'weakly connected' because they show a strong orientation *neither* to a media world *nor* to a public world independent of media. Here is one example:

> Some weeks I think I really don't know what's going on in the world and you make more of an effort to switch the news on and other weeks, you think, oh, I'm not really interested
>
> (Marie, 34, p/t accounts clerk, Midlands rural)

Strikingly the weakly connected diarists (of whom we had six) were very far from being social loners; indeed they were *more likely* to be oriented overall by family and social networks than by anything else (from work to the local civic sphere to individual values). This brings out that the reasons for disconnection are complex and not necessarily, taken in themselves, negative.

Long-term shifts?

Discussion about democratic (dis)engagement in political science has often proceeded without interest in the details of media consumption, and even when it has noticed media consumption, this has generally been in a minimal way, as in the post-Putnam debate (where to put it crudely, the claim has been as follows: watching a lot of TV is bad; reading a newspaper is generally good).

Our research has tried to offer a more nuanced account, through both the diary- and survey-based phases of our project, of how, and under what conditions, *particular types* of media consumption may make a difference to democratic engagement. This is not the place to elaborate on the detailed differences between particular types of media use. Instead we want to make three points about possible long-term shifts, before moving onto some wider disarticulations which shape what kind of difference media consumption can make.

First, a common error in considering how media affect the conditions of democratic engagement is to think about media technology in the abstract, not necessarily in a deterministic way but simply in a way that ignores the long-term nature of the processes by which media technologies get embedded in daily practice. This point was made forcibly in relation to television and early home computers in the 1980s and early 1990s,[36] but the point returns in a new form with the Internet. It is *habit*, and the possibility of *new habits* of public-oriented media consumption, that offers the best route into thinking about how online practice might change the possibilities of public connection. If Internet-related practices are to improve the general preconditions of democratic engagement, then Internet-related habits must be articulated in a stable way with habits of political socialization (whether the latter remain stable or are themselves changing).

Clearly there are some grounds for optimism here, expressed, for example, in a recent article by Tony Benn:

> A combination of satellite television stations, Google and Yahoo, laptops and mobile phones have made it possible for the public to get an understanding of what is going on that is totally different from what they are being told. That is how the World Social Forum has come into being.[37]

But the question is how representative such possibilities are of the general conditions under which people become oriented towards a public world, or not. While online resources clearly create possibilities of accelerated and enhanced mobilization, these possibilities must be set against not only the continued social stratification of Internet access and use, but against the highly individualized context in which online use is growing for most people most of the time. Here the overview of some of the most experienced of US Internet watchers is useful:

> Even with higher band width and richer format, this mode [the internet] does not fit well with the way people get politically socialized. Rather, it is our view that the internet is a form of syntopia – an extension of but still heavily integrated with other face-to-face and mediated channels and processes.[38]

In other words, the Internet is primarily a space where individuals can better link together the various things they need and want to do *as individuals*, but not a space through which individual actions become socialized in new ways, in spite of early optimists such as Howard Rheingold[39] who argued precisely that. Oscar Gandy put it more mordantly when he suggested that 'as a result of the aura of personalization that surrounds these new media, individuals may actually feel better about knowing less and less about the world around them'.[40]

Things are not of course entirely closed. Take the increasingly widespread practice (among those lucky enough to have relatively unregulated access to the web through their work computers) of web surfing during work breaks. Web surfing in the lunch hour can have many uses, as our diary data brought out. Some people (for example, our diarist Jonathan, a 23-year-old university administrator from a West London suburb) used it for news-gathering:

> Referred to the internet throughout the day (BBC/SKYNEWS) which had main stories on Oliver Letwin's new policy of cutting tax and public spending. Still hear echoing stories of WMD, Iraq and Hutton
>
> (diary, 16 February 2004)

Others (including Beccy, already quoted) used the Internet to gather information for social diversion (for example celebrity news or music magazine websites: ananova or nme.com). Can we imagine any policy shifts that might encourage the first type of Internet use so that new social habits of online news consumption emerge that can replace the old but, perhaps, demographically threatened habits of watching the TV news or reading the daily newspaper? Perhaps we cannot yet, but our point is that it is the balance of such media *habits*, and their articulation (or not) with wider habits of *political socialization*, on which policy-makers need to focus. In other words, media technologies only become effectively embedded in practices of political socialization when the practices that articulate one to the other become banal, taken-for-granted; hence the importance of practice theory in analysing this process. We return to this point later.

A second key point concerns the scale on which the apparent disruptions to public connection are occurring. Touraine poses the general issue very powerfully, but he frames it only as a conflict between global media/cultural flows and local sites of (in)action. But we would like to question whether the 'global' is as automatically salient for everyone as Touraine implies. Certainly one of our diarists, Kylie (a 24-year-old unemployed single mother living in an inner city council estate in South London), exhibited vividly the clash between, on the one hand, very limited local possibilities of action – she tried and failed to get neighbours to sign a petition for a local childcare group – and, on the other hand, an intense emotional involvement in 'distant suffering'[41] on a global scale, suffering about which she knew she had no possibilities of acting effectively at all.[42] But the more general picture emerging from our survey (Table 7.1) was that when people were asked to name an

Table 7.1   Would you describe this issue (the one you named) as local, national or international? (%)

	Gender		Age			SES		All
	Male	Female	18–34	35–54	55+	ABC1	C2DE	
Local	12	11	11	12	12	10	13	12
National	46	48	46	45	50	48	46	47
International	41	36	39	41	35	39	36	38

Note: Base $N = 789$.

issue that had been of importance to them over the past 3 months and then say how they categorized that issue, the largest group (47%) described the issue they had mentioned as a national issue, with 38% saying it was an international issue and only 12% saying it was a local issue.[43] This suggests not only that the international, in news terms, at least, remains outweighed by national issues, but that there is a gap different from Touraine's between the scale on which people can act (still local) and the types of issues they follow (rarely local, but not necessarily global either).

This may, however – our third point – simply illustrate that international comparison is here essential. While the issue of disengagement from democratic politics is almost universal among 'mature' democracies,[44] including the problem (if that is what it is)[45] of falling trust in politicians, the dynamics of engagement may vary greatly between countries.

The picture now emerging from the US project that is twinned with ours[46] is very different. That study found evidence of much greater salience for Internet use among the US diarists: many moved easily between old and new media to get the information they needed, admittedly in the intense context of a highly contested presidential election in November 2004. The US diarists also appeared to have a stronger sense of having a local context for taking civic action, with religious organisations (almost entirely absent in our UK study) important here. This takes us to the wider context in which mediated public connection matters.

Wider disarticulations

Even if our diarists had mediated public connection (as we call it), and even if this was stabilized by socially reinforced values (the value of 'keeping up to date') or by everyday social talk, that does not mean they were any closer to becoming active in the public world. People's public dis/connection is separate from, and its consequences more broadly shaped by, wider *disarticulations* of a supra-individual or structural nature. These are the gaps between talk and action, and between individuals' interest in civic action and their possibilities of, indeed disengagement from, political action.[47]

First, on *talk*, our evidence was that most of our diarists had opportunities to talk about public issues (our survey data pointed to a similar conclusion). There were, as is well known, some social constraints on talking about politics and serious public issues, particularly at work and on social occasions. However, many people talked about enjoying a debate, although there was a small minority of diarists who did appear to be constrained by not having friends or family willing to discuss public issues with them at any length (Jonathan was one of them). But in thinking about the wider context in which diarists' public connection operates, restrictions on talk were not decisive. More important, and more surprising to us, was *the almost complete absence of a connection between diarists' reports of talk and any reports of action*. In fact, we found only one case of discussion leading to action: our diarist Christine (a 46-year-old business events coordinator from a Northern suburb), who mentioned talking to her friends at a party about the lack of local recycling, and then jointly lobbying the council to start local recycling collections.

This is certainly not because most of our diarists lacked opinions on things where action might be taken, or were apathetic; nor, on the whole, were they reluctant to share opinions socially and subject them to disagreement. Indeed, many diarists reported having been involved at some time or other in at least low-level public actions. However, the fact remains that there is a near-complete absence of evidence in our data of talk leading directly (or, even, indirectly) to an associated active response, even though we met diarists on up to three occasions, and throughout expressed our interest in hearing about their everyday conversations linked to the issues they mentioned.

Clearly we are not suggesting talk and action are never linked! Indeed, the evidence of our survey complicates the picture.[48] A clear association emerged in our survey between having opportunities to talk about public issues and taking at least some action on that issue. When we put this alongside our diary data, we conclude that what our survey shows is that it is general opportunities for talk (and the conditions that sustain them) that are important in facilitating public connection. However, this is not the same as saying that talk is directly or necessarily articulated to action in the way that notions of 'deliberation' in political theory propose: such evidence was singularly lacking from our diary findings, and this absence remains significant, insofar as political science generally implies that public engagement, deliberation and practical involvement are very broadly, or should be, mutually reinforcing.[49] The lack in diarists' reported talk of a link to public action, that is, to direct involvement in the public world, supports Pattie *et al.*'s[50] suggestion that there is a decline in Britain's deliberative culture.

Other disarticulations arise when we turn to *action*. Once again there is no space to discuss what types of action our diarists took, but most had taken at least some limited public action at some point, although only a small minority had done anything that involved coordination with others. It is worth noting in passing that we did not find consumer-type action particularly prominent among our diarists: perhaps the most striking cases were Christine's initiative against the local lack of a recycling service and three diarists' decision to stop buying the *Daily Mirror* in protest against its notorious front-page use of staged photos of alleged abuse of Iraqi prisoners by British soldiers.[51] We want, however, to concentrate on two other points.

First, we found almost no cases where diarists appeared to recognize *in their local situation* a supportive context for public action.[52] The only clear exception was, again, Christine, who likewise was the only diarist with an explicit philosophy of activism and a belief in the importance of getting involved; a diarist who had once been an exception was Patrick, previously a councillor (although he was now disenchanted with local politics). This absence of the local as an action-context in our UK study contrasts sharply with the evidence emerging from the linked Illinois study where a local civic context was present for many diarists. We can only speculate as to the reasons, but we cannot believe it has no link to the long-term war of attrition by central government against local government in the United Kingdom in recent decades.[53]

Second, we found evidence of a gap between some diarists' civic activism (which was strong) and their cynicism about its possible linkage to the world of politics and policy-making. Particularly interesting here is the perspective of Edward (a 64-year-old retired chief executive of a financial services company living in a wealthy Northern suburb). Edward, from a position of privilege, was one of the most civically active of our diarists, serving as a local magistrate in his retirement.[54] Leaving aside his all-too-typical cynicism about politicians, his concern was that the *active experience* of him and others 'on the ground' in an area crucial to government policy (penal policy) was not taken into account in the formulation of government policy:

> [government's] all a top thing – it's not at the bottom at all. The reality at the bottom is still totally different. You still have the courts clogged up with police witnesses who have to wait forever in court for cases which don't go through for one reason or another. . . . You'll probably never see all of this, of course: nobody does. But it happens all the time. But that's of no concern to politicians. What the politicians are concerned with is that very top layer of presentation through the media of one sort or another to the public.
>
> (Edward)

The disjuncture here is not between an individual and a distant public world, but between an individual who *is already* civically active and the public world of government. If those who are engaged and active fail to see a wider public context in which their practice has meaning and value, then there is, potentially, a major problem.

A similar gap between existing practices of, or potential for, civic engagement and clear political disengagement has recently been noted by the report of the UK commission chaired by Dame Helena Kennedy QC.[55] Their recommendations include greater citizen involvement in policy deliberation and implementation.[56] Whether such recommendations can succeed, even if taken up by government, is uncertain but the report's value lies in addressing the fracturing of the wider context in which democratic engagement (like mediated public connection) can be sustained. Again, as noted in the previous section, this UK crisis must be placed in comparative perspective. The parallel US study, carried out admittedly at a very different point in a particularly contested electoral cycle, found US diarists did generally have a context in which to act out their public engagement. Important differences would also, we suspect, emerge from European comparisons.[57] It is only through such comparisons that in the long-term we can grasp the subtle differences in how banal practices are articulated in different countries with very different histories of democratization.

Conclusion

Media consumption, we have argued, has for a long time occupied an ambiguous position in relation to the consumption/citizenship divide. We argued at the outset, first, that media comprise a distinctive type of consumption because of the double articulation they involve and, second, that media consumption has links both with citizenship or public engagement and with everyday non-political, non-civic pleasures. As a result, media do more than challenge the consumption/citizenship divide. Nor can media be understood if we force that divide into a 'consumer-citizen' or 'citizen-consumer' couplet. These ambiguities are inherent in media's contribution to contemporary societies,[58] and we have explored them in the realm of public engagement through our recent research. This has clarified how, by attention to the organization of everyday life – and the hidden articulations that link actions together into 'dispersed practices' – we can understand better the subtle role that 'ordinary' consumption plays in sustaining citizen engagement.

The consumer/citizen contrast, however, still has its uses, pointing to crucial dilemmas in an era when, first, our sense of where, and in what way, we 'belong' is troubled and, second, as our fieldwork has brought out, crucial contexts for public action are atrophied, at least in contemporary Britain: contexts of deliberation and contexts for effective citizen participation in policy generation. The consumer/citizen distinction reminds us of the only possible direction in which solutions to such uncertainties and fractures can be found; that is, by turning *towards* a broad notion of politics – wider than traditional politics but grounded still in a notion of publicness,[59] as the zone where issues that affect us in common are, or should be, addressed – and away from a narrow market-based vision of the 'consumer'. As with our diarist

Beccy, there is no difficulty in finding an individualistic rationalization of staying distant from a world of public issues, or expressing this in consumerist language. But such rationalizations ignore the key difference between politics and markets, as expressed by Jon Elster:

> The notion of consumer sovereignty is acceptable because, and to the extent that, the consumer chooses between courses of action that differ only in the way in which they affect him. In political choice situations, however, the citizen is asked to express his preference over states that also differ in the way in which they affect other people ... This suggests that the principles of the forum must differ from those of the market.[60]

While he oversimplifies what is at stake in consumption, Elster at the same time expresses a fundamental point. Of course consumption practices may generate many issues for the 'forum', but they do so on condition that their status is transformed from matters of purely individual concern to actions relevant to all of us as members of a shared public world where shared but limited resources are at stake. 'Public', as Josh, one of our diarists, put it, is 'anything that doesn't just involve one person.'

In sustaining such a distinction media consumption plays, we have argued, a vital role, but one we must keep always in context. Consider the wider explanation Beccy gave for her 'consumerist' solution to the quandary of public connection:

> You need to be able to turn the tv off, as awful as it is ... you do, in life you do have to do what you've got to do and if you've had a bad day at work you've got to do whatever ... it takes ... to make you go back there the next day.

There is a much wider space – not just the space of economic action but also the space where democratic possibilities are put into practice, or not, at work as well as at home – which shapes the meaning that following the world through media has.[61] If, as John Dewey argued, the idea of democracy, to be effective, must extend beyond interfaces with the state to include 'all modes of human association, the family, the school, industry, religion' then it is clear that media consumption, important though it is, can only be one part of the solution to contemporary citizenship's problems.[62]

8
The Moral Force of Consumption and Capitalism: Anti-slavery and Anti-sweatshop

Michele Micheletti

Introduction[1]

Can consumption and capitalism play a moral force globally? This chapter says yes. It uses historical scholarship on anti-slavery centuries ago and current research on the anti-sweatshop movement to show how consumption and capitalism can be morally charged to improve the lives of others. In making this argument, it also puts forward the idea that the contemporary anti-sweatshop movement is the moral equivalent of the anti-slavery movement. Historians view the anti-slavery movement as a landmark, something new in history, and 'outstanding development of a general humanitarian movement'[2] that formed an important part of '[a]n unprecedented wave of humanitarian reform sentiment [including such citizenship rights' movements as women's suffrage] that swept through the societies of Western Europe, England, and North America in the hundred years following 1750.'[3] Phrases like 'against all odds' and 'sea change of opinion' are used to signify the movement's uphill struggle in using common consumer goods to shift mentality on slavery.[4] Scholars who investigate the anti-sweatshop movement consider it to have a transformative air about it,[5] yet they have not explicitly drawn the parallel between it and the anti-slavery movement.[6] Activists evoke the word 'slave' – chocolate slaves, fruit slaves, and slave labor – in their rhetoric to condemn corporate policies and practices and to get citizens to think twice about their consumer preferences and choices. Another interesting parallel discussed in this chapter is the important role of capitalism for both the movements.

This chapter is organized in four sections. The first section shows how and why capitalism can be a moral force and, therefore, is, in certain circumstances, vital for humanitarian movements. It uses historic scholarship on anti-slavery, new conceptualizations of political responsibility, and contemporary ideas about anti-sweatshop institutional designing to make this point. The second and third sections discuss the anti-slavery and anti-sweatshop movements respectively. They emphasize the commonalities between the movements regarding their communication of values, reliance on capitalism, appeals to consumers, and use of the marketplace as an arena of citizen's political action. The concluding section discusses why common consumer goods are important objects for humanitarianism and can, therefore, be important for shaping and deepening citizenship.

Capitalism as hotbed of humanitarianism

Historians agree that the rise of capitalism was a trigger or hotbed for value change, value practice, and a new sense of political responsibility on the practice of slavery. They debate fiercely why this is the case. Some historians argue that the rise of capitalism spurred on anti-slavery ideas and values through the medium of class interest.[7] For them, actors and class relations are the pertinent aspect of capitalism triggering value change hostile to slavery.[8] Others find capitalist market logic as most significant because it forced a new understanding of causation and responsibility on market actors. Both positions indicate how capitalism can, in certain circumstances, kindle thinking about responsibility for the treatment of workers in the production apparatus.

The social actor perspective provides two important insights. First, the economic changes associated with the rise of capitalism 'caused a shift in values which in turn made slavery appear much worse.'[9] This shift involved an other-oriented, public virtuous perspective that included a general conviction that free labor is morally and economically superior to slave labor and that this belief should be a universal one, no matter how it affected private interests. Second, self-interested industrial workers as well as small Northern farmers in the United States feared and then opposed slavery's system of cheap labor because they could not compete with it without severe economic sacrifice.[10] Self-interested private virtues, in this case wanting to survive economically, spilled over and became other-oriented public virtue, in this case general opposition to slavery.[11]

For market-oriented historians, the important trigger is the cognitive style nurtured in capitalism. They show how capitalism taught a ' "widening of causal horizons" and heightened awareness of the remote consequences of both one's acts and (equally important in moral matters) one's inactions.'[12] New class society and older traditional society social actors used these developments as the basis – the hotbed – for humanitarian political action that dismantled slavery 'precisely at a time when capitalist ideas were in the ascendant, and large-scale production of all kinds of goods were beginning.'[13] For market transactions to work, market actors – production owners, traders, shopkeepers, consumers, and others – had to learn forethought, calculation, and gratification denial. This taught them two important lessons: promise-keeping and attention to the remote consequences of their actions.[14]

The inculcation of these norms dovetailed nicely with cultural trends in eighteenth-century Great Britain and spilled over into other spheres. Later they became the theoretical root of rational choice theory in economics and political science, the economic theory of democracy, and social exchange theory, and, as discussed below, are now used to formulate new conceptions of and institutions for political responsibility.

Insights from capitalism's role for the anti-slavery cause are the grounds for arguing that capitalism's social actors, preconditions, and market mechanisms are again functioning as a moral force and paving the way for social justice humanitarian sensibility in the new millennium. There are striking parallels between the rise of capitalism and the rise of global capitalism. The treatment of slaves in the eighteenth and nineteenth centuries and the treatment of workers in outsourced manufacturing in the 1990s and 2000s are not unsimiliar. Both groups of workers labored and labor under substandard working conditions and suffered and suffer from lack of human respect, denial of payment for work, and non-living wages.[15] No wonder that the words 'slave' and 'slavery' are evoked in the discourse of this millennium's humanitarian crusade against sweatshops. An important similarity between the times is the creation of new social actors from capitalism's and later global capitalism's rise and the focus on consumer goods as a tool in the struggle for social justice. Three significant new actors in the rise of global capitalism are the highly fickle (choosey) price-running consumer, the political consumer who uses her wallet as a political vote, and consumer-oriented (buyer-driven) transnational corporations, or what is now being called 'globally integrated enterprises' (GIE), whose thinking and practice is less defined by state borders and who fashion their strategy, management, and operations in pursuit of a new goal: 'the integration of production and value delivery worldwide.'[16] Another common characteristic is the mobilization of workers on the basis of self-interests to fight against capitalist reliance on cheap labor to provide Western consumers with affordable goods. Slavery made cane sugar affordable, thus moving it from a luxury item to one purchased and consumed almost daily. Sweatshop labor in the global garment industry does the same by offering Western consumers a variety of clothing styles and fashion at affordable prices.[17] Also, like the self-interested farmers and industrial workers in anti-slavery times, in the late 1990s North American unions and their members protested against garment manufacturers' decision to close their US plants and outsource their manufacturing to developing countries as a way of cutting costs to make clothing even more affordable. These and others developments show clear similarities between slave trade and free trade.

The lessons that market actors learned in the rise of capitalism have developed to fit changing capitalist conditions. They have been used and tuned repeatedly to fit the times. In industrial society, promise-keeping and responsibility were fitted to the consumer market in the form of consumer rights and protection against unfair and deceptive corporate market practices. For decades now, legislation in varying degrees in Western and other nations requires corporations to provide consumers with information on their products about ingredients, safety, using and washing instructions, and country-of-origin label.[18] False advertising is also generally prohibited. Currently, these market exchange prerequisites give consumers and consumer-oriented actors a hook to hold corporations accountable for their sweatshop policies, practices, and products and to broaden both the consumer and the corporate causal horizon of responsibility for wrongdoings in global manufacturing. Examples of reactions to corporate promise-breaking include publicity campaigns, consumer mobilization, boycotts, buycotts, and lawsuits against corporate giants for falsely advertising their corporate social responsibility. The anti-sweatshop movement has found broken responsibility promises in corporate social responsibility reports, codes of conduct, and commercial advertisements.[19]

Global garment corporations are sensitive to this kind of organized consumer humanitarianism. This is the case because the rise of the global capitalist market makes these new buyer-driven market actors highly vulnerable to anti-sweatshop criticism. Market restructuring in the form of buyer-driven commodity chains and lean retailing means that they must survive in increasing competitive consumer settings and respond rapidly to changing consumer demands for what the large transnational corporation H & M has advertised as 'fashion and quality at the best price.'[20] To do this, buyer-driven corporations rising from global capitalism invest huge resources in their corporate identity (logotype, image, and culture) to create lifestyle choices for fickle, price-running consumers (who also have risen from global capitalism) and, thereby, increasingly put themselves into the hands of political consumers and consumer-oriented movements, which have been formed and revitalized in global capitalism.[21] They must rapidly create and satisfy fluctuating and fickle consumer taste for affordable clothing that reproduce their images, values, and lifestyle settings. Their promise to deliver their image-made current fashion and quality (including a good material product as well as an imagined feeling of identity and community) at the best price forces them to rely on the sewing hands of individual garment workers rather than garment-making machinery. This puts buyer-driven transnational garment corporations in a bind: 'The catch is that the more successful corporations have become at branding our culture and creating a certain reputation for themselves, the more vulnerable they are to disruptions of that image through exposés linking their products to sweatshop conditions.'[22]

Transnational garment corporations are, thus, in a social justice trap. Buyer-driven corporate promise-making to consumers and their consumer-dependence gives the evermore encompassing anti-sweatshop movement opportunities to use the rise of global corporate capitalism to infuse consumer choice with social justice humanitarian sensibility. For buyer-driven garment corporations, the only way out of their sweatshop woes is to concede to anti-sweatshop demands. Global clothing and shoe corporations – like slave-driven production centuries ago – have boxed themselves into a humanitarian sensibility corner. The diverse social actors forming the encompassing anti-sweatshop movement are winning because they use market logic to force social responsibility on market actors.

Capitalist market logic also appears in scholarly efforts to end sweatshops. Social justice and workplace-related wrongdoings in the global garment industry trigger a new conception of political responsibility. Some writers focus on the role of competitive incentives in transnational power and bargaining relations for taming corporate globalization.[23] Others like the late political philosopher Iris Marion Young have pondered sweatshop woes and the anti-sweatshop movement to fuel her social connection model of global political responsibility. She stood on the shoulders of political philosophers (Arendt, Rawls, and others) and used their thinking to formulate the connections between universalizing social justice and establishing responsibility for wrongdoings in corporate policy and practice. Her moral argument is that Western consumers and corporate actors – democratic citizens – have obligations of justice to garment and other workers because of the social processes and connections (the consumer goods and economic transactions) tying them together to distant others (the workers sewing our clothes, building our shoes, weaving our rugs, picking our food, and providing us with other products).[24] In Young's words, 'Our actions are conditioned by and contribute to institutions that affect distant others.... Because our actions assume these others as condition for our own actions,...we have made practical moral commitments to them by virtue of our actions. That is, even when we are not conscious of or actively deny a moral relationship to these other people,...we have obligations of justice in relation to them.'[25]

The use of capitalist logic to broaden causal horizons to build the new millennium's social justice humanitarian sensibility does not stop here. In applied political science, scholars take capitalist logic as their explicit point of departure to design institutions to rid the world of sweatshops. Ratcheting Labor Standards (RLS) is one such idea about 'how open competition can save ethical sourcing.'[26] RLS has four basic principles – transparency, competitive comparison, continuous improvement, and sanctions – that are reminiscent of the norms generated from the rise of capitalism. RLS involves all market actors – corporations, retailers, consumers, and stakeholders like labor unions, consumption-oriented groups, and economic journalists – and develops ongoing corporate commitment (promise-keeping) to social responsibility and corporations' promise-making to review their ethical practices in internal reports and external audits. It then asks corporations to take a natural step (a ratchet up) and commit themselves to implementation strategies and documentation of implementation practice. The institutional designers see their work as creating both a competitive market and a driving force for anti-sweatshop humanitarian sensibility. The linchpin is corporate competition over market share and the need to protect reputations and safeguard logotypes under conditions of fierce competition over choosey, fickle, and brand-sensitive consumers. This is said to create an innovative market spiral with the following components: corporations strive for superior social practices; monitoring firms seek to establish themselves by excelling in auditing skill and experience; and monitoring data informs increasingly sovereign consumers about the sweatshop politics of products. Thus, continuous social justice improvement is the natural (market logical) step from competitive comparison because market actors are, by nature, motivated to increase their market share and profitability.

Anti-slavery movement

Anti-slavery scholarship reveals that old and new social actors creatively used the hotbed of capitalism for their social justice project. The heterogeneous actors forming the anti-slavery movement – different Christian churches, former slaves, women suffragists, liberals, socialists, pacifists, workers, farmers, political parties, individual consumers, and others – first needed to raise consciousness before they could call boycotts and sell anti-slavery goods. The reason is obvious. Anti-slavery was 'unthinkable until a tremendous task of altering people's views of reality had been accomplished,' which depended 'upon reaching the hearts and minds of vast number of people.'[27] Anti-slavery activists managed to show and convince a sufficient number of people that they were morally connected with distant others, that is the slaves hidden in the production of common consumer goods. The key was 'moral suasion' or what we today would term 'communicative political action' in the form of consciousness-raising and opinion formation. Some movement actors, as the Quakers who started and sustained the crusade, were ingenious political communicative activists. As early as the 1600s, traveling abolitionist Quaker ministers stumped anti-slavery in their existing communications network, which previously generated both social and financial capital in their communities.[28] This fusion of the public and private was an ideal setting to ready Quakers and the new social actors formed in the rise of capitalism for an anti-slavery mentality, political culture, and consumer lifestyle.

Today we would slot the anti-slavery movement as a consumer-oriented transnational advocacy network, which used lifestyle politics, deliberation to change and shape values as well as a repertoire of conventional and unconventional methods to boomerang their political cause about human rights on governments and other politically charged institutions.[29] Anti-slavery activists distributed pamphlets, gave public lectures, published official declarations, petitioned and lobbied government, interrogated political candidates, engaged in civil disobedience, raids, and legal battles, and used the retail market – the nexus between production and consumption – as an arena for politics.[30]

Moral suasion also entailed confronting individuals directly with the immorality of slavery by bringing slave reality into their everyday settings. The aim was to bring the distance up close. From our contemporary horizon, this consciousness-raising and value change task seems insurmountable without the mass information technology of photographs, television, and most importantly the Internet. Yet anti-slavery activists were innovative in their use of moral logic and moral chocks 'that triggered personal transformations and motivated bold collective action.'[31] The moral logic was that slavery was a sin, and for religious people abolition was personal redemption; they were blessed with the mission of converting slaves to Christianity, a mission which post-colonial historians view as Christian and racist hegemonic action.[32] Moral shocks took the form of life stories and novels (e.g., *Uncle Tom's Cabin*); common consumer goods (primarily sugar, tea, and cotton) formed the lens for ordinary people to understand tangibly (see, feel, taste, and wear) how their daily lives were connected with and responsible for slavery. The new 'world of print,' speeches, and book tours offered people who had direct experience with slavery venues to tell their life stories (in today's anti-sweatshop vocabulary testimonials) of fear, flogging, hunger, slave-women raping, and Christian hypocrisy. They gave slavery a human face; two examples are Olaudah Equiano (1789) and Frederick Douglass (1845). Other publicists, appealing to younger generations, wrote books that told the story of slave children separated from their parents and mistreated by their masters. Moral shocks created moral outrage and an urgency for the anti-slavery cause that mobilized hundreds of thousands of Anglophones.[33]

To confront ordinary people with slavery in other ways, activists even grafted anti-slavery onto popular culture, where it resonated well with the times. Popular tunes were given anti-slavery lyrics; anti-slavery became 'startling and quotable language'[34] and was pictorially represented on handicraft goods and in newspapers and broadsides. Possibly what may be considered as the world's first culture jam[35] (see Plate 8.1) occurred in this struggle, when abolitionist poet John Greenleaf Whittier changed the message of 'S.S.' (slave stealer, a common admonishing label) to 'Salvation to the Slave' in his poem 'The Branded Hand.'[36] These examples of discursive political consumerism are the forerunners of anti-sweatshop campaign buttons, slogans, apparel, songs, and culture jamming. More confrontational movement actors spiced up abolition by creating spectacular events. Publicist William Lloyd Garrison publicly burned the American constitution and called on people in the northern slave-free states to boycott voting because the constitution was 'a covenant with death and an agreement with hell.'[37] Over time, it became increasingly difficult for people to avoid the slavery issue in their everyday activities. Distant slaves became a very near and personal moral issue for pondering and action.

Plate 8.1 'The Branded Hand,' Philadelphia, *ca.* 1845
Source: African American Odyssey, Library of Congress, John G. Whittier.

Once awareness of the cause had begun to establish itself, activists also asked people to act as political consumers, that is boycott slave-made consumer goods and infuse their consumer choices with anti-slavery values. They used the market mechanism of supply and demand to press for change. Boycotts of selected slave-grown consumer goods were called to give ordinary people the chance to take personal responsibility for humanity. As has been documented in more contemporary boycotts,[38] dissatisfaction with government led citizens to use their consumer power for market-based political action. The British Parliament's rejection of an abolition bill in 1792 triggered a large consumer boycott of slave goods that mobilized between 300,000 and 500,000 British consumers.[39] Anti-slavery shopkeepers even made a point of advertising that they sold no-slave sugar 'produced by the labour of freemen,' and, thereby, encouraged consumers to use their wallets politically and 'buycott' for social justice. A poet stressed the responsibility of ordinary consumers for slavery by labeling tea 'the blood-sweetened beverage.' The private was fused with the public, and as later repeated time and again in history, women came out in force. Interestingly, here we also see a flicker of self-interest, as women learned from the anti-slavery movement's vocabulary to articulate awareness of their own oppression. Later in the early 1900s, food boycotts by women in the United States, Sweden, and elsewhere would also promote women's political agency in ways that did not always meet with the satisfaction of husbands and the male-dominated labor movement and communist party.[40]

Capitalists who were sympathetic with the cause found that they could profit from it. They began manufacturing and marketing anti-slavery goods for the burgeoning consumer market 'at a time when social emulation and emulative spending already had a powerful hold over the lives of many middle-class men and women.'[41] Middle-class people with sentiments against slavery purchased the British Wedgwood medallion 'Am I not a Man and Brother' grafted on the already fashionable cameo jewelry available on the consumer market and a variety of anti-slavery tokens, medals, jugs, plates, dinner services, artifacts, satirical prints, paintings, and printed images. Anti-slavery businessmen commercially exploited the growing abolition sentiment in Britain that was held by people wanting to play a part by shopping for justice. Their efforts fit well with the growing commercialization of politics that began in eighteenth-century Britain[42] and illustrate how grand political projects must mobilize a variety of actors with diversified motives and action repertoires in order to gain strength and become successful.

Anti-slavery was innovative politics for its day. Scholars call the movement's activities ingenious and sophisticated.[43] Over time, it changed the social meaning of slavery and functioned as a role model for other struggles for political and human rights. Slavery proponents at the time reacted viciously to the movement's successes by orchestrating riots against the anti-slavery press and leaders in the Northern states. They also desperately tried to bring the public more in line with self-interest by proclaiming that sugar abstinence (a popular form of boycotts at the time) was unhealthy. The British government officially abolished slavery in 1833 and the United States in 1865. Anti-slavery's moral and market suasion showed that it had teeth to persuade governments to enact progressive legislation.

Anti-sweatshop movement

Like the anti-slavery cause, the anti-sweatshop movement has its roots in both other-oriented public interest and self-interested private virtues. For the other-oriented Third World solidarity movement, the cause was fair trade to promote and empower Third World industry and actors. The alternative trade movement began in the 1950s with Third World stores (presently called worldshops) selling goods and now fair trade labeled goods produced in developing countries. For self-interested unions and particularly North American ones in the 1960s and 1970s, the problem was domestic unemployment caused by textile and shoe factory moves to low-wage Third World countries. Initially the union movement's focus was purely protectionism, which had led critics of fair trade to question the general motives underlying the movement.[44] By the new millennium, old civic society's trade unions, international humanitarian groups, and religious communities had teamed up with new civil society's student, women's, environment, and global social justice and fair trade groups in a moral stance against sweatshops in the global garment industry. This heterogeneous movement protests the same kind of problems as anti-slavery, which in contemporary language is termed 'dangerous working conditions,' 'non-living wages,' 'forced overtime,' 'child labor,' 'sexual harassment,' and 'corporate neglect.' Their general goal is sweatshop abolition, meaning the promotion of unionization, decent work, worker empowerment, fair globalization, and trade justice in the global garment industry and, more recently, every consumer-oriented productive area that deny workers human rights and a living wage.[45]

All movement actors exert effort to make consumers, the global public, governments at different territorial levels, and corporations aware of the sweatshop politics of apparel and now all kinds of sweat-made consumer goods generally. Like the anti-slavery movement centuries ago, they are multi-targeted in character. They ask people to pressure all levels of government and particularly transnational corporations and retail marketers to end sweatshop practices. Their focus on market mechanisms and use of moral logic and moral shocks in their activities aims at changing the social meaning of fashionable and affordable apparel. Like anti-slavery, it too turns to the market because governments have not been able to provide a proper solution to sweatshop problems. However, unlike anti-slavery, it has no current hope in local, regional, national, or supra-national governmental regulatory policy making. The reason is the absence of a proper governmental venue, due to the strong forces of corporate globalization and weak ones of political globalization.[46] Its early use of consumer boycotts and present use of new market-based regulatory tools (labeling schemes, codes of conduct, and monitoring institutions) show how capitalist market mechanisms are used to create rule-making and this millennium's social justice humanitarian sensibility.

As with the anti-slavery movement, it began its crusade by morally persuading the public about the wrongness of sweatshops. Activists from religious communities, universities, unions, international humanitarian groups, newly created anti-sweatshop consumer-oriented groups, corporate watchdogs, and an array of other civil society groups used and continue to use moral shocks to open the eyes of Western consumers, citizens, corporations, and governments to the moral wrongs of sweatshops and their responsibility to sweatshop workers. Its efforts are numerous and varied in character. Different anti-sweatshop groups have scandalized transnational apparel corporations with public revelations and reports of child labor, workers killed in factory fires, bad wages, unfair treatment, gender discrimination, and general transnational corporate neglect. Movement fact-finding missions, slick publications, political cartooning, cultural resonating techniques, comic books, street theater, spin doctored Internet communication, publicized sweatshop workers' testimonials and organized tours in Western consumer society, and direct confrontations with transnational apparel corporations have brought and continue to bring sweatshop problems closer to home. As illustrated in Plate 8.2, culture-resonating tactics – focus on well-known brand names, humor, new song lyrics for Christmas carols, celebrity endorsement, holiday campaigns like Santa's toy sweatshop and Fair Trade Valentine's Day Action Kit, culture jamming, anti-sweatshop personal political apparel ('T-shirt activism'), alternative fashion shows, and so on – show how private consumer choice is hooked up with global social justice. Consumers are asked to feel, see, and wear the bad treatment of workers in domestic and foreign garment-

Culture jams of the Nike Corporation that uses the word "slave" to
urge consumers to see the connection between popular affordable
fashion and corporate sweatshop practices.

Plate 8.2 'End Slave Labor'
Source: Designer Joe Biel, Microcosm Publishing, 1990.

making sweatshops and to compare this treatment with the image that global
garment corporations create for their products with the help of their marketing strategies. In particular, the movement takes advantage of the Internet to
show the plight of garment workers in clickable videos, mobilize support for
urgent sweatshop alerts, offer DIY-toolkits for individualized collective
action, sell anti-sweatshop goods, and discuss sweatshop solutions.

Again, universities, students, higher education, and the urban consuming
middle class play a central role. Although anti-slavery scholarship generally
points out that individuals belonging to these groups are a privileged few
with both economic and intellectual means of empowerment, their role in
humanitarian movements, as witnessed by the anti-sweatshop cause, should
not be dismissed on these grounds as insignificant or less worthy. Outraged
university students have held sit-ins, engaged in civil disobedience, demonstrated against university contracts with transnational garment corporations,
and demanded that university officials add sweat-free clauses to their procurement policy and agreements for sportswear for their athletes and on their
logoed wear that they sell profitably to the general consuming public.
Moreover, these students created their own movement organization,
United Students Against Sweatshops (USAS), considered to have started a
new student movement, and which for years now is a central anti-sweatshop
player with good ties to North American trade unions and even US-based
global garment corporations.[47] Religious groups (again including the
Quakers) have disrupted shareholder meetings with anti-sweatshop resolu-
tions. Soccer moms joined their high-school daughters in noisy demonstrations outside retail stores. More traditional, professional associations for
safeguarding workers' and human rights have learned how to put bite in
their moral message by focusing on celebrity logo owners and, thus, using
cultural resonance to publicize their anti-sweatshop messages.[48] Union members in North America have mobilized against domestic and increasingly
global sweatshops, thus complementing at least in part their protectionist
motivation with an other-oriented one for opposing corporate globalization's
outsourced manufacturing practices. Anti-sweatshop groups quickly respond
to abridgments of universal workers' rights in urgent e-mail alerts and call on

consumers to mobilize against sweatshop practices in e-mails to corporate leaders, questions to retailers, and other discursive political consumerist activities.

Like heterogeneous anti-slavery, which disagreed about whether ending the slave trade or abolition (i.e., ending slavery *and* freeing slaves) was its main goal and had different motives for supporting the cause, the diversified groups forming the anti-sweatshop movement argue about the proper remedy to rid the world of sweatshops. For some, global agreements and unionization of garment workers are *the* answer.[49] For others, what are needed are independently monitored corporate codes of conduct that follow universal guidelines formulated by the International Labor Organization.[50] A third group growing in number competes with mainstream corporations by selling no-sweat apparel.[51] They want to show that companies can make a profit without using sweatshops. Anti-sweatshop activists dropped the idea of a labeling scheme for no-sweat clothes as a solution because of the complexity in the global garment industry. At first, most groups supported consumer boycotts, but now they generally view them as doing more harm than good for garment workers.[52] As all transnational garment corporations now have codes of conduct (a development which is a victory for the movement), anti-sweatshop actors monitor their promise-keeping and level of ambition and implementation like a hawk.

Today discursive political consumerism dominates as an anti-sweatshop tactic. It gives preeminence to communication (opinion formation, dialogue, deliberation, negotiation, and culture jamming) to convince corporations, consumers, and others that they have moral obligations of justice to the distant others whose sweat lies behind our consumer goods.[53] Clean clothes groups worldwide use attention-gathering global events to rub in their message. They have, for instance and reminiscent of anti-slavery's spectacular US constitution-burning event, threatened to burn publicly newly released corporate social responsibility reports unless corporations acquiesce to more movement demands.[54] Interestingly, the two examples of spectacular events (use of a national constitution respective corporate social responsibility report) also show clearly the differences in political settings during the rise of capitalism (the nation-state) and the rise of global capitalism (the global market). Anti-sweatshop activists also use popular global sporting events to communicate their message. Examples include actions in association with the World Cup of Football and the 'Fair Play at the Olympics' campaign, which publicized 'the real cost of the game' and garment workers' need of a sporting chance to make a decent wage and live a decent life.[55]

Today the word 'sweatshop' is a well-known part of contemporary vocabulary with over 3 million hits in an early March 2006 Google search. Garment corporations are forced to relate to it; politicians talk about it; social justice groups have it as their master frame; new sweat-free companies use it to market worker-friendly apparel; pollsters put it in their surveys; cartoonists create comic strips around; and in 1 year in the late 1990s over 700 articles published in the *New York Times* included it.[56] The word resonates well culturally: Jay Leno joked on the Tonight Show on a hot Southern Californian summer day in 1998 that 'It's so hot out I'm sweating like a 10-year-old Malaysian kid in a Nike Factory.' Quite remarkably, MIT-media lab master's student Jonah Peretti started his celebrity career in contagious media when his 2001 culture jamming 'Nike Email Exchange' traveled rapidly through e-mail inboxes to an estimated 11–12 million people globally.[57] He used the innovative prize-winning buyer-driven Nike iD web site specially created for customized and personalized online consumer marketing[58] to order a pair of customized shoes with the word 'sweatshop' on them. When Nike repeatedly refused his request, he wrote back with the culture jam that used Nike's image-making slogan in an anti-sweatshop way: 'Your web site advertises that the NIKE iD program is "about freedom to choose and freedom to express who you are." I share Nike's love of freedom and personal expression. . . . My personal iD was offered as a small token of appreciation for the sweatshop workers poised to help me realize my vision. I hope that you will value my freedom of expression and reconsider your decision to reject my order.' The consorted efforts of the anti-sweatshop movement are changing the social meaning of fashionable and affordable clothes and, therefore, step-by-step changing global garment corporations. They use capitalist logic and corporate vulnerabilities to make consumers increasingly conscious about the hidden politics – the slave-like treatment of global garment workers – behind clothing labels and fashionable affordable apparel.

Shaping good citizens through consumption, capitalism, and consumer goods

The anti-slavery cause developed into an encompassing humanitarian movement that included a diverse array of individuals, civil society groups, and networks. To gain successes in its social justice work, it used the new market logic of capitalism and called on the new social actors of capitalism to make slavery the antithesis of contemporary times. Scholarship on anti-slavery shows how slavery went against basic norms (laws) of capitalism on promise-keeping, forethought, and the economic incentive relationship between work and ownership. Interestingly, Adam Smith, the eighteenth century's important economic thinker, condemned slavery and slave trade as unnatural economic practice because they opposed his basic law of human motivation, namely people work to acquire private property.[59] Scholarship also clearly shows how anti-slavery wove together a variety of different and, at times, competing or contradictory reasons for opposing slavery, including enlightenment thought, desires to Christianize slaves, workers' protectionism, pure moral stances about the value of all human life, venues for women's political action, spillover effects from the cognitive style nurtured in capitalism, political and social mobility, and crass self-interested econom-ics.[60] That the movement was built on the mobilization of people from different walks of life and representing a mixture of personal motives does not surprise scholars of politics and social movements. Nor should one be alarmed by the fact that the movement did not stamp out slavery completely, that anti-slavery sentiment did not necessarily imply a stance against racism, and that all the reasons for engaging in anti-slavery were not morally clean and publicly virtuous . Most grand movements are constructed in this way. As research on political compromises convincingly shows, grand political work that binds actors together in long-term political projects for change is based on the tugging, pulling, and exchange of interests as well as the interaction of morally and morally dubious motives to find sufficient common ground for widespread collective agreement. It would be naively utopian to think other-wise.[61] As put by American progressive political activist Saul Alinsky, 'the only time you stand up in righteous moral indignation is when it serves your purpose.'[62] The challenge for movements is to find ways to convince ordinary citizens that humanitarianism serves *their* particular purposes.

Today another grand and encompassing humanitarian movement is show-ing its head. Corporate globalization, a new rise in capitalism, has generated a platform for anti-sweatshop social justice humanitarian sensibility. Actually, anti-sweatshop is not completely new. Crusaders in early industrial society mobilized support to eradicate domestic sweatshops with the help of labor unions, consumer actions, at least one market-based labeling scheme, and governmental regulatory legislation.[63] Today corporate globalization has made the focus on government action an unrealistic alternative. Instead, the contemporary movement uses production and consumption (unions, worker- and consumer-oriented organizations, transnational networks, glo-bal consumer society, and the new social roles of fickle price-running con-sumers with shopping money to spare, political consumers, and vulnerable buyer-driven corporate brands) to bring home the message that there are global injustices and violations of universal workers' and human rights involved with reliance on sweatshops to produce common consumer goods. The cause is crafted with the help of a variety of motives – with some more publicly and others more privately virtuous, and a third kind represent-ing tactical awareness of this window of opportunity to change economic power relations and move societal positions forward. A crucial motivational argument that calls on everyone (worker, corporation, consumer, investor, and stakeholder) is the ties, bonds, obligations, and responsibilities created in market transactions. The practice of capitalist consumption builds this move-ment that asks everyone who shops (or wants to do so) to broaden their causal horizon of personal responsibility and become agents of justice.[64] Thus, the global consumer market – just like the capitalistic market of centuries ago – has hatched a new wave of humanitarian sensibility. Perhaps further research will answer an important finding from this study, namely why it is the case that capitalism's formative moments, as illustrated by the rise of capitalism and the rise of corporate globalization, make capitalist actors particularly receptive to humanitarian sensibilities.

Anti-slavery and anti-sweatshop show clearly that consumer goods can, in certain settings, become an everyday tool of citizenship. For centuries now, consumer goods have played a vital role in struggles for minority group rights, civil rights, workers' rights, and social justice. They have also been an important venue for women's political participation. Citizens have been called on to boycott tea, sugar, coffee, buses, grapes, fruit, shoes, wine, computers, tourism, corporations as well as other goods and services. They have used consumer boycotts to send political messages about environmental and human rights violations to foreign governments.[65] As institutional or collective consumers, even governments, civil society associations, and corporations are encouraged to, and in fact at times support, buycotts by reforming their procurement policies to include environmental and social justice purchasing criteria and values. The fusion of citizenship and consumption has even reached the electoral arena. Supporters of the Democratic Party frustrated with the outcome of the US presidential election in 2000 and 2004 created the political consumerist network 'BuyBlue.org' that asks citizens to 'put their money where their mouth is' and impact society positively by voting with their wallets, which means 'supporting businesses that abide by sustainability, workers' rights, environmental standards, and corporate transparency' and boycotting others without these values and which offer economic support to politicians deemed inappropriate for democratic office.[66] Citizens also team up in networks with social movements, policy-makers, think tanks, corporations, scholars, and others to develop market-based regulatory schemes that use economic transactions as their base for binding citizenship to the capitalist commodity chain of foreign production, transnational corporations, and consumption. Eco-labels, organic labels, fair trade labels, marine and forest stewardship certification as well as joint efforts to create independent monitoring institutions against garment sweatshops are examples of how citizens use consumption and capitalism to initiate incremental change in corporate policy and practice.[67] Discursive political consumerism complements consumer boycotts and buycotts by using brand names as a lens to communicate the obligations of justice embedded in the production – consumption commodity chain of attractive value-ladden, image-making, lifestyle-oriented consumer goods.[68]

This chapter used the anti-slavery and anti-sweatshop causes to show how market transactions can teach obligations of justice. This is a form of citizenship or civic education. Consumer goods are a good pedagogic object to put the social connections of market transactions directly in the hands of citizens. This education sensitizes citizens to the hidden politics of products and shows them numerous opportunities to use supermarkets, shopping malls, the Internet, and e-commerce to broaden the causal horizon of their personal

responsibility for others.[69] All categories of citizens up and down the commodity chain from the everyday shopper to citizen representatives, procurement officers, and corporate citizens are included in this educative program
to learn to see the hidden social and environmental costs of Western products
in a global perspective. Some citizens decide not to care about these connections; others just think about them; a growing number take action in a variety
of ways. When thinking and acting, they engage in cross-border exchanges
and dialogue on the relationship between capitalist production and consumption, environmentalism, and social justice.[70] Working on the social
justice and environmental problems associated with consumption practices
is an important way for citizens to activate themselves to engage in individualized and collective efforts to manage and (hopefully) contribute to a
solution to consumer-related global crises and contradictions. Thinking
about and acting on how we relate, purchase, and use consumer goods is
thinking about and acting out our responsibilities to fellow citizens locally
and globally and for future generations of citizens both near and far. Learning
about capitalism's mechanisms and consumer goods has probably always
been citizenship education. Yet it seems that this form of civic education
takes on special significance in certain settings and under certain circumstances. Anti-slavery and anti-sweatshop are two instances when citizenship
and consumption fuse into political responsibility-taking for the footprints
left by developments in capitalism and consumer cultures.

Part 3
Prospects

9

Exit *Homo Politicus*, Enter *Homo Consumens*

Zygmunt Bauman

Symptoms abound and multiply of the slackening public interest in the officially recognized paraphernalia of democracy (indeed, in all its acknowledged principal mechanisms): falling participation in elections and referendums, shrinking membership of established political parties, or rising ignorance of the issues on the political agenda and of the persons claiming the right and the will to articulate and resolve them.

In Britain, the facts speak for themselves. It is worth recalling that in 1997, New Labour was backed by only 31% of those qualified to vote. Voter turnout at this election was the lowest since 1945. 'The 1997 general election excited less interest than any other in living memory', as the authors of a Nuffield College study of this event concluded. Even the highly hyped public relations campaign surrounding devolution in Scotland and Wales failed to engage the public's interest. Voter participation in these 'history-making' elections in 1999 indicated that the public regarded it as yet another stage-managed event. The majority of the Welsh electorate stayed at home – only 46% of them bothered to vote. In Scotland, a high-profile media campaign, designed to promote voter participation, led to a 59% turnout. On the same day, polling booths in England attracted only 29% of registered voters for the 6th May local elections. The June 1999 UK elections to the European Parliament represented an all-time record low. Only 23% turned out to vote. In one polling station in Sunderland, only 15 people turned up out of the 1000 entitled to vote.[1]

A very recent survey, conducted at the start of the 2005 electoral campaign, suggests that 'contrary to popular perception the British public is not apathetic about politics. That is the conclusion of a new report from the Electoral Commission and the Hansard Society, which found that 77 per cent of those polled by MORI were interested in national issues.' It immediately adds, however, that 'this high level of basic interest is compared to the minority 27 per cent who feel that they actually have a say in the way the country is run.'[2]

Judging from the precedents, one could surmise that the actual number of people going to the electoral booths would fall somewhere between those two figures and come perhaps closer to the lower of the two. Many more people declare their interest in whatever has been vetted in public as a 'national issue', than consider it worth the effort of walking to the polling station in order to give their vote to one of the competing political parties. Furthermore, in a society oversaturated with information, headlines serve mostly to efface from public memory the headlines of the day before; the issues which the headlines recast as 'public interests' can only claim the most ephemeral life-span and have but a meagre chance to survive from the date of the opinion poll to the date of the election. Most importantly, the two things – the interest in national issues and the participation in the extant democratic process – just do not congeal in the minds of the rising number of citizens. The second does not seem to be a relevant response to the first. Perhaps it is considered altogether politically irrelevant.

The 'Guardian Student' website of 23 March 2004 informed us that 'three quarters (77 per cent) of first-year university students are not interested in taking part in political protests ... while 67 per cent of freshers believe that student protest isn't effective and doesn't make any difference, according to the Lloyds TSB/*Financial Mail on Sunday* Student Panel.' It quotes Jenny Little, editor of the student page in the *Financial Mail on Sunday*, who says,

> Students today must cope with a great deal – the pressure to get a good degree, the need to work part-time to support themselves and to get work experience to ensure that their CVs stand out from the crowd ... [and let me add: managing their swiftly rising debts – ZB]. It's not surprising that politics falls to the bottom of the pile of priorities for this generation, though, in real terms, it has never been more important.

In a recent study dedicated to the phenomenon of political apathy,[3] Tom Deluca suggests that apathy is not an issue in its own right, but 'more a clue about the others, about how free we are, how much power we really have, what we can fairly be held responsible for, whether we are being well served ... It implies a condition under which one suffers'.

Political apathy 'is a state of mind or a political fate brought about by forces, structures, institutions, or elite manipulation over which one has little control and perhaps little knowledge.

Deluca explores all those factors in depth to paint a realistic portrait of what he calls 'the second face of political apathy' – the 'first face' being, according to various political scientists, an expression of contentment with the state of affairs or exercise of right to free choice, and more generally (as stated in the classic 1954 study by Bernard Berelson, Paul Lazarsfeld and William McPhee, later rehashed by Samuel Huntington, and obliquely opted for by Anthony Giddens, welcoming the advent of 'consumer activism') as a phenomenon that is 'good for democracy' for the reason of 'making mass democracy work'.[4]

And yet if one wants to decode in full the social realities to which rising political apathy provides a clue and which it signals, one would need to look further still than that 'second face' which Deluca rightly claims to have been unduly neglected or only perfunctorily sketched by the mainstream scholars of political science. One would need to recall also a few other factors: first, the power rapidly evaporating from the state-centred political institution into the no-man's land of supra-national 'global space'; second, the subsidiarizing of a growing part of politics once administered by the state into the individually run and serviced 'life politics'; and third, the 'outsourcing'of a rising section of life-relevant functions from the state to the consumer markets. The meeting of power and politics in the offices of the nation state (the only meeting point allowed in the era of territorial sovereignty) interpellated the residents of the state realm as citizens. The splitting of the power-politics union and the resulting impoverishment of the no-longer sovereign nation state of both power and politics, as well as the takeover of most relevant life-servicing functions by the markets, cast the residents as consumers first and foremost.

The void left behind by citizens massively retreating from the extant political battlefields is, to the acclaim of some enthusiastic observers of new trends, filled by ostentatiously non-partisan and altogether un-political 'consumer activism'. This, however (contrary to the enthusiasm with which it has been greeted by some observers eager to theorize it into a new revolutionary breakthrough in democratic participation), engages a yet smaller part of the electorate than can be mobilized in the heat of election campaigns by the orthodox political parties (who are no longer trusted to represent their voters' interests and so are fast falling out of public favour). Frank Furedi warns, 'Consumer activism thrives in the condition of apathy and social disengagement. Consumer activists regard their campaigns as a superior alternative to parliamentary democracy. Their attitude to political participation expresses a strong anti-democratic ethos.'[5] It needs to be seen clearly that the consumerist critique of representative democracy is fundamentally an anti-democratic one. It is based on the premise that unelected individuals who possess a lofty moral purpose have a greater right to act on the public's behalf than politicians elected through an imperfect political process. Environmentalist campaigners, who derive their mandate from a self-selected network of advocacy groups, represent a far narrower constituency than an elected politician. Judging by its record, the response of consumer activism to the genuine problem of democratic accountability is to avoid it altogether in favour of opting for interest group lobbying.

'There is little doubt that the growth of consumer activism is bound up with the decline of traditional forms of political participation and social engagement': such is Furedi's verdict based on his thoroughly documented study.[6] 'Consumer activism' is a symptom of the growing disenchantment with politics. To quote Mark Lawson, 'as there is nothing else to fall back on it is likely that people then give up on the whole notion of collectivism and therefore any sense of a democratic society and fall back on the market (and, let me add, their own consumer skills and activities) as the arbiter of provision'.[7]

And yet quite a few writers, for example Thomas Frank, the editor of the Chicago *Baffler*, note the spectacular rise of 'market populism' in the United States since the beginning of the 1990s.[8] Markets, the story goes, convey more faithfully what democracy is ultimately about: human choices. As the representation of popular choice, markets are spot on and can be trusted; and they could be relied on as well to deliver what people demand. Since that is the case, any interference with the markets cannot but be an assault against democracy and a step towards tyranny. Markets are 'naturally' democratic – and in order to perform their democratic job best they need to be free from political supervision and immune to all 'extraneous' (that is, political) regulation. In a bizarre reversal of the views that informed and guided the efforts to expand political democracy through most of the modern era, 'market populism' proclaims politics to be the 'public enemy number one' of democracy, and the market to be democracy's best friend and most reliable (if not the sole) support.

What market populists gloss over are the devastating social consequences of uncurbed and uncorrected market activity: the fact that markets are the prime factories of social inequality. For great numbers of people, clustered towards the bottom of the social pyramid, this means precisely a denial of their 'consumer rights', a drastic cut in options, dwindling choice, and in the end the nebulousness of freedoms even if they have been formally granted; while for the majority it spells the prospects of a perpetually insecure life haunted by an uncertain future. Democracy was conceived and promoted precisely as a means of countering these and other negative effects of unrestrained markets, and in its fully fledged form came close to succeeding in that.

Market populists are also uniquely 'economical with truth' when it comes to locating the enemies of the consumers' freedom. They cast them all, fairly and squarely, in the camp of politics, whereas the sins of the market are absolved before they are confessed. Admittedly, the market is not unique in loading dices, manipulating human choices, and, above all, limiting them in advance to the range defined by its own, not the customers' preferences; politics, with good reason, may be charged with similar misdeeds. But in its struggle to recast humans as consumers, first and foremost, and to strip them of all alternative or complementary social qualities and entanglements (and so of any means to compensate for the harm suffered in the sole dimension in which they are called/allowed to operate, let alone to prevent such harm being done), the market reveals itself as a past master of social disqualification.

The production of consumers is one of the most wasteful industries on record. Quality control is strict and merciless; rejection is swift, with sharply reduced chances of rehabilitation; and the ranks of the condemned – of flawed consumers or consumer invalids – swell with every successive advance of the market. As to the volume of insecurity to which players are exposed, the market game has no equals – while democracy, let us recall, was advanced by people seeking remedy for the horrors and fears of insecurity, and was kept on course by people craving to join the ranks of the happy ones who had already managed to obtain it.

Mindful of such criticism, other writers suggest that, in addition to (or alongside) consumer activism, other alternative, unorthodox yet even more promising instruments have become available, and are increasingly deployed to replace the inept and unreliable political tools formerly used by state and political parties in their pursuit of democratic objectives. They vest their hope of democratic renaissance in the Internet.

Many academics have greeted the Internet and World Wide Web as the wondrous alternative and replacement for a fading political democracy more enthusiastically and less critically than they did the market. Nor is this surprising when one considers that virtual space has become the natural habitat of the current and aspiring members of the knowledge classes: of those for whom, to quote Thomas Frank, 'politics becomes in the first place an exercise in individual auto-therapy, an individual accomplishment, not an effort aimed at the construction of a movement' – a means to inform the world of their own virtues, as documented by iconoclastic messages stuck to car windows or by ostentatious displays of conspicuously 'ethical' consumption. Theorizing of the Internet as the new and improved form of politics, of World Wide Web surfing as a new and more effective form of political engagement, and of the accelerated connection to the Internet and rising speed of surfing as advances in democracy look suspiciously like so many glosses on the evermore common life practices of the knowledge-class, and above all on their keen concern with an honourable discharge from the 'politics of the real'.

Like all other consumer products, Internet-produced and Internet-stored information is well in excess of the consumer's capacity to absorb and digest, not to mention make use of, it. As Ignazio Ramonet points out, during the last 30 years more information has been produced in the world than during the previous 5000 years, while 'a single copy of the Sunday edition of the *New York Times* contains more information than a cultivated person in the eighteenth century would consume during a lifetime'.[9] Just how difficult, nay impossible, to absorb and assimilate, and so endemically wasteful, such a volume of information is one can glean from Eriksen's observation that 'more than a half of all published journal articles in the social sciences are never quoted', and many articles are never read by anyone except the 'anonymous peer reviewers' and copy editors.[10] It is anyone's guess how small a fraction of the articles' contents ever manages to find its way into social-science discourse.

'There is far too much information around', Eriksen concludes.[11] 'A crucial skill in the information society consists in protecting oneself against the 99.99 per cent of the information offered that one does not want.' We may say that the line separating meaningful message (the ostensible object of communication) from background noise (its acknowledged adversary and obstacle) has all but disappeared. In a cut-throat competition for the scarcest of scarce resources – that is, the attention of would-be consumers – the suppliers of would-be consumer goods desperately search for the scraps of consumers' time still lying fallow. The tiniest gaps between moments of consumption need to be found that could hopefully still be stuffed with more information. Perhaps in the course of their desperate searches for the bits of information they need, some section of those at the receiving end of the communication channel would come by chance across the bits which they do not need yet the suppliers wish them to absorb; and perhaps they would be sufficiently impressed to pause or slow down to absorb them rather than the bits they sought. Picking up fragments of the noise and converting them into a meaningful message is by and large a random process. 'Hypes' – those products of the public relations (PR) industry meant to separate 'desirable objects of attention' from the non-productive (read: unprofitable) noise (like the full-page commercials announcing a premiere of a new film, launching of a new book, the broadcasting of a TV show heavily subscribed by the advertisers, or an opening of a new exhibition) – serve to divert for a moment, channel and condense in one direction, the continuous and desperate yet scattered search for 'filters'. They focus attention, for a few minutes or a few days, on a selected object of consuming desire.

All the more resounding for that reason is Jodi Dean's blunt verdict that the present-day communication technologies are 'profoundly depoliticizing', that 'communication functions fetishistically today: as a disavowal of a more fundamental political disempowerment or castration', that the technological fetish is

> 'political' ... enabling us to go about the rest of our lives relieved of the guilt that we might not be doing our part and secure in the belief that we are after all informed, engaged citizens ... We don't have to assume political responsibility because ... the technology is doing it for us ... (It) lets us think that all we need is to universalize a particular technology and then we will have a democratic or reconciled social order.[12]

Reality stands in stark opposition to its sanguine and cheerful portrait painted by the 'communication fetishists'. The powerful flow of information is not a confluent of the river of democracy, but an insatiable intake intercepting its contents and channelling them away into magnificently huge, yet stale and stagnant artificial lakes. The more powerful that flow is, the greater the threat of the river bed drying up.

The world servers store information so that the new liquid-modern culture can substitute forgetting for learning as its major driving force; and they suck in and store the imprints of dissent and protest so that liquid-modern politics can roll on unaffected and unabated, substituting sound bites and photo opportunities for confrontation and argument. The currents flowing away from the river are not easily reversed and returned to the river bed: there might be many factors that allowed Bush and Blair to go to war under false pretences, but the *dearth* of websites calling their bluff was not among them.

As far as 'real politics' is concerned, on its way towards electronic warehouses dissent is sterilized, defused, and made irrelevant. Those who stir waters in the storage lakes may congratulate themselves for their fitness-testifying verve and sprightliness, yet those in the corridors of real power are hardly forced to pay attention and can only be grateful to state-of-the-art communication technology for siphoning off their potential troubles and dismantling the barricades erected on their way before they had time to settle.

Real politics and virtual politics run in opposite directions, and the distance between them grows as the self-sufficiency of each benefits from the absence of the other's company. The age of simulacra did not cancel the difference between genuine stuff and its reflection, between real and virtual realities; it only dug a precipice between them – virtually easy, but in reality increasingly difficult, to bridge.

It seems there is as yet no viable substitute for the extant mechanisms of political participation and democracy. At any rate, consumer markets and communication technologies look quite unpromising as serious contenders for that role. They are symptoms of withdrawal from public engagement and, simultaneously, of the massive loss of faith in the effectiveness of public action and the responsibility for the state of public life. They are, to put it bluntly, the signs of the citizen's retreat.

The secret of every durable, that is successfully self-reproducing, social system is the recasting of its 'functional prerequisites' into the behavioural motives of its actors. To put it a different way, the secret of all successful 'socialization' is forcing/persuading/cajoling the individual actors to *wish to do* what the system *needs them to be doing* in order to self-reproduce and persist over time. This may be done directly and explicitly, mustering approval and active support for the system's brand, as with the 'state' or 'nation' in the 'solid' phase of modernity, in the 'society of producers' – through a continuous campaign variously dubbed 'spiritual mobilization', 'civic education', 'ideological indoctrination', 'defence of values', or, sometimes, 'brain washing'. Or it may be done obliquely and implicitly, through the training or drilling of individual actors in certain behavioural patterns, including those of problem-solving. Once these patterns are observed (and they must be because of the gradual erosion of alternative choices and of the skills needed to practice them) and recast into no-longer-reflected-upon habits, they come to sustain and reproduce the system – as is the usual mode in the 'liquid' phase of modernity in the society of consumers.

The tying together of 'systemic prerequisites' and individual motives, typical of the society of producers, required the devaluation of the 'now'; particularly, of the pursuit of immediate satisfaction and, more generally, of enjoyment (or rather of what the French mean by the virtually untranslatable concept of *jouissance*). By the same token, that tying together had also necessarily to enthrone the precept of procrastination or 'deferred gratification' – to endorse the sacrifice, that is, of specific present rewards in the name of imprecise future benefits, as well as the sacrifice of individual rewards for the future benefit and well-being of the 'whole' collective (be it society, state, nation, class, gender, or just a deliberately under-specified 'we'). In a society of producers, the 'long term' is given priority over the 'short term', and the needs of the 'whole' over the needs of its 'parts'. Likewise, the joys and satisfactions derived from 'eternal' and 'supra-individual' values are cast as superior to the fleeting individual raptures, while the happiness of a greater number is put above the plight of a smaller one, and are lauded as the only genuine and worthy satisfactions amidst the multitude of seductive, but false, contrived, deceptive, and ultimately degrading 'pleasures of the moment'.

Wise after the fact, we (men and women whose life is conducted in the liquid-modern setting) are inclined to dismiss that way of dovetailing systemic reproduction with individual motivations as wasteful, exorbitantly costly, and, above all, abominably oppressive since going against the grain of 'natural' human proclivity and propensity. Sigmund Freud was one of the first thinkers to note this fact.[13] Gathering his data, however, as he had to from a life lived on the rising slope of the society of mass industry and mass conscription, even he – despite his lively imagination – was unable to conceive of an alternative to the coercive suppression of instincts. He thus subscribed to what he observed to be the generic status of necessary and unavoidable features of all and any civilization – of civilization 'as such'.

The demand for instinctual renunciation would not, Freud concluded, be willingly embraced. The majority of humans, he wrote, would obey many of the cultural prohibitions (or precepts) 'only under the pressure of external coercion' – and 'it is alarming to think of the enormous amount of coercion that will inevitably be required' to promote, instil, and make safe such necessary civilizing choices as that of a work ethic (that is, a wholesale condemnation of leisure coupled with the commandment to work for work's sake whatever the material rewards), or the ethics of peaceful, nay friendly, cohabitation proposed by the commandment 'Thou shalt love thy neighbour as thyself.' ('What is the point of a precept enunciated with so much solemnity', Freud asks rhetorically, 'if its fulfilment cannot be recommended as reasonable?') The rest of Freud's case is too well known to be restated here in any detail: civilization must be sustained by repression, and repeated rebellions – as well as the continuous struggle to contain or pre-empt them – are inescapable. Dissent and mutiny cannot be avoided since all civilization means constraint and all constraint is repulsive. Freud thus argues that replacement of the power of the individual by the power of the community constitutes the decisive step of civilization. The essence of it lies in the fact that members of the community restrict themselves in their possibilities of satisfaction, whereas the individual knew no such restriction.

Let us leave aside the caveat that 'the individual' who is not already a 'member of community' may be a yet more mythical figure than Hobbes' pre-social savage of the *bellum omnium contra omnes*, or just a rhetorical device deployed 'for the sake of an argument', like the 'original patricide' that would crop up in Freud's later work. For whichever reason the particular wording of the message was chosen, the substance of the message is that putting the interests of a supra-individual group above individual inclinations and impulses, or placing long-term effects above immediate satisfactions in the case of work ethics, is unlikely to be willingly acknowledged, embraced, and obeyed by the *hoi polloi*, and that civilization (or, for that matter, human peaceful and cooperative cohabitation, with all its benefits) must rest therefore on coercion, or at least on a realistic threat that coercion would be applied were the restrictions imposed on instinctual urges not punctiliously observed. By whatever means, the 'reality principle' must be assured an upper hand over the 'pleasure principle' if civilized human togetherness is to persist.

Freud re-projects that conclusion on all types of human togetherness (retrospectively re-named 'civilizations'), presenting it as a universal law of life in society. But whatever answer is given to the question of whether or not the repression of instincts was indeed coterminous with the history of humanity, one can credibly suggest that it could have been discovered, named, put on record, and theorized upon only at the dawn of the modern era; more to the point, only following the disintegration of the *ancien régime* that immediately preceded it. It was that disintegration, the falling apart of customary institutions, that sustained a by-and-large monotonous reproduction of *Rechts*- and *Pflichts-Gewohnenheiten*; that laid bare the human-made artifice hiding behind the idea of the 'natural' or 'Divine' order, and so forced a reclassification of that order as one that was no longer 'given' but a task to be undertaken; in other words, that recategorized the '*logic* of *Divine* creation' as an *achievement* of *human* power. The point here, then, is that although prior to the advent of the modern era there was equally ample room for coercion, there was no space for the self-assured and prosaic manner in which Jeremy Bentham managed to assimilate obedience to the law with a confinement so restrictive that it left no choice other than work or death. 'Power of community' did not have to *replace* 'the power of the individual' to make cohabitation feasible and viable; power of community was in place long before its necessity, let alone its urgency, was discovered. Indeed, the idea that such replacement was a task, to be performed by one or another (collective or individual) power holder, would hardly occur to either 'the individual' or 'the community' as long as that was the case. Community, as it were, held power over the individual (a total, all-encompassing kind of power) as long as it remained *un-problematical*, and not a task that (as all tasks) could be fulfilled or left undone. To put it in a nutshell, the community held individuals in its grip as long as it remained *unaware* of 'being a community'.

Turning the subordination of individual powers to those of a 'community' into a 'need' waiting 'to be met' reversed the logic of modern development; though, at the same time, by 'naturalizing' what was in fact a historical process, it instantly created its legitimation and the etiological myth of an aggregate of free-floating, solitary individuals who once upon a time came to be transmogrified, through civilizing effort, into a 'community' claiming the authority to repress any individual impulse found contrary to the requirements of secure cohabitation.

Community might be as old as humanity, but the idea of 'community' as a *sine qua non* of humanity could be born only together with the experience of its crisis. That idea was patched from the fears emanating from the disintegration of the self-reproducing social settings retrospectively called *ancien régime* and subsequently recorded in social-scientific vocabulary under the name of 'traditional society'. The *modern* 'civilizing process' (the only process calling itself by that name) was triggered by the state of uncertainty occasioned, so it was suggested, by the falling apart and impotence of 'community'.

'Nation', that eminently modern innovation, was visualized in the likeness of 'community': it was to be a new community, community writ large, community-by-design, community made to the measure of the newly extended network of human interdependencies and exchanges. What was given the name of the 'civilizing process' later, at the time when the developments to which that name referred were fast grinding to a halt or apparently going into reverse, was an ongoing attempt to re-regularize or re-pattern human conduct no longer subjected to the homogenizing pressures of self-reproducing pre-modern institutions. Ostensibly, that process was focused on individuals: the new capacity of self-control (and, more generally, self-constraint) by newly autonomous *individuals* was to take over the job done before by the no-longer available *social* controls and coercive constraints. But the genuine stake of the bid was the deployment of the self-controlling capacity of individuals in the service of re-enacting or re-constituting 'community' at a higher level. Just as the ghost of the lost Roman Empire hovered over the self-constitution of feudal Europe, that of lost community was a spectral presence at the constitution of modern nations. Nation-building was to be accomplished through the use of patriotism – an induced (taught/ learned) readiness to sacrifice individual interests to the interests shared with other individuals ready to do the same – as its principal raw material. As Ernest Renan famously summed up that strategy, nation is (or rather can only live by) the daily plebiscite of its members.

Setting about restoring historicity to Freud's a-temporal model of civilization, Norbert Elias explained the birth of the modern self (that awareness of one's own 'inner truth' coupled with responsibility for its self-assertion) by the *internalization* of *external* constraints and their pressures. The nation-building process was inscribed in the space extending between supra-individual panop-tical powers and the individual capacity to accommodate the necessities which those powers set in place. The newly acquired individual *freedom of choice* (including the choice of self-identity), resulting from the unprecedented under-determination of social placement caused by the demise or radical weakening of traditional bonds, was to be deployed, paradoxically, in the service of the *suppression of choices* deemed detrimental to the 'new totality': the community-like nation state.

Whatever its pragmatic merits, the Panopticon-style, 'discipline, punish, and rule' way of achieving the needed/intended manipulation/routinization of behavioural probabilities was cumbersome, costly, and conflict-ridden. It was also inconvenient, and surely not the best choice for the power holders, as it imposed severe and non-negotiable constraints on their own freedom of manoeuvre. It was not, however, the sole strategy through which systemic stability, better known as 'social order', could be achieved and made secure. Having identified 'civilization' with a centralized system of coercion and indoctrination (later reduced, under Michel Foucault's influence, to its coer-cive wing), social scientists were left with little choice except, misleadingly, to describe the advent of the 'post-modern condition' (that coincided with the entrenchment of the society of consumers) as a product of a 'de-civilizing process'. What in fact happened, though, was the discovery, invention, or emergence of an alternative method of manipulating the behavioural prob-abilities necessary to sustain the system of domination recognized as social order. This method was less cumbersome, less costly, and relatively less conflict-ridden, but above all it provided more freedom, and so more power, to the power holders. Another, and apparently more convenient, way of promoting the 'civilizing process' was found and set in place.

This new variety, practised by the liquid-modern society of consumers, arouses little, if any, dissent, resistance, or rebellion as it re-presents the *obligation* to choose as *freedom* of choice. By the same token, it overrides the opposition between 'pleasure' and 'reality' principles. Submission to stern demands of reality may be lived through as an exercise of freedom, and indeed as an act of self-assertion. Punitive pressure, if applied, is seldom naked; it comes disguised as the result of a false step or lost (overlooked) opportunity. Far from revealing the limits of individual freedom, it hides them yet more securely by obliquely retrenching individual choice in its role as the main, perhaps even the only, 'difference that makes a difference between victory and defeat' in the individual pursuit of happiness.

The 'totality' to which the individual should stay loyal and obedient is no longer experienced as a denial of individual autonomy. Nor does it require obligatory sacrifice of the kind demanded by universal conscription and the duty to lay down one's life for the national cause. Instead, it takes the form of highly entertaining, invariably pleasurable and relished festivals of commu-nal togetherness and belonging, held on the occasion of a football world cup or a cricket test. Surrender to the 'totality' is no longer a reluctantly embraced, cumbersome, and often-onerous duty but figures as 'patriotainment' – an avidly sought and eminently enjoyable revelry.

Carnivals, as Mikhail Bakhtin memorably suggested, tend to be interruptions in the daily routine: the brief exhilarating intervals between successive instalments of dull quotidianity; a pause in which the mundane hierarchy of values is temporarily reversed, the most harrowing aspects of reality are for a brief time suspended, and the kinds of conduct considered shameful and prohibited in 'normal' life are joyously and ostentatiously indulged. If it was the individual liberties denied in daily life that were ecstatically tasted during the old-style carnivals, now it is the burden and anguish of individuality that is thrown off through dissolution in a 'greater whole', willing to surrender its rule and submersion in the tides of indistinguishability. The function (and seductive power) of liquid-modern carnival lies in the momentary resuscitation of the sunk-in-coma togetherness. Such carnivals are *séances* during which people hold hands and summon the ghost of deceased community. Not an insignificant part of their charm is the awareness that the ghost will pay but a fleeting visit and will promptly go away when the *séance* is over.

It does not mean that the 'normal', weekday conduct of individuals has become random, un-patterned, and uncoordinated. It only means that the non-randomness, regularity, and coordination of individually undertaken actions can be, and as a rule are, attained by other means than the solid-modern contraptions of enforcement, policing, and chain of command deployed by a totality bidding to be 'greater than the sum of its parts' and bent on training/drilling its 'human units' into discipline.

In a liquid-modern society of consumers, *swarm* tends to replace the *group* – with its leaders, hierarchy of authority, and pecking order. Swarm can do without all those trappings and stratagems without which a group would neither be formed nor be able to survive. Swarms need not be burdened by the tools of survival; they assemble and disperse and gather again from one occasion to another, guided by shifting relevances and attracted by changing and moving targets. The seductive power of shifting targets is as a rule sufficient to coordinate their movements, making redundant all command or other enforcement 'from the top'. As a matter of fact, swarms do not have 'tops'; it is solely the direction of their current flight that casts some of the self-propelled swarm units into the position of 'leaders' to be 'followed' – though only for the duration of a particular flight, or a part of it.

Swarms are not teams; they know not of the division of labour. They are (unlike *bona fide* groups) no more than 'sums of their parts (self-propelled units)'. They can be visualized best as Warhol's endlessly replicated images with no original, or with an original discarded after use and impossible to trace. Theirs is but a 'mechanical solidarity' (to continue this revision of Durkheim), in which each unit, on its own, re-enacts the moves made by any other while performing the whole of the job, from beginning to end and in all its parts. (In the case of consuming swarms, the job so performed is the job of consuming.) Or one could compare the way in which coordination is achieved to Heidegger's *das Man* or Sartre's *l'on*. One would then, however, have to correct or complement their understanding of the solid, imperturbable, and overwhelming powers of the impersonal 'It' (a conception held prior to the 'liquification' of modernity) with that offered by Siegried Kracauer. A thinker ahead of his time – thanks to his gift for spotting the most inchoate, incipient, and prodromal symptoms of future trends – Kracauer noted that 'the term "climate of opinion" happily connotes the instability of opinions and their resemblance to the weather'.[14]

In a swarm, there are no specialists – no holders of separate (and scarce) skills and resources whose task would be to enable/assist other units to complete their jobs or to compensate for their individual shortcomings or incapacities. Each unit is a 'Jack of all trades', and needs the complete set of tools and skills necessary for the entire job to be fulfilled. In a swarm, there is no exchange, no cooperation, no complementarity – just the physical proximity and roughly coordinated direction of the current moves. In the case of the human, feeling/thinking units, the comfort of flying-in-swarm derives from the trust in *numbers*. This is the belief that the direction of flight has been properly chosen since an impressively large swarm follows it – the supposition that so many feeling/thinking humans could not be simultaneously fooled. As a means of providing self-assurance and a sense of security, the swarm is the next best (and no less effective) substitute for the authority of group leaders.

Swarms, unlike groups, know not of dissenters or rebels – only, so to speak, of 'deserters', 'blunderers', or 'maverick sheep'. The units that fall out from the main body in flight are just 'straying', 'lost', or 'fallen by the wayside'. They are bound to forage on their own – but the life of solitary mavericks is unlikely to last long, as the chance of their finding a realistic target on their own is much smaller than if they were to follow a swarm. And as they tend to pursue fanciful, useless, or dangerous targets, their risks of perishing multiply. The society of consumers tends to undermine group formation and to favour instead that of swarms. Consumption is a supremely solitary activity (perhaps even the archetype of solitude) – even when it happens to be conducted in company. No lasting bonds emerge in the activity of consumption. Such bonds, as they manage to be formed in the act of consumption, do not tend to outlast the act; they may keep the swarm units together for the duration of their flight (that is, until the next change of target), but are self-evidently short-lived, because bound by occasion, and in other respects thin and flimsy, having little bearing, if any, on the subsequent moves of the units and throwing scarcely any light on the units' past histories.

What kept the household members around the family table and allowed the latter to function as an instrument of integration and assertion of familial permanence and solidarity was in no small measure the *productive* element in consumption: the gathering at the dinner table was but the last (distributive) stage of a lengthy productive process that started in the kitchen and even beyond – in the family field or workshop. What bonded the diners into a group was the cooperation in the course of productive labour that preceded it, not the shared consumption of its results. We may suppose that the 'unintended consequence' of 'fast foods', 'takeaways', or 'TV dinners' (or perhaps rather their 'latent function' and the true cause of their fast-rising popularity) is either that they make the gatherings around the family table redundant – and so put an end to shared consumption – or that they symbolically endorse the ways in which commensality and communal consumption have been freed of their onerous bond-tying and reaffirming propensities, since these have become irrelevant or even undesirable in the liquid-modern society of consumers.

Consumer society promises to gratify human desires in a manner undreamt of by any other society in the past. But the promise of satisfaction remains seductive only as long as the desire stays *ungratified*; more importantly, as long as the client is not 'completely satisfied' – as long as the desires that motivate consumers to further consumerist experiments are not thought to have been truly and fully gratified. Just as the easily satisfied 'traditional worker', who wished to work no more than necessary to allow the habitual way of life to continue, was the nightmare of the budding 'society of producers', so the 'traditional consumer', guided by yesterday's familiar needs and immune to seduction, were she/he allowed to survive, would sound the death knell for a mature society of consumers, consumer industry, and consumer markets. Setting the targets low, assuring easy access to the goods that meet the targets, and believing in objective limits to 'genuine' and 'realistic' desires are precisely the major adversaries of consumer-oriented economy and are earmarked for extinction. It is the *non*-satisfaction of desires, and the firm and perpetual belief that each act of satisfaction *leaves much to be desired and can be bettered*, that are the flying-wheels of the consumer-targeted economy.

Consumer society thrives as long as it manages to render non-satisfaction (and so, in its own terms, unhappiness) permanent. One way of achieving such an effect is to denigrate and devalue consumer products shortly after they have been hyped into the universe of the consumers' desires. But another, yet more effective, way is more covert: this is the way of providing for every need/desire/ want in such fashion that it cannot but give birth to new needs/desires/wants. What starts as a need must end up as a compulsion or an addiction. And it succeeds in this all the better, the more the disposition to treat shopping as a panacea for all problems, pains, and anxieties is not only tolerated but actively encouraged and allowed to become habitual. But there is yet another reason for its success: *the realm of hypocrisy, stretching between popular beliefs and the realities of the consumer's life, is a necessary condition for the properly functioning society of consumers*. If the search for fulfilment is to continue, and if the new promises are to be alluring and ensnaring, promises already made must be routinely broken, and the hopes of fulfilment regularly frustrated. Each single promise *must* be deceitful or at least exaggerated, lest the search loses its intensity or even grinds to a halt. Without repetitive frustration of desires, consumer demand could quickly run dry and the consumer-targeted economy would run out of steam. It is the *excess* of the sum total of promises that neutralizes the frustration caused by the superfluity of each one of them, and stops the accumulation of frustrating experiences before it has sapped the confidence in the ultimate effectiveness of the search.

In addition to being an economics of excess and waste, consumerism is for this reason also an economics of deception. As with the excess and waste, deception does not signal its malfunctioning. On the contrary – it is a symptom of its good health and of its being on the right track; a distinctive mark of the sole regime under which the society of consumers may be assured of survival.

The regular discarding of what is offered to the consumer as a promised source of gratification is paralleled by the rising mountains of dashed expectations. Among the expectations, mortality is high; and in a properly functioning consumer society, it must be steadily rising. Life-expectation for hopes is minuscule, and only an extravagantly high fertility rate may save them from thinning out and extinction. For the expectations to be kept alive, and for the new hopes to promptly fill the void left by those already discredited and discarded, the road from the shop to the garbage bin needs to be short and the passage swift.

There is more, though, that sets the society of consumers apart from all other arrangements – even the most ingenious – for skilful and effective 'pattern maintenance' and 'tension management' (to recall Talcott Parsons' prerequisites of the 'self-equilibrating system'). The society of consumers has developed to an unprecedented degree the capacity to absorb all and any dissent it inevitably, and in common with other types of society, breeds – and then to recycle it as the major resource of its own well-being and expansion. Richard Rorty said of technology that whatever (critical) programme may be developed for the twenty-first century, it is unlikely to include the detechnologization of the world, simply because nobody can think of a way to counter the effects of bad, old technological-bureaucratic initiatives except through the development of new and better technological-bureaucratic initiatives.[15] By analogy, one may say the same of the wondrous all-ingesting-and-digesting, all-assimilating, all-re-making-after-its-own-likeness capacity of the consumer markets.

The society of consumers derives its animus and momentum from the disaffection it itself expertly produces. It provides the prime case of a process which Thomas Mathiesen has recently described under the name of 'silent silencing' (of potential system-born dissent and protest) through the stratagem of 'absorption' – meaning that 'the attitudes and actions which in origin are transcendent (that is, threatening the system with explosion or implosion – Z.B.) are integrated in the prevailing order in such a way that dominant interests continue to be served. This way, they are made unthreatening to the prevailing order.'[16] I would add that they are concerted into a major resource of the reproduction of that order.

10
Consumer Citizenship in Post-national Constellations?

Michelle Everson and Christian Joerges

Introduction

The relationship maintained between the law and the figure of the consumer is a highly complex and contradictory one. As is often noted, the consumer is not a monolith, but is instead only one of many roles played by any one human agent – as worker, producer of goods or economic agent – always with varied personal aspirations in mind.[1] By the same token, the law is never simply law, but is also highly differentiated, breaking down into distinct areas of contract law (distributional) regulatory law, labour law or competition law, each with its own, sometimes contradictory, policy goals. Accordingly, and at this simple level, the notion of an identifiable and coherent 'law of the consumer' is inevitably elusive as different human agents interact with distinctly programmed bodies of law, experiencing the law either as a weapon with which to pursue their own preferred patterns of consumption or as a constraint upon their own economic behaviour.

The complexity of the consumer–law relationship, however, is also augmented by virtue of the fact that law, when viewed as an autonomous social institution, not only faces the almost insurmountable challenges of co-ordinating its various social steering mechanisms (e.g., distributional law versus competition law), but is also always prone to manipulation and direction by the extra-legal forces of politics and economics. Beyond simple and simplistic notions of consumer protection, 'consumer law' is thus surely a chimera: we cannot conceive of law as playing a supporting and sustaining role for consumption; instead, consumption is a simple fact to which law simply responds, always doing so imperfectly.

Or is it? Perhaps uniquely amongst social institutions, law is not simply a steering mechanism, but also aspires to normative status; it is not simply about social steering, but about 'good' social steering. Applying this statement down to the level of consumption, and deploying Habermasian terms, law's encounters with the consumer are thus always also about the legal effort to translate the 'fact' of consumption into a normative 'good' of consumption. Complex, contradictory and flawed though they might be, legal encounters with the consumer are also indelibly marked by a legal aspiration to establish a framework of consumption that appropriately reflects the social, political and ethical mores of the society to which it applies.

In the following we chronicle the efforts of law to sustain consumption as a normative good. At the same time, we identify an inevitable challenge to the legal normativisation of consumption within the forces of globalisation. As our initial section demonstrates, legal encounters with the consumer were historically contained within nation states and, more importantly, national welfare states, which allowed the law to draw upon the integrative powers of the national community in order to avoid schism over the positive meaning of consumption. Beyond the borders of the nation state, however, the law of the European Union (EU) and, more recently, the law of the World Trade Organisation (WTO) have struggled to identify sustainable normative contours for global consumption.

The inadequacy of post-national law and its inability to identify the legitimate demands for protection and sustenance of the post-national consumer can largely be traced to the famous query posed by Jürgen Habermas of whether democracy can survive globalisation.[2] At another level, however, as our very brief discussion of the recent WTO panel report on the dispute between the United States and the EU on genetically modified organisms (GMOs) exemplifies, the failure of law to establish a coherent normative good of post-national consumption can also be argued to derive from law's generic inability to free itself from forces of extra-legal manipulation – in this case, forces of 'science' and global economic rationality.[3]

A brief history of national legal encounters with the consumer

The legal relationship with the act of consumption is complex and flawed, inevitably characterised by conflict between the varied roles played by any one individual and by the challenges faced by any one legal order, both in integrating its disparate distinct policy goals (competition *vs.* regulation, and so on) and in insulating itself from extra-legal manipulation. Nonetheless, as a brief review of legal encounters with the consumer at national level demonstrates – above all, examination of the three legal ideal-types of the sovereign-consumer, the citizen-consumer and the enabled-consumer – national law has long been engaged in the act of integrating and ameliorating conflicting approaches to consumption, in order to give rise to a 'national' good of consumption.

The freedom to consume: Formal law and the 'sovereign-consumer'

The notion of US 'consumerism', or unbridled commitment to freedom of consumption above all other social interests, has a modern air to it.

Nonetheless, consumerism – or, in its positive formulation, the concept that the act of consumption possesses its own egalitarian force – has deep historical roots within national legal orders and, more particularly, within nineteenth-century (European) legal notions of contractual justice and equality, which, although unable to recognise consumers as a distinct legal class, nonetheless assumed that contractual partners were fit and able to determine their own destinies. This contractual conception of consumption furnishes us with our first glimpse of an abiding form of encounter between law and the consumer, which is governed not by any legal desire to identify and support consumers within the economy, but rather by a happy coincidence between law's ancient mission to preserve its own (pre-political) legitimacy through the maintenance of 'formal legal rationality' and the economic and social rationales and theories that once underpinned emerging European nation states.

As Max Weber teaches us, the modern law of the Western nation state was to be distinguished from its natural forebears by virtue of its refusal to embody or promote any one substantive vision of the legitimate nature of human organisation. Instead, the legitimacy of law derived from its neutral mission to provide a formal framework of norms within which all human agents were assumed to be willing and able to act of their own volition.[4] The cornerstone of such a theory of legal legitimation was in turn formed by a private law doctrine of contractual privacy, which precluded any legal intervention within economic exchange relationships that might be motivated by interventionist efforts to secure the particular status of any one contractual party (as consumer, and so on). In other words, the inspirational power underlying a formally rational legal refusal to recognise the consumer as a distinct legal class lay in the belief that once a formal legal framework had been established that would apply equally to *all*, regardless of status, the individual autonomy and creative power of all citizens would be assured, leaving them free to pursue productive economic activity in service of the economy.

By the same token, formal rationality was to find much favour within emerging nation states, dedicated both to the destruction of status-based relationships, which had seemingly retarded the economic and social development of their hierarchical forebears, and to the promulgation of the new and integrative powers of the national economy. In other words, classical economic theory, the growing political preference for bourgeois patterns of social organisation and the national imperative for creative economic development acted in concert to support and sustain formal legal notions of contractual autonomy, which assumed that individual volition, or individual 'economic sovereignty', formed both the legitimate basis for law and served the foundation of an egalitarian society. Within such an egalitarian society, the legally secured economic freedom 'to act within the market' would both sustain and be sustained by national solidarity and would further unleash creative forces of political and economic consolidation. The imputed social distinctions of the feudal economy had been superseded. As a consequence, formal law would refuse directly to recognise a distinct class of consumers. Nonetheless, a freedom to consume would be enshrined within the legal order and be further supported by the ideology of the emerging nation state, which deemed the 'talented' character of the 'national (economic) citizen' to be both a force for the creation of egalitarian society and a potent weapon to ensure national economic evolution.

The inspirational power that lies behind formal egalitarian conceptions of 'the freedom to consume', or the notion of contractual sovereignty, provides us with an explanation for the fact that traces of the nineteenth-century conception of formal equality can still be found in most European private legal orders.[5] Most strikingly, however, 'the freedom to consume', and, with it, a notion of the 'sovereign consumer', now finds its most powerful contemporary expression within the 'consumerism' that is attributed to a peculiarly US conception of the nature of world trade orders.[6]

Alternatively, whilst the simple assumption that individual autonomy can be secured by the blanket application of one set of legal norms to all parties may appear outmoded, both within law and within wider society, the inspirational roots of consumer sovereignty still live on within a rhetoric of consumer choice, that is, in its modern form, underpinned by a legal framework of individual legal rights. Seen in this light, US consumerism is not simply an expression of 'cultural rootlessness', a 'meaningless' consumerism within which the urge and ability to purchase unravels any deep-seated cultural or social perceptions about the nature of 'valued' goods, but is, instead, an echo of the egalitarianism and belief in the self-determining powers of the identity politics that marked the birth of the modern Western state.[7] To the 'consumerist' legal order, the notion of rights is determinative: evident weaknesses in formal legal rationality – abuse of power within contractual relations – can be compensated for by the recognition in higher (constitutional) law that all *must* be treated equally, regardless of race, religion or national origin. By the same token, modern neo-classical economic theory, together with the self-determining and socially creative purchasing power of once disregarded minorities – women, blacks and gays – imbue the consumerist economy with an egalitarianism all of its own. In this scenario, 'valued goods' are, thus, not the simple creation of unthinking and possibly prejudicial traditional values and social relations, but are, rather, an immediate market response to the needs and self-expressed identities of 'sovereign consumers'.

Freedom from harm: Material law and the 'citizen-consumer'

Although the notion of the 'sovereign-consumer' may be thought to be most closely identified with the US legal arena, ample evidence for the complexity of legal encounters with the consumer can likewise be derived from history and from the simple fact that the United States is also the cradle of a notion of 'consumer protection', which often places the status of the sovereign consumer in doubt. It was thus President John F. Kennedy who, in the wake of the thalidomide crisis, began to encourage lawyers to review their age-old refusal to regard consumers as a distinct class requiring legal protection. Consumers were no longer to be seen as isolated purchasers of goods, but were instead to be viewed as persons 'concerned with the various facets of society which might affect them directly or indirectly as consumers'.[8]

Thalidomide cruelly exposed the myth that the modern industrial economy might simply be viewed as a forum for egalitarian economic exchange. By the 1960s, economic exchange was characterised by large-scale imbalance in the relative bargaining powers of producers and consumers of goods. Above all, thalidomide revealed a wide-ranging disjunction between the profit motive driving modern production and the legitimate interests of consumers in the safety of consumer goods. The time had come for the re-evaluation of the place of the consumer within national society and, with this, for the re-consideration of the underlying notion that unfettered exchange could *per se* sustain an egalitarian and 'just' society. Kennedy's sentiments directly addressed the dilemma of the conflicting identities and interests of modern consumers. Certainly, consumers possessed an interest in plentiful and cheap goods; however, as producers, workers, family members and simple national citizens, they also maintained a simultaneous interest in the sustainable production of safe goods, produced with due respect for the legitimate concerns of the workforce and society as a whole.

Immediate public outrage coalesced into a demand for prompt regulatory intervention. Accordingly, 'explicit' legal recognition was at last given to the notion of the 'consumer'. More strikingly, however, within the context of European welfare states, the shift in emphasis from an isolated 'freedom to consume' to an integrated conception whereby the state would act to ensure 'freedom from harm' also formed the backdrop for a new legal encounter with the 'citizen-consumer'.[9] Consumption could not and would not be viewed as an autonomous act. Instead, consumption would be regulated in the light of the shared concerns of the citizens of the nation state. The state, the representative of the joint interests of its citizens, would consequently intervene widely in acts of economic exchange in order to balance the character of the consumer against that of the worker, producer or family member.

The egalitarianism of the post-war welfare state within Europe, which secured the equality of its own citizens through large-scale redistribution, was in large part facilitated by a belief in Keynesian theories of economic organisation. At the same time, however, it also necessitated a re-evaluation of the legitimate bases of national law. Where once the formal legal order had derived its own internal legitimacy from its ability to impose one universal and pre-political framework of legal norms upon society, the law of the welfare state now demanded that law cede to purposive political direction in order to treat different groups within society in different ways. The consumer would henceforth be recognised as a distinct class of citizen in need of particular protection; at the same time, the needs and interests of consumers would also be balanced against the needs and interests of the entire population.

Legal encounters with the 'citizen-consumer' are consequently also marked by a high degree of what Max Weber termed 'legal materialisation'. In stark contrast to the formal legal notion of the 'sovereign-consumer', the citizen-consumer entails a series of positive values, which cannot be legitimated by a simple internal legal dedication to the maintaining of contractual autonomy, but must instead find their approbation in democratic discourse and the subjection of law to subsequent political direction. In turn, the normative parameters of consumption within the paradigm of the 'sovereign-consumer' are no longer conditioned by law's internal paradigms of formal rationality, or the abstract theories of classical economics, but are instead intimately entwined with democratic process; more precisely, democratic process within the national welfare state.

This democratisation of the process of the legal identification of a normative good of consumption was undoubtedly of major benefit to the populations of post-war Western economies. Nonetheless, legal materialisation and democratisation of consumption also brought its own complex of far-reaching contradictions. Above all, legal materialisation heightened the social steering difficulties faced by national legal orders. As legal autonomy ceded to political direction, disjunction between the policies pursued by partial segments of the legal order only intensified (competition law *vs.* labour law and so on), giving rise, in its turn, to 'irrationality' or incoherence within each national framework for consumption. Equally, as each national regulatory framework for consumption fell victim to its own incoherencies and contradictions, national regulation began to form an immutable barrier to consumption across national boundaries. Regional and global trade was inexorably foreshortened and as much as the emergence of the figure of the citizen-consumer heralded the evolution of the democratic effort to determine a normative good of consumption, it also bore with it the seeds of its own destruction. Increasing and economically stagnating differentiation between national economies inexorably led to demands for economic liberalisation and rationalisation within the ambit, first, of regional organisations of economic integration such as the EU, and, secondly, within a global legal-economic order such as the WTO.[10]

Legal proceduralism and the 'enabled-consumer'

Our final, 'ideal-type', encounter between law and the consumer cannot be exemplified through broad brush-stroke reference to any one national legal order. Instead, the notion of the 'enabled-consumer' can only be found fleetingly within various legal orders and the writings of legal theorists.[11] By the same token, the concept of the 'enabled-consumer' is not a product of politics or economics, but is, instead, a manifestation of a legal preoccupation with the integrity and coherence of law. As a brief discussion of the sovereign-consumer and citizen-consumer clearly demonstrates, Max Weber was correct to comment that law would be forever caught on the horns of a dilemma. Formal rationality within law, and with it the notion of a sovereign-consumer, might draw its legitimating powers for apolitical notions of contractual autonomy. By the same token, however, it would always falter in the face of demands that social values be incorporated within it: what price my freedom to consume (and express my own identity politics) if I am thus exposed to the potential harms and dangers of unfettered economic exchange? Equally, material rationality within law, for all its underlying democratic pedigree, is also subject to its own limitations: the notion that law can be directed by one (national) democratic will to furnish one (national) vision of the normative good of consumption is an illusion, subject always to distorting irrationality as law struggles to translate conflicting political goals within its limited and fragmented social steering capacity.

To lawyers engaged in the eternal waltz between formal and material conceptions of law, the struggle to identify the legitimate bases of law is an existential one, and, within the specific context of legal encounters with the act of consumption, leads to a conclusion that the law should never claim to have identified one final and 'legitimate' ideal-type consumer. The process of legal transformation of the act of consumption into a normative good of consumption is not one that can be satisfactorily performed through simple recourse to the panacea of sovereign purchasing power; nor is it one that can be said to have been performed by means of the subordination of law to one political, economic or social set of consumption values. Instead, the only sustainable source of legitimacy that might be identified for law during its encounters with the consumer is procedural in nature. Law should not attempt to predetermine the normative good of consumption. Instead, it can only ever attempt to ensure that the social, economic and political parameters within which each individual act of consumption occurs have been drawn up, and are continually re-drawn up, with due regard for each and every interest upon which the act of consumption impacts.

Procedural law is the law of political discourse; an open-ended law which founds its legitimacy in the fact that substantive values are not the product of law, but rather the product of the political discourse which law enables and facilitates. As noted, procedural law is largely the product of legal theory minds and can only be identified in a real world of consumption in limited circumstances. Nonetheless, and at national level, procedural conceptions of enabled consumption have always been recognised and may yet find their true applicative value at supranational and global level.

The consumer within the post-national constellation

'Markets are always socially embedded.' In our context, it is particularly useful to reconstruct the three paradigms of legal encounters with the consumer in Polanyian terms.[12] Formal, materialised and proceduralised law are, after all, simply different modes of 'instituting' the economy within a given social context. Certainly, legal formalism does this only in an indirect manner since it may be argued to represent little more than an unthinking marriage between law and classical *laissez-faire* economics. Nonetheless, even formal law implies a degree of social 'embeddedness', either since it is also founded in notions of egalitarianism (contractual autonomy and identity politics) or, more simply, since it provides the stable legal framework within which market relations are established. The status of 'materialisation' and 'proceduralisation' processes – each being necessary democratic responses to irreversible technological and economic change – is beyond doubt: we can be certain that each is a positive effort to embed the market within its social context. However, a large degree of doubt necessarily arises in relation to the impact of Europeanisation and globalisation upon all of these historical accomplishments of the constitutional nation state.

No one commentator may be found who argues that European market integration has fully prized the European economy out of its 'socially embedded' setting, and our review confirms that analytical categories deployed within the national setting retain much of their analytical strength and normative plausibility at EU level. Similarly, it would be frivolous to expect that a globalised market could ever function in the absence of institutionalised mechanisms to ensure consumer faith in the reliability and safety of goods offered across national frontiers. Post-national constellations, however, do exhibit *differentiae specificae*; the most important of which are the lack of institutions comparable to those used by nation states to ensure the social embeddedness of markets, and the challenges post-national organisations face when seeking to organise transnational political processes that might act as functional equivalents. These differences and difficulties are more obvious at the international than at the European level. We therefore deal with both levels of governance separately.

The European constellation: The rule of law on trial?

The European legal integration process is commonly divided into three eras: a formative 'integration through law' period under the guidance of the European Court of Justice; a second, highly dynamic, era characterised by the effort to complete the internal market and to strengthen European competitiveness; and a final period of consolidation entailing adaptation of EU competences and decision-making rules in order to respond to the functional challenges posed by these new ambitions.[13] The first two eras are relatively easily captured within our existing paradigms. It is only in the third (current) integration phase, which encompasses the effort to democratise the integration project, that the challenges of the post-national constellation have become more fully apparent.

Modest beginnings

At its outset, the European integration project was conceived of as a wholly economic undertaking. However, the new member states of the Community were all social and welfare states with institutionalised 'mixed economies'.[14] As a consequence, the integration project came with its own in-built tension between a (limited) European level of governance, dedicated to economic freedom and open markets, and a national level of governance, at which nation states retained comprehensive powers to organize their own economic and social affairs. Fritz W. Scharpf has conceptualised the enforced division between national social policy and European market-building competences as the decoupling of 'interdependent' policy spheres.'[15] However, this problem remained latent for nearly two decades, and particularly so in relation to consumer policy, which was then dominated by notions of the sovereign-consumer and was thus of marginal importance within the European post-war economy.

By the 1970s, however, 'freedom from harm' was firmly on the political agenda and the European Commission were to adopt their first ambitious and innovative consumer policy programme in the mid-1970s.[16] The innovative element within the programme was its reliance upon 'soft law' ('communications'), which compensated for the fact that the Community had no genuine powers or competences in the field it had now entered – a soft law approach which has now become the norm. The ambition of the programme was to be found in its many 'hard law' measures. These were often presented as a means of overcoming competitive obstacles to the completion of the common market in the effort to overcome national sensibilities that might be used to block European regulation under the then applicable unanimity voting requirements. Following the move to (qualified) majority voting (1987 Singe European Act) as well as the introduction of Article 100(a), guaranteeing a 'high level of protection' for European consumers, European consumer policy was further strengthened. Nationally embedded concepts of the consumer and the national regulatory programmes that sustained them were accordingly exposed to the rationalising gaze of the demand that all barriers to trade within the Community be dismantled. Primary European law, though not inherently concerned with visions of the consumer, was thus forced not only to confront embedded national attitudes to consumer law and culture, but also to investigate the character of the European consumer in order to justify its deregulatory interventions.[17]

Ambitious endeavours

The Delors Commission's 'White Paper on Completion of the Internal Market' of 1985 proved a turning point in EU history.[18] Following years of stagnation, the integration project developed a new dynamic. The programme was presented and widely perceived as a confirmation of Europe's commitment to economic efficiency through market-building. However, what began as a collective effort to improve European competitiveness through new de-regulatory strategies inevitably entangled the EU within a greater number of policy fields and soon necessitated the evolution of far more sophisticated regulatory machineries.[19] In particular, the European legislator and the European Commission (EC), concerned now with 'social regulation', were irresistibly drawn to issues of health and safety, labour policy and the environment.

What was the consequence for the European legal understanding of consumption? Seemingly, it was now beyond doubt that 'high standards of protection' (or freedom from harm) should form an element within the European 'social (market) model' such that the purposive national materialisation paradigm (and citizen-consumer) would appear to have been transferred from the national to the European level. This impression, however, was to be of *breve durée*. Europeanisation under the guidance of Jacques Delors' White Paper had been a modernising and innovative initiative. To expect this initiative to be a European cure to the failures experienced during interventionist programming at national level was at best naïve. At the national level, the response to these failures had been (at least in legal theory terms) 'proceduralisation'; Europe was bound to follow suit, but likewise lacked the plethora of institutions and dense communicative practices through which proceduralisation was embedded within national societies. The alternative it chose was officiously announced in 2001 in its White Paper on Governance.[20] We now turn to that new trend.

Between de-formalisation of Community rule and a new austerity of economic liberalism

Unsurprisingly, the adoption at EU level of a rhetoric and practice of 'governance' was triggered by scandalous malfunctioning within the EU's regulatory machinery, which caused great anxiety amongst European consumers, visibly politicised the internal market and propelled the once obscure area of consumer policy into the arena of high politics.[21] The economy had mutated into a polity and the White Paper sought to meet this new challenge, defining governance as 'rules, procedures and behaviour, that affect the way in which powers are exercised at European level – particularly regarding, openness, participation, accountability, effectiveness and coherence' (p. 8). The intense resonance of the new programme was easily explained: governance was an immediate necessity – BSE was only one of many challenges that Europe faced. The 'integration through law' paradigm, founded in a creaking legislative process, was outmoded and the internal market still lacked an

appropriate institutional framework. Europe was now in dire need of continuous management of its political economy, but still had no genuine and
centralised European administration. The governance movement was inevitable and necessarily built upon the strengthening of co-ordination between
governmental and non-governmental actors. But what did it accomplish?

Returning to our paradigms of legal encounters with the consumer, developments within European private law seemed to re-affirm a return to the
liberal beginnings of the market and the re-emergence of the 'sovereign-consumer'. Following announcement of its 2003 'action plan' on European contract
law, the Commission began to prioritise consolidation of the patchwork
of European consumer protection directives.[22,23] Most significantly, Directive
2005/29, 'concerning unfair business-to-consumer commercial practices', constructed the European consumer as a market actor with economic interests whose
'transactional' performance European law should seek to promote through the
'smooth functioning of the internal market' (recital 3).[24] With recent European
Court of Justice (ECJ) judgements taking the same neo-liberal line, Europe's
future would appear to be in the hands of its 'talented economic citizen'.[25]

What is true in the field of contractual consumer legislation, however,
surely cannot be true in the classical 'materialised' field of protection of
health and safety? Surely, Europeans cannot simply be regarded as 'shoppers'
when anxious about their health or unwilling to consume genetically modified food? Yet, although pursued with great vigour, this policy goal would
also seem to have been de-politicised. The recently established European
Food Safety Authority (EFSA) provides a telling example. According to its
founding statute, '[i]t is necessary to ensure that consumer *confidence* and
the confidence of trading partners is secured through the open and transpar-
ent development of food law' (preamble (22)).[26] This would seem to indicate
that the authority has nothing to do with politics, or with the control *over* the
market by the consumer, but is rather, in a technocratic-scientific market-
driven logic, designed to secure the position of the consumer (rather than
citizen-consumer) *within* the market. Equally, this technocratic logic would
seem to be confirmed by the statute's commitment to principles of scientific
neutrality, with its scientific members undertaking 'to act independently *of
any external influence*' (Article 37(2)).

'Scientification' is a very visible characteristic of evolving European risk
regulation. The intensification of European consumer policies is occurring in
tandem with a reliance on novel – increasingly de-formalised – modes of
governance, characterised by their reliance upon 'soft law' and their use of
flexible management and cognitive openness as a substitute for the normative stubbornness of purposive (material) legal intervention. Expertise and
flexible management is only seemingly at odds with a return to orthodox
formalism in contract law. There is no paradox and no contradiction: each act
to depoliticise the national citizen-consumer. Legal formalism within contract law replaces political contestation over social impacts of private

contracting with the objective mechanisms of market process. Expert governance appears to replace political contestation over socially acceptable exposure to risks with reference to the objective standards of sound science.
'Sound science and the market' are natural allies.

However, bleak as this assessment may be, the European scenario is also more
complex. Once again the status of EFSA is telling. Alternatively, its scientific
attributes must also be contrasted with an envisaged role for the agency's
leading technocrats that is to be exercised as follows: 'The members of the
Management Board, the Advisory Forum and the Executive Director [of the
EFSA] shall undertake to act independently *in the public interest*' (Article 37(2)).

The notion of 'in the public interest' provides the key: the embedding of
Europe's agencies not only within a technocratic market-driven logic, but also
within a sphere of conflicting political interests. The distinction made in the
design of European agencies between 'political' decision-making functions,
undertaken by the Commission, and strict technocratic activities, delegated to
bureaucrats and scientific expertise, is a false one. More importantly, it is seen to
be a false one: the present policy orientation of the European Commission was
undoubtedly imposed upon it by the failure of the Draft Constitutional Treaty.
This failure had a destructive impact on the cohesion of the Union and, under-
standably, also upon confidence in its regulatory endeavours. The resort to
'sound science and the market' is therefore quite comprehensible. However, it
is also unlikely to restore the faith of consumers in Europe. Europe's law recognises this fact: the turn to sound science and expert management in the realm of
health and safety is embedded in European-wide communicative networks of
politically accountable actors and in an evermore active civil society. The new
formalism in private law remains embedded in mature legal systems, which
have learned to live with competing rationalities and politicised consumers. The
European polity is still developing and the transformation of the European
shopper into an enabled-consumer is still underway.

Globalisation as regression: The WTO panel report on the GMO dispute

Returning to Karl Polanyi, we can conclude that European consumer markets
have yet to find their final 'social embeddedness' within the dense legal
frameworks that now structure the internal market. However, politicisation
impulses have not fully receded and neither austere economic liberalism nor
erosion of the rule of law will ever succeed in 'dis-embeddeding' the European
consumer. The international constellation is nonetheless different.
Certainly, the social-embeddedness imperative also operates here; however,
its powers are necessarily of a different kind. Globalisation has created its own
legal frameworks for international trade – frameworks within which national
and European health and safety regulation have already proved to be powerful transformative accelerants.

The irritating impacts of national consumer regulation are most visibly demonstrated by the transformation of the old General Agreement on Tariffs and Trade (GATT) regime into the new WTO legal system established in 1994. The main objective of the GATT was the reduction of protective trade tariffs. From the 1970s onwards, however, intensification of domestic economic regulation, especially in the fields of health and safety, consumer and environmental protection, led to a shift of emphasis to non-tariff barriers to free trade. The most important reforms introduced by the WTO included overhaul of procedures of dispute settlement and the conclusion of special agreements concerning non-tariff barriers to free trade such as the *Agreement on the Application of Sanitary and Phytosanitary Measures* (SPS) and the *Agreement on Technical Barriers to Trade* (TBT). These agreements aim to balance the global economic objective of free trade with the domestic regulatory concerns of WTO members. There are obvious parallels with the European experience, but there are also important differences. WTO members did not confer 'positive' regulatory powers upon the organisation, although they did agree that WTO law should restrain the exercise of domestic regulatory powers. WTO law has no powers comparable to EU re-regulatory powers; the co-originality of market and regulation postulated by Polanyi must find a different mode of expression. Currently, the most important supplement to domestic regulatory restraint is the intense process of quasi-legal norm-production at the international level by both non-governmental and governmental actors, especially so in the field of product safety.[27]

The GMO case and its object

Our discussion of the global encounter of law with the consumer focuses on one single case: the dispute between the EU, the United States, Canada and Argentina on the legitimate or otherwise use of GMOs in foodstuffs. While foodstuffs generally are such highly politicised products that no legal system has ever failed to subject them to a degree of regulatory supervision, GMOs are likewise the most technologically advanced and controversial of all food-stuffs, if not of all consumer products. This is so for a variety of reasons: highly technologically advanced GMO production is led by the United States, but has also been mastered by countries such as Brazil and India, giving rise to very ambivalent socio-economic implications as development imperatives clash with agrarian employment concerns.[28] The most intensive debate, however, focuses on risks posed by GMOs. Both GMO sceptics and adherents agree that there is little evidence that GMO food poses a positive risk to health.[29] Nonetheless, a major concern remains that non-GMO crops will be contaminated by GMOs released into the environment. Likewise, conflict rages on the meaning of consumer anxiety and choice: do we have a 'right to know' what we are eating;[30] might governments demand GMO labelling since the majority of their citizens refuse to accept them;[31] is the EU correct

to have 'perfected' its authorization procedures by means of the establishment of an ethical advisory body?[32]

The GMO conflict is long running: the present legalised stage commenced
in spring 2003, as the United States (supported by Argentina and Canada)
requested formal dispute settlement. The complainants argued that the EC
had imposed a *de facto* moratorium on approvals of biotech products, tolerat-
ing 'national marketing and import bans' on biotech products. The panel was
established in March 2004, announcing and postponing its report several
times. A preliminary report was published in February 2006 and, following
responses, a final modified report spanning some 1087 pages was published
in September 2006.[33]

Two core Issues

The WTO reports are highly formalised examples of law, reconstructing the
arguments of dispute parties and *amici curiae* and furnishing intensely technical *lege artis* interpretations of the SPS and TBT agreements from which their
authority derives. We do not comment upon the multitude of issues covered,
but restrict our observations to questions of how WTO law constructs its
encounters with the global consumer and what, in its view, is the nature of
the social embeddedness of the global GMO market. We single out and
differentiate its two core and entwined points of reference: the supremacy
of science; and the de-legitimation of politics.

Supremacy of science

The United States and the EU differ in their regulatory approaches to
GMOs in two significant aspects: whereas the United States focuses on
the health risks posed by food, the EU follows a more comprehensive
approach, placing an additional and greater emphasis upon environmental
risks.[34] US authorities will approve products *unless* evidence exists con-
firming existence of risk. By contrast, the 1992 Treaty on European Union
constitutionalised the 'precautionary principle', so that all legislative,
administrative and judicial decision-making within Europe must respect
the notion that *any* indistinct hazard must be guarded against (Article
174(2) EC Treaty). Rules and principles governing resolution of conflict
between the two legal orders are to be found in the SPS Agreement;
unsurprisingly, they are founded within the authoritative supremacy of
science.

As noted, the WTO has no 'positive' legislative competences and instead
recognises the regulatory autonomy of its members. It seeks to ensure com-
patibility of domestic regulation with a free trade commitment by asking
members to exercise restraint in the application of domestic law and, when
this fails, seeks to resolve conflicts through reference to a meta-rule to which
all the parties can be expected to subscribe. As such, WTO law mirrors the old
European model of overcoming obstacles to trade in domestic regulation: this

model first identified legitimate policy objectives for national regulation (such as health, safety and environmental protection) and then required member states to provide scientific evidence that these regulatory concerns were, in fact, real.[35] Resorting to scientific authority, Europe invoked a non-partisan authority that national regulators could tolerate. Naturally, Europeans remained aware that risk assessment and management also entailed political and ethical issues.[36] Nonetheless, science and techniques of risk assessment do possess meta-political validity – even where scientists fail to agree, disagreements are always conducted within a shared and constantly re-assessed scientific logic.

Inevitably, the successful EU model was to find persuasive force as a conflict-mediating strategy within the international arena: technically complex and potentially harmful products cannot be assessed without the help of expertise; *vice versa*, where WTO members refuse free access to their markets, they can surely be expected to justify such restrictions with scientific evidence. This is exactly what the SPS agreement provides for.[37] Nonetheless, a vital question remains: what happens when science 'runs out' and scientists agree that general hazard cannot be transformed into specific risk since they cannot hope to gather sufficient data with which to conduct a scientific risk assessment (scientific uncertainty)? Although such a situation does not necessarily herald the end of methodologically disciplined discourse, scientific debate is nonetheless inexorably curtailed should one party to the conflict adopt a version of the precautionary principle in which the quest for scientific evidence is rejected *a priori*. As the travails of European Courts readily document, the transition from scientific discourse to ethical precaution is exceedingly difficult to pinpoint.[38] Nonetheless, it appears that it would be far too much to expect of a WTO body even tangentially to declare that its own mandate ends where science has no answers on offer.

In the Hormones Case, the WTO Appellate Body found that the '[precautionary] principle has not been written into the SPS Agreement as a ground for justifying SPS measures that are otherwise inconsistent with the obligations of Members set out in particular provisions of that Agreement'.[39] The panel in the GMO case followed suit in a slightly different way. Recalling 'that, according to the Appellate Body, the precautionary principle has not been written into the *SPS Agreement* as a legitimate ground for justifying SPS measures', the panel went on to explain that 'even if a member follows a precautionary approach, its SPS measures need to be 'based on' a ('sufficiently warranted' or 'reasonably supported') 'risk assessment' (paragraph 7.0365, note 1905). Initially leaving aside the mental machinations that must attend any effort 'to prove the unprovable' or 'make known the unknown unknowns', it is readily apparent that the WTO panel will simply not recognise the constitutional commitment of any of its members to precaution.

De-legitimation of Politics

Returning, though, to 'unknown unknowns', we can surely object that resort to science in the face of knowledge indeterminacy is akin to invoking an emperor without clothes – where science is uncertain, its invocation as a conflict-settling legal meta-rule makes no sense whatsoever. A variety of legal responses is certainly conceivable. The most compatible with the panel's logic is a 'broad' understanding of 'science' and 'risk assessment'. Recognising uncertainty deriving from incomplete knowledge, the Appellate Body in the Hormones case appeared to fall into line with the more conservative interpretations of the precautionary principle promoted by the ECJ, who in their most important judgement to date have argued as follows: the precautionary principle must not be understood as legitimating 'a purely hypothetical approach to risk, founded on mere suppositions which are not yet scientifically verified', but requires 'a risk assessment which is as complete as possible in the particular circumstances'.[40] Equally, uncertainty can also be tackled through extension of risk assessments to production processes and/or to their use. However, the vagaries of phrasing ('as complete as possible'), plus ever-widening spatial/temporal risk assessment parameters, necessarily imply that non-scientific criteria will also have their impact upon risk evaluations.[41] Once these implications are clear, however, it becomes evermore difficult to justify *a priori* exclusion of socio-economic considerations on the social costs and benefits of new technologies from the legal process. Re-phrasing: since legal orders cannot refuse to reach a decision simply because science provides no guidance, a resort to non-scientific criteria must surely suggest itself. Socio-economic considerations, such as the impact of new technologies on the agricultural sector, cannot be dismissed as utterly irrational, even though the closed market-building logic of the WTO would love to do so.

Uncertainty has two further implications: first, where uncertainty prevails, differences in problem assessments are unavoidable; secondly, such diversity requires a framework within which it can be managed. The EU is well equipped in this regard. The European Treaty explicitly recognises the national right to impose higher levels of consumer protection than those foreseen in legislative acts (Article 95(5) and 153 ECT); meanwhile the precautionary principle infers that member states retain autonomy in cases of uncertainty; equally, all relevant secondary legislation contains (exit) safeguard clauses for states in disagreement with the majority response (including directives on GMO authorisation).[42]

Naturally, diversity within a system predicated on the establishment of a *common* market is hard to accept, and the ECJ – forever seeking uniform standards – has limited recourse to safeguards to cases where evidence 'indicates the existence of a specific risk', excluding reasons 'of a general nature'. Further, the ECJ confirms that safeguards must be understood in 'in the light of the precautionary principle' and that they may therefore justify a temporary derogation, but *only* where 'it proves impossible to carry out as full a risk assessment as possible...because of the inadequate nature of the available scientific data'.[43] However, even here, the ECJ has categorically refused immutably to subject European governments to the 'objective' standards promoted by the proponents of sound science. No such shyness is visible in the GMO panel findings, which insist upon the exclusive legitimacy of a decisional scientific yardstick, which – all indeterminacy notwithstanding – overrules precautionary reservations: if you cannot prove that GMOs are not safe, you have no reason to reject them.

This final tendency is firmly entrenched within efforts to de-legitimise political process and is most apparent in the panel's treatment of defensive European submissions. Europe's GMO framework did not appear out of the blue. It was many years in the making. The first directive appeared in 1990;[44] yet, political debate and revisions continued and a final common platform for a new framework directive was agreed upon by European Environmental Ministers only in June 1999, with the details taking even longer to fill in.[45] Such intense political debate was nonetheless devalued by the WTO panel, who – although they did not directly question its quality – found a convenient and indirect means of de-legitimising it. Having once decided that the SPS agreement was applicable to the authorisation of GMOs, the panel could then point to Article 8 SPS Agreement, the provisions of which require that applications must not be treated with 'undue delay'. The right of applicants seeking authorisation for their products trumps all others; it is simply irrelevant that time may be needed to debate domestic political and ethical issues. The panel found that the completion of the approval process had been 'unduly delayed' in 24 cases. It, accordingly, requested the EU to bring the measures 'into conformity with its obligations under the SPS Agreement', effectively asking the EU to complete the approval process for the outstanding applications.

The panel's critique of EU member state autonomy in relation to safeguard measures was equally indirect but effective. French, German, Austrian, Italian, Luxembourgoise and Greek bans on the marketing and import of EU-approved biotech products were held incompatible with WTO law. The panel took it upon itself to include EU procedures within its own jurisdiction: although it did not directly address provisions allowing EU member states to impose SPS measures in deviation from the EU norm, it nonetheless opined that since the EU's scientific committee had already adjudged relevant biotech products to be safe, the named states had failed to undertake risk assessments that would 'reasonably support [their] prohibitions' under the SPS Agreement. The competence to determine exactly what constitutes a proper risk assessment under SPS provisions is thus usurped by WTO law, regardless of its lacking a regulatory or political framework.

The EU has decided not to appeal against the panel report. With Commission Trade Spokesman Peter Power declaring, '[t]he impact of that judgment is entirely of historical interest', we now ask why the EU is so sanguine.[46]

'Sound science' the consumer-citizen choice: The global consumer?

Global consumption is wholly dependent upon the establishment of global regimes that ensure trust in the free trade of complex and potentially hazardous goods. To this extent, the WTO panel report can be read as explicit confirmation that the global market will also be 'socially embedded'. However, in this, its most recent encounter with the global consumer, the global legal order reaches for a very distinct regulatory framework and seemingly strictly delimits the degree of social market embeddedness that will apply to global trade. Inexorably, the market is de-politicised as the global consumer is assured that 'sound science' is its appropriate guardian global angel. What form of global consumer, then, are we dealing with? Presumably, de-politicisation of the market and regulation through science both serve an agenda of consumer choice such that global law would seem to be promoting the 'sovereign-citizen' so beloved of nascent national economies (and the EU). But, will this citizen evolve to share the egalitarian traits of its (post-feudal) historical counterpart or, indeed, the imputed identity-liberating characteristics of contemporary 'consumerism'? This is an unlikely scenario, given the WTO's disregard for individual equality rights.

All is uncertainty and time alone will tell. What is clearer, however, is that a global legal order has allowed itself to be colonised by the logics of science in its encounters with the global consumer; a circumstance that might not endure should consumers cease to be satisfied with commercial freedom of choice and aspire instead to contribute actively to the political structuring of a global market. Karl Polanyi, after all, may also be read as arguing that no market can ever escape from complex embedding within its own social context. Certainly, the global arena is unlikely ever to be characterised by the complex materialisation processes witnessed at national level. Nonetheless, as history and EU experience teaches us, global lawyers may yet be called up to restructure their encounters with evermore politically vociferous and 'enabled' global consumers.

11
Sustainability, Well-Being and Consumption: The Limits of Hedonic Approaches

John O'Neill

[I]s it possible to decouple improvement in people's quality of life (or their overall level of life satisfaction) from increases in consumption?[1]

In his report *Redefining prosperity* for the Sustainable Development Commission, Jonathan Porritt appeals to recent findings in hedonic research on subjective well-being to suggest that a decoupling of consumption and the improvement of well-being is possible. That decoupling offers a way of moving towards a low consumption economy that is necessary for sustainability:

The recommended prescription as far as radical environmentalists are concerned is simple: people in the rich world must not just consume in more socially and environmentally responsible ways, but must be persuaded to consume less. To bring that about, the hypothesis is advanced that people who have reached a certain level of material comfort and security can (and should) be persuaded that their future quality of life resides in freeing themselves of the trappings of consumerism and in opting instead for low-maintenance, low-throughput, low-stress patterns of work, recreation and home life.[2]

His argument for the possibility of the decoupling of consumption and the improvement in well-being starts from much-cited claims about the relation of life-satisfaction and gross national product depicted in graphs such as Figure 11.1. The graph has been central to a great deal of recent work on hedonic welfare that includes other contributions from writers such as Kahneman, Frey, Lane and Layard. Beyond a certain level overall growth in real income has not been matched in a growth in reported happiness. While relative income is closely correlated with differences in reported happiness, so that those with higher incomes tend to report higher life-satisfaction, the growth in GNP is not correlated with a change in subjective happiness. Porritt takes these findings

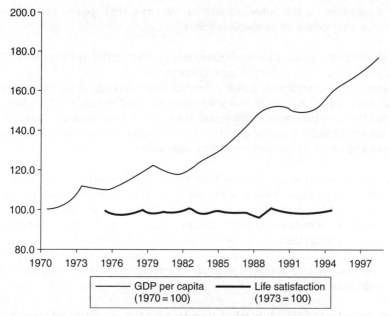

Figure 11.1 UK life-satisfaction and GDP per capita, 1973–1997[3]
Source: N. Donovan and D. Halpbern, *Life Satisfaction* (London, 2002).

to offer the basis for a redefinition of prosperity which divorces prosperity from ever-increasing levels of consumption and which instead focuses on the real determinants of well-being.

Porritt draws on three main arguments that are common within recent hedonic research to support his conclusion. The first is the hedonic treadmill argument that as people get more they want more and hence their overall life-satisfaction remains stable:

> As Richard Easterlin puts it: 'Even though rising income means people can have more goods, the favourable effect of this on welfare is erased by the fact that people want more as they progress'. He refers to this effect as 'the hedonic treadmill', as our desire for more constantly outstrips what we already have.[4]

The second argument is the comparative status argument that people's levels of life-satisfaction depend on their relative rather than their absolute incomes so that increases in aggregate absolute wealth do correlate with improvements in happiness:

> Comparisons of the perceived happiness of rich and poor in different countries demonstrate time after time that it's where people place

themselves on the ladder of relative affluence that counts, rather than what they consume in absolute terms.[5]

Both of these arguments suggest there is something self-defeating about the current pursuit of ever-increasing consumption.

Porritt's third argument is that given the self-defeating nature of that pursuit we need to turn to research on what actually determines well-being. What the literature on hedonic research suggests is that the major correlates of subjective welfare are the quality of work, familial relationships, and wider social and political relationships in a community:

> People can be happy with very little wealth and few possessions, or miserable with plenty... Most research indicates that peoples' quality of life is determined far more by the quality of their working life, their family life and their overall social relationships – all seem to be more important relatively than the amount of consumption they are able to enjoy. And if that consumption is increasingly eroding the quality of those other aspects of overall wellbeing, then it is clearly far less beneficial than it might at first sight appear.[6]

Recent hedonic research is taken then to offer the possibility of a redefinition of prosperity that offers the possibility of easing the transition to a sustainable society through a decrease in consumption which does not rely in making unrealistic demands on people to give up improvements in the quality of life. Porritt's line of argument here is a popular and attractive one. Indeed it might appear to be particularly attractive in the context of citizenship and consumption. Work of Frey and Stutzer has suggested a correlation between reported subjective welfare and political participation.[7] However, despite the obvious attractions of the conclusions, I will argue in this paper that there are major problems with the hedonic route to them.

The revival of hedonistic accounts of welfare is often presented as a return to Bentham.[8] Porritt's deployment of the hedonist's argument could be fruitfully understood as a call to go back further, not to Bentham but to Epicurus. It picks up on themes that were central to the Epicurean traditions, that the desire for wealth without limits is founded upon error – the wealth required for happiness is limited:

> Natural wealth is both limited and easy to acquire. But wealth [as defined by] groundless opinions extends without limits.[9]

However, such claims about the limits to wealth required for well-being are not confined to the hedonic tradition. They were central also to Aristotle's account of the goods required for a flourishing life:

[T]he amount of household property which suffices for a good life is not unlimited, nor of the nature described by Solon in the verse "There is no bound to wealth stands fix for men". There is a bound fixed.[10]

Both the Epicurean and the Aristotelian traditions stand in contrast to more recent desire satisfaction accounts of well-being which tend to concur with the lines in Solon's verse. However, while both traditions concur in their conclusion about the limits of goods required for the good life, they differ in how they arrive at that conclusion. They start from different accounts of the well-being. The Epicurean offers a subjective state account – happiness is a matter of having the appropriate mental state. The Aristotelian offers a more objectivist account – well-being is a matter of what one can be and do.

In the following, I want to suggest that despite the attractions of the hedonic theory that Porritt offers, a broadly Aristotelian account of the good life offers a better starting point to understanding the limits of goods required for the good life. In the following section, I suggest that the central empirical results of recent hedonic research have been open to misinterpretation and are consistent with an Aristotelian framework. In particular it offers a clearer basis for distinguishing different versions of the treadmill arguments and assessing their plausibility. In the following section, I argue that the Epicurean framework is less able to provide the basis for an understanding of commitments over generations that is required if we are to move towards sustainability. In contrast the Aristotelian position, in particular as developed in republican tradition, provides a surer basis for understanding the conditions for a citizenship across generations. The conditions for intergenerational citizenship require not simply changes in levels in consumption, but also the creation of a common world that extends over generations.

Welfare, treadmills and thresholds

Porritt's argument appeals to recent hedonic research on 'subjective well-being'. In the literature in the hedonic tradition, welfare is a matter of having the right mental states of pleasure and the absence of pain, of feeling good and not feeling bad. It refers to a subjective state: 'Hedonic psychology... is the study of what makes experiences and life pleasant and unpleasant. It is concerned with feelings of pleasure and pain, of interest and boredom, of joy and sorrow and of satisfaction and dissatisfaction.'[11] Elsewhere, Kahneman, Wakker and Sarin refer to 'subjective hedonic experience' as 'experienced utility'.[12]

The surveys on life-satisfaction to which Porritt refers are taken in much of the hedonic tradition to capture either directly or indirectly subjective welfare in this sense. Frey and Stutzer make the claim thus:

Behind the score indicated by a person lies a cognitive assessment to what extent their overall quality of life is judged in a favourable way . . . People evaluate their level of subjective well-being[13]

The passage shifts between two distinct claims. The first sentence claims that the score indicates respondents' subjective assessment of their welfare. The second sentence claims that the score indicates respondents' assessment of their subjective welfare. The move from the first claim to the second involves an illicit shift in the scope of the adjective. The two claims are distinct. An assessment of subjective welfare is an assessment of psychological states – feeling good and not feeling bad. A subjective assessment of welfare need not be about psychological states in that sense at all.

Consider questions that are typically employed in surveys on subjective welfare:

i Taking all things together, would you say you are very happy, quite happy, not very happy, not at all happy?
ii All things considered, how satisfied are you with your life as a whole these days? Please use this card to help with your answer.

1	2	3	4	5	6	7	8	9	10
Dissatisfied									Satisfied[14]

The answers do indicate respondents' subjective assessments of their happiness or the quality of their lives. However, it does not follow that they are assessing their subjective well-being. The concept of happiness or satisfaction need not only refer to psychological states. It is also sometimes used to evaluate a person's projects or life as a whole. If asked 'how happy are you with your job?' or 'how happy are you with your life?' or 'how satisfied are you with your life as a whole?', it is not clear that what a person is being asked to sum up are particular moments of feeling good or feeling bad. Rather the natural interpretation is to understand it as an evaluation of how well a person's projects or life is going according to their own lights. This conception of happiness takes us somewhere closer towards Aristotle's conception of eudaimonia, although it does not take us all the way.[15] The conception is more objective in nature in the sense that it is what a person can actually do or be that matters, not merely their subjective states. It is a conception that has been revived by Sen and Nussbaum in characterising well-being in terms of capabilities to achieve valuable functionings, where functionings refer to 'the various things a person may value doing or being' and capabilities to 'substantive freedoms to achieve alternative functioning combinations'.[16] The surveys are quite open to being understood in eudaimonic terms, to be a person's assessments of how far central valued functionings have been achieved. There is no reason to assume that they capture assessments of hedonic welfare.

We need to distinguish then between the following:

1. a subjective assessment of subjective well-being; and
2. a subjective assessment of objective well-being.

There are good reasons to assume that life-satisfaction surveys may tell us more about 2 than about 1. These subjective assessments of well-being need themselves to be contrasted with objective assessments. We need to distinguish 1 and 2 above from the following:

3. an objective assessment of subjective well-being;
4. an objective assessment of objective well-being.

A distinction between the subjective and the objective assessments of subjective well-being is drawn in the hedonic literature by Kahneman. Kahneman calls 'objective happiness' the aggregate utility derived from a record of actual point-by-point records of the quality of an experience during some episode. 'Subjective happiness' is used to refer to the person's assessment of that utility score of the episode.[17] Both are about subjective welfare. What distinguishes objective welfare is the method by which it is assessed.[18] Subjective and objective happiness can, Kahneman claims, depart from each other. The departure is illustrated by widely discussed experiments in which episodes of painful experiences prolonged by additional but less intense pain receive better global subjective valuations than shorter episodes without the additional period of pain.[19] Retrospective assessments of an episode of painful experiences are a function of the peak intensity of the experience and the intensity of the last moment of the period, and not of the duration of episodes. They depart from an objective assessment that is founded on records of point-by-point painful experiences during that episode. Whether one can go further and claim subjects make an error is a question I will return to shortly. It may be that the structure of the episode matters, not simply aggregate utility.

A similar distinction between subjective and objective assessments of well-being is to be found within the eudaimonic tradition. It comes to the fore in particular in the problem of adaptive preferences. Sen employs the concept to reject the use of pleasures and preferences as guides to well-being. 'Our desires and pleasure-taking abilities adjust to circumstances, especially to make life bearable in adverse situations.'[20] The same point applies also to subjective assessments of functionings themselves. A deprived person's subjective assessments as to how well their lives are going may be adjusted through lower expectations to fit the circumstances they find themselves in. In assessing the distribution of well-being, objective characterisations of different capabilities to achieve functionings may be a better guide than self-reported assessments. There are weaker and stronger senses in which we can talk of an objective characterisation in this context. On a weak reading it might be simply taken to be that characterisation a person would endorse if they were to judge in ideal conditions of full information and equal expectations. Something like that reading is endorsed by Sen. The stronger reading would be that of Aristotle or Marx, which relies on an account of what it is to be a flourishing human being from which certain central human functionings can be derived. Whether one opts for the weaker or stronger reading, a distinction needs to be drawn between subjective assessment of objective well-being and objective assessment of objective well-being.

Once the distinctions between subjective and objective assessments of well-being are drawn, the relationship between reported satisfaction and dissatisfaction and actual changes in welfare becomes more complex. The fact that people do not report improving welfare does not mean welfare is not improving. Consider the treadmill phenomena at the centre of much recent hedonic research. A distinction needs to be drawn between two different treadmills, the hedonic treadmill and the satisfaction treadmill.[21] The claim that there is a hedonic treadmill is a claim directly about subjective welfare. For some pleasures, those involved in many forms of addiction being notable examples, increased consumption of a good is required to maintain a particular level of pleasure. One has to up the hit or else the pleasures decline. Not all pleasures are subject to this effect.[22] Part of the classical Epicurean discussion of pleasures was concerned to distinguish those pleasures which are thus subject to a treadmill effect from those that are not.

While the hedonic treadmill directly concerns levels of subjective well-being, the satisfaction treadmill in contrast concerns changes in subjective assessment of well-being. People's assessment of their welfare can be subject to a treadmill effect. As they get more their assessment of how well they are doing does not alter. Now this could be because they correctly assess that there has been no improvement in welfare. However, it also can be in virtue of a revision of their standards for assessing their welfare. As they get more their aspirations change and the standards by which they judge their welfare are raised. If there is a satisfaction treadmill in which aspirations change to meet improved circumstances, it does not follow that levels of welfare have stayed the same. On an objective assessment welfare may have improved. Nor does the satisfaction treadmill show that there is anything self-defeating with shifting standards of assessment as such. That people aspire to do and become more with their lives as their conditions improve is as such to be expected and is consistent with the claim that their lives have improved over various dimensions. Thus from within the hedonic framework itself the satisfaction treadmill need not be a problem. And it raises a question as to whether improving satisfaction levels should be the primary aim of public policy. Thus, for example, Kahneman suggests otherwise: 'Policies that improve the frequencies of good experiences should be pursued even if people do not describe themselves as happier or more satisfied.'[23]

The problems have more bite from within the eudaimonic framework. The fable of the fisherman and his wife who move from hovel to palace with no increase in life-satisfaction offers a classic tale of the satisfaction treadmill. Their welfare on an objective account improves even if they fail to recognise that this is so. The bite comes in an obverse point – that in some conditions an increase in dissatisfaction with life conditions is a sign that things are going better rather than worse. In the context where dissatisfaction is a corollary of improved knowledge and the failure of adaptation of preferences to conditions of deprivation then it is to be welcomed. For example, it would not be a sign of failure of literacy programmes for Third World women that it increased their dissatisfaction with their life. More generally, where the contented slave, wage earner or housewife becomes discontented with their lot, it is better for them that this is so and not just in virtue of other possible improvements this might bring. It is not just in the case of a failure of adaptation that increasing dissatisfaction might be a sign that things are improving. A similar point holds in some perfectionist contexts where a person is exercising capacities that are part of what it is for a life to be improving but becomes increasingly dissatisfied as they do so. Consider a pianist who starts being greatly satisfied with their initial developments, but who, as they continue to develop technically and artistically, becomes evermore critical of their performance. Their increasing dissatisfaction is a symptom of increasing accomplishment. Something of the same perfectionist thought underpins Mill's observations that it is better to be Socrates dissatisfied than a fool satisfied. To make these points is not to say that dissatisfaction and the subjective assessment of welfare do not matter. There is clearly a danger of paternalism in employing objective criteria for judging how well a person's life goes that are not endorsed by that person. An endorsement constraint on what makes a person's life go well is consistent with an objective theory of well-being. One cannot improve an individual's life by supplying resources that are by some objective criteria valuable to the individual, but not themselves recognised and accepted as such by that individual: a person's life cannot go better in virtue of features that the individual does not endorse as valuable. However, that endorsement is a necessary condition does not entail that it is sufficient. The mere fact of satisfaction does not as such entail that life is going well as the fact of adaptive preferences illustrates.

What these points illustrate is the care that needs to be exercised in interpreting life-satisfaction data. In particular, the graphs on life-satisfaction to which Porritt appeals do not as such show that life has not improved during the period in which reported life-satisfaction has remained static. The simple lack of a correlation between increasing levels of consumption and increasing life-satisfaction does not of itself entail that increasing levels of consumption have not improved well-being. There is more that needs to be said to defend those conclusions. One needs some account of the nature of the shifting standards of appraisal of welfare and how they themselves are to be judged.

Some shifts of standards are signs of improved knowledge or understanding. The perfectionist standards noted above can be of this kind. So also are those that undermine adaptive preferences to poor conditions. Others may be self-defeating or founded upon errors as to what the constituents and determinants of a good life are. It is these that give some force to appeals of the kind Porritt makes. Three arguments have particular import in this regard: those about satiability and limits, those about positional goods and those about the determinants of well-being.

Consider first satiability and limits. The significance of the treadmill argument for sustainable consumption is not that aspirations shift upwards as conditions change, but that there are no limits to the upward spiral: 'our desire for more *constantly* outstrips what we already have'.[24] Whatever people get they will always want more. There is no point at which one can say 'enough'. Now there is a strong case for the claim that on certain dimensions of well-being, to have more no longer improves well-being. Moreover, one objection to the unqualified identification of well-being with preference satisfaction to be found in many standard texts in welfare economics is that it fails to recognise the possibility of such limits. If wants have no limits then neither does the improvement of well-being. As I noted above, the claim that there are limits to the wealth required for a good life is common to both the Epicurean and the Aristotelian tradition. Where they differ is in how they reach this conclusion. On the Aristotelian account the limits of wealth are determined by the needs wealth satisfies. Consider non-instrumental or categorical needs. Things needed in this sense are those which are necessary for human life to flourish at all – without which a life would be blighted.[25] For example, a person needs a certain amount of water, food and shelter, and also certain social relations if they are to flourish at all. A feature of such non-instrumental needs is that there are thresholds such that if a person goes below or above them their well-being will suffer. One can have too much or too little of a particular good. Wealth that is concerned with meeting needs has bounds: 'the amount . . . which suffices for a good life is not unlimited'.[26] A case for limits can be developed from within a hedonic account in terms of limits on particular goods required to give pleasure to agents, but the difference is that those limited goods are not themselves constitutive of well-being. Whether the hedonic case can be made depends on the account of the causal determinants of the relevant psychological states. However, for reasons I outline below, the determinants of well-being are better understood in constitutive terms.

Arguments about positional goods point towards the collectively self-defeating nature of certain shifts in aspirations. As Hirsch notes, where goods are valued as positional goods, their general pursuit is self-defeating. Each agent makes an individual choice for a good that is affected by the same choice by others and hence there is no increase in life-satisfaction.[27] Layard offers a hedonic version of the argument. Income operates as a social measure of relative worth with respect to some reference group with whom people compare themselves. Since comparative position is what matters, as overall wealth grows overall happiness does not improve. The race for status and relative income is self-defeating if we are concerned with improving happiness in society as a whole.[28] This line of argument is powerful, but has no essential tie to a hedonic account of well-being. The argument is to be found in the work of the classical economists who assume an objective state account of well-being.[29]

The third argument to which Porritt appeals in recent hedonic research is that the pursuit of consumer goods in modern market economies involves an error about what the determinants of happiness are.[30] The central determinants of happiness are the security and intrinsic worth of work, health, the quality of familial relationships and the quality of wider social relationships in a community, political participation and levels of personal and political freedoms. However, while Porritt appeals to the hedonic tradition in giving an account of these determinants of well-being, in characterising them he shifts, after some hedging comments, to the more objective needs-based conception of well-being developed by Max Neef.[31] That he does so is not surprising since many of the central determinants of hedonic welfare reappear in the standard lists of the constituents of well-being in the eudaimonic tradition.[32] The convergence should not be surprising given that the survey data on life-satisfaction are themselves open to eudaimonic interpretations. Where the differences between the hedonic and the eudaimonic traditions lie is on how the items on this list should be interpreted, as causal determinants of the appropriate psychological states or as constituents of well-being.

The central problem with the hedonic account here is precisely that it does treat these items as determinants and not as constituents. For the hedonist, social relationships, working life, political participation, personal autonomy and the like matter for well-being in virtue of standing in a contingent causal relationship to a psychological state. The result is that these are either treated purely as a means to an end – autonomy is good, for example, simply because it makes you feel good[33] – or as distinct values that are not themselves central to the well-being of the agent.[34] Neither looks plausible. We value a variety of other goods – relationships with others, accomplishment, interesting work, autonomy – as central welfare goods in themselves, not merely as an external means to good feelings. Indeed, we feel good about fostering such goods because we believe they are value. We do not just value being in the right subjective states. This is part of the point of Nozick's well-known experience machine. We would not plug into an experience machine that would promise us a lifetime of blissful experience because 'we want to *do* certain things, not just to have the experience of doing them' and 'we want to *be* a certain way, to be a certain sort of person'.[35]

Well-being, narrative and citizenship over generations

A central weakness in the hedonic account of well-being when it comes to sustainability is it cannot offer an adequate account of a citizenship across generations. Why should hedonism have a particular problem with regard to inter-generational citizenship? An initial important observation to make is that nothing in hedonism rules out concern for future generations. A hedonist account of well-being combined with a suitable ethical theory can entail strong obligations for future generations. Thus the classical utilitarian claim that we should maximise hedonic well-being is normally taken to be blind to the time when any agent affected by an act exists. In classical Epicurean texts one finds passages that appear to suggest concern for future generations. Consider one of the arguments Lucretius offers to purge the fear of death:

> There is need of matter for the growth of later generations, all of which, nevertheless, shall follow you when they have lived their lives; and in like matter generations before you have died, and others shall die hereafter. Thus without end one springs from another, and life is granted to no one as possession but as a loan.[36]

Our very deaths are a condition of the welfare of those who follow and should be accepted as such. With some special pleading, the appeal to 'need of matter for the growth of later generations' could be given even an environmental interpretation as suggesting claims about sustainability.

The problem for hedonism is not that it rules out concern for future generations, but rather the nature of the concern it calls upon. The problem is the obverse of its solution to the problem of consumption, which appeals to our own quality of life. When it comes to concern for future generations in contrast it has to make it a purely ethical matter that is not tied to how well one's own life is going. The problem appears in the famous mirror argument in Lucretius that follows immediately after the passage I have just quoted:

> See likewise of how little concern to us were the ages of eternal time that passed before we were born. Nature holds this up to us as a mirror of the time that will be after our death.[37]

As far as our own well-being is concerned, life before we existed is a mirror of life after we die. Neither matters to us in so far as our own well-being is concerned. If well-being consists in having the right mental states of pleasure and the absence of pain, then neither what happens before nor what happens after we die can affect our well-being. We may have concerns for future generations, but these will be purely ethical concerns for others. The future is irrelevant as far as our own lives go.

There is a more general point to be made here about the role of time in hedonic accounts of well-being. Hedonic accounts assume that the welfare values of different moments of time are separable. Many assume they are additively separable. Informally, to say they are separable is to say that the value of what happens at some point in time, t_i, is independent of the value of what happens at another point, t_j, and to say that they are additively separable is to say that the total value of an episode over a period of time is the sum of these independent values. As Ramsey puts it, 'enjoyments and sacrifices at different times can be calculated independently and added'.[38] Some care is needed here. Consider Kahneman's account of objective happiness. Kahneman's account of experienced utility does allow for one kind of non-separability. Kahneman takes the objective experienced utility of an episode to be a function of the instant utilities, that is the pleasure or pain experienced at each moment. And the experienced pleasure at one moment can be affected by what happens before and the expectations of what happens after. The temporal location of a moment of pleasure or pain can make a difference to the level that is experienced at that moment. However, the value of the experienced utility at that moment itself is independent of the value of the experienced utilities at other times.[39] The total value is thus just the sum of those values. If one assumes a subjective state account of welfare, then one can treat the value of events in time as separable. Whether or not the event was pleasurable or painful can be ascertained independently of what happened before or after. The objective characterisation of the subjective well-being of a person over a period of time will be the sum of those independent values.

This account fails to capture the way that the values of moments of pleasure and pain are themselves a matter of the overall narrative structure of episodes in people's lives. The problem is already apparent to some degree in Kahneman's experiments on episodes of pain. What appears to matter to patients in these contexts is the structure of the episode, in particular how they end. In this case the narrative structure is so minimal that it may be unclear how much it should count. But elsewhere the narrative structure of our episodes, and endings in particular, do matter to our evaluation in much more clear-cut ways. Consider the following example:

A. A newly married couple, couple A, go on a two week honeymoon. The holiday begins disastrously: they each discover much in the other which they had not noticed before, and they dislike what they find. The first two days are spent in an almighty row. However, while they argue continuously over the next seven days, they begin to resolve their differences and come to a deeper appreciation of each other. Over the last five days of the holiday they are much happier and both feel that they have realised a relationship that is better than that which they had before their argument.

The holiday ends happily. Sadly, on their return journey, the plane that carries them explodes and they die.

B. A newly married couple, couple B, go on honeymoon. The first twelve days proceed wonderfully. On the thirteenth day their relationship deteriorates badly as each begins to notice and dislike in the other a character trait which they had not noticed before, at the same time realising that the other had a quite mistaken view of themselves. On the last day of the holiday they have a terrible row, and sit on opposite ends of the plane on the return journey. They both die in an explosion on the plane.[40]

Which holiday goes better? From the hedonic perspective it looks like holiday B. On any simple summing of goods over moments of pain and over moments of pleasure, holiday B contains far more of the good, less of the bad. This looks to be true even if the short moments of pleasure in A and the short moments of pain in B are particularly intense because of where they feature in the sequence of experiences. However, a few of my more hedonistically inclined students and colleagues aside, most people I have given the example to claim that holiday A is better. What matters is the shape of the episode. What counts in favour of holiday A is the narrative order of events. Crucial to that order is the way in which the story ends. People's lives have a narrative structure, and the ending of a narrative is crucial to the genre to which a person's life, or an episode of that life, belongs – tragic, comic, pathetic and so on. Our evaluation of how well a person's life goes depends on the narrative we can truly tell of it. The temporal structure of a life matters. It matters not just to the overall valuation but to the value we place on different moments in the episode. The value of those moments is not simply a matter of the intensity of the experience at any moment but their place in the larger structure of an episode. In holiday A, the argument at the start of the holiday is not simply a moment of pain. Rather, taken in context, it might be taken to be a 'turning point' in the relationship, one which clarifies the relationship and lays the foundation for the ensuing happiness. Within the context of the individuals' entire lives, it has another significance. For that reason one can also talk of the earlier event having been 'redeemed' by the later reconciliation to which it gave rise. Likewise, the moments of experienced happiness in holiday B are not just pleasures to be valued simply as such. Rather, within the context of the whole story, they are moments of illusion, when each person has a false view of the other, an illusion shattered by the final argument. Had their lives continued, the argument also may have become something else, but the ill fortune of untimely deaths robs the participants of such a future. The values of different moments in an episode are not separable in the way that hedonism assumes. Whether moments of pain and pleasure are goods or evils depends on their context of a life as a whole. Their value is not reducible to levels of intensity considered in isolation.

The shift in welfare valuation here relies on a move to a different account of the constituents of well-being. Well-being is not just a matter of subjective experiences. It is a matter of what one can do or be in one's life. For example, relationships to others matter as such, not just in virtue of the experiences they bring. What matters in the episodes outlined is not just experiences of the relationships to others, but how those relationships actually are. What matters in holiday B is not just the experiences of pleasure but their actual significance in the development of a relationship. What matters for our welfare is the good, not simply the experience of the good. What lies behind the rejection of any simple sum of experiences is an appeal to a more objective account of well-being. If how well our life goes is a matter of what we can actually do or be, then for a number of our central relationships and projects we cannot ascertain the value of moments independent of a larger narrative structure in which they occur. A personal relationship that begins in contention and through that ends in reconciliation is valued more than one that begins in apparent harmony and ends in discord. The way in which the earlier moments of contention and harmony are to be understood and appraised depends on the larger narrative. If a person suffers great difficulties in a central project of their lives and ultimately succeeds, the suffering is redeemed in a way that is not the case if the attempt fails. The outcome matters to how the present suffering is to be evaluated. The use of the concept of redemption in everyday non-religious contexts depends on that possibility. The way matters turn out matters. Our lives are not a series of events such that at any moment we can say whether our lives now are going well or badly. The future determines what appraisal we can give to the present.

In shifting from subjective states to what we can do and be we have shifted to a more objective Aristotelian account of the well-being. The points about the way our appraisal of well-being is subject to the way lives actually turn out lies behind Aristotle's partial endorsement of Solon's dictum that we can call no man happy until he is dead.[41] Aristotle shows some ambivalence about accepting the further entailment of this account, that Solon might be too quick in stopping at the point of death. For if what we actually can do and be that matters, then what happens after our deaths can matter to how well our life can be said to go now. We engage in projects and belong to communities such that how well our lives can be said to go can depend on what happens to the projects and relationships that occur beyond our lifetime. Hence, the way the future will be and that we have a stake in creating a particular future can matter to us. Consider the activity of doing science. The status of scientific works depends on their relation to both a particular past and a particular future. In relation to the past, the assessment of a piece of scientific work makes reference to a particular history of problems and theories to which it makes a contribution. Its success or failure depends on its capacity to solve existing problems where others fail. However, it also depends on a projected relation to the future in terms of its capacity to solve not just existing problems, but also problems not envisaged by its author, and its fruitfulness in creating new problems to be solved and new avenues of research. The existence of future scientists educated in a discipline and able to continue work within it matters for current scientific activity. The same points apply in the arts. The greatness of many works of art lies in their continuing to illuminate human problems and predicaments in contexts quite foreign to that in which they were originally constructed. Likewise, many of the qualities of a work of art may only become apparent in virtue of its relation to future works. In that minimal sense, Eliot is right: 'the past should be altered by the present as much as the present is directed by the past'.[42] Similar points apply to more 'prosaic' activities. They apply to everyday working activities, where these involve skilled performances which are embodied in objects and landscapes. That they do so is central to Arendt's criticisms of consumer society to which I return below.

The significance of these points is central to the civic republican criticism of emerging commercial society in the eighteenth century. The disruption of historical narrative by market norms lay at heart of debates about land and commerce in Britain in the seventeenth and eighteenth centuries. Early critics of emerging commercial society were concerned in part with the effects of the mobilisation of landed property by commerce on the conditions of community and projects across time. The eighteenth-century civic humanist criticism of commercial society was founded on the belief that the civic virtues had their basis in stable ownership of landed property. The material foundation of a good society lay in 'real property recognizable as stable enough to link successive generations in social relationships belonging to, or founded in, the order of nature'.[43] Commercial society, by mobilizing land, undermined that link between generations.

The republican theme has remained a refrain in political theory since, developed in different terms in particular within the socialist tradition. The theme is central to the work of Polanyi. Polanyi's account of land and labour as fictitious commodities, as items that are treated as if commodities, is concerned in part with the consequences of the disruption of social ties of place:

> To allow the market mechanism to be sole director of the fate of human beings and their natural environment ... would result in the demolition of society ... Nature would be reduced to its elements, neighbourhoods and landscapes defiled, rivers polluted.[44]

The separation of workers from the land and the subsequent mobilisation of labour break ties of 'a human community to the locality where it is'.[45] The consequences of this disruption in part explain the power of the conservative reaction to economic liberalism that opposed the mobilisation of land.[46] Another version of the theme is also echoed in the socialist tradition, in particular in the more associational guild traditions. Historical community over generations is disrupted by the mobilisation of labour across occupations. The necessity of the mobility of labour was central to the defence of the market economy by its early defenders like Adam Smith whose work was aimed against guilds and the practice of lengthy apprenticeship as a barrier to the movement of labour. One response is that the disappearance of continuity in craft and work weakens ties across generations. The relation of craftsman and apprentice is undermined, and with it the sense in which success in craftwork is tied to past and future. The craftsperson has a particular relation to those who come before and will follow: 'Not only his own thoughts, but the thoughts of the men of past ages guide his hands; and, as a part of the human race, he creates.'[47] The view is echoed in Weil's comment:

> A corporation, or guild, was a link between the dead, the living and those yet unborn, within the framework of a certain specified occupation. There is nothing today which can be said to exist, however remotely, for the carrying out of such a function.[48]

The mobilisation of labour in market society, like its mobilisation of land, disrupts ties of community across generations.

As I have argued elsewhere, to make these points is to raise a problem rather than a solution.[49] The return to stable ownership in land and limited mobility of labour is neither possible in modern conditions without excessive authoritarianism, nor is it desirable. The mobilisation of land and labour was a source of liberation from personal servitude and narrow horizons. The theme is central to Marx's response to the nostalgia for pre-capitalist social relations and forms of craft labour.[50] The problem of creating intergenerational citizenship is one of creating the economic, social and cultural conditions for the existence and expression of narrative identity that extends across generations and is at the same time consistent with autonomy and independence. The problem of intergenerational community is a particular version of the problem about individualism and community which has been at the centre of social and political theory for the last two centuries. How is it possible to develop forms of community which no longer leave the individual stripped of particular ties to others, but which are compatible with the sense of individual autonomy and the richness of needs that the disintegration of older identities also produced? The problem emerges in the responses from the classical economists to the civic republican criticism of the mobilisation of land which themselves invoke the republican virtues of independence. Versions of the problem are to be found in the work of Hegel and Marx. Variations on the theme are repeated in the debates between liberals and communitarians. The question about the conditions for community that crosses generations creates a particular temporal version of that problem. The question was central to the republican tradition: what are the conditions which develop a sense of intergenerational citizenship in modern conditions?

A dimension of this problem that is of immediate concern to this volume is the theme in the republican tradition that citizenship depends upon the existence of a common public realm that is shared between members of a community. Correspondingly, intergenerational citizenship requires a public world that is durable over generations. The theme is central to Arendt's critique of consumer society. Arendt starts with the classical thought that we engage in common activities that extend beyond our lives: 'Through many ages – but now not any more – men entered the public realm because they wanted something of their own or something they had in common with others to be more permanent than their earthly lives.'[51] A 'common world that can survive the coming and going of the generations' is both a condition and a consequence of that sense of the significance of a life moving beyond death. The critique of consumer society that Arendt develops in *The Human Condition* centres on the loss of this common world. The world of consumption is tied to the activity of labour. Labour, encompassing those activities required as part of our biological necessities, issues in objects that lack permanence, that are consumed and produced again as part of the natural cycles of our private existence. Work in contrast produces a public and stable realm of human artifice, of those fabricated things to be used that form the common world. Work creates not a world of consumer goods but of use objects that have a durable public existence independent of the worker and are the conditions of a shared public life:

> Viewed as part of the world, the products of work – and not the products of labor – guarantee the permanence and durability without which the world would not be possible at all. It is within the world of durable things that we find the consumer goods through which life assures the means of its own survival. Needed by our bodies and produced by its labouring, but without stability of their own, these things for incessant consumption appear and disappear in an environment of things what are not consumed but used, and to which, as we use them, we become used and accustomed. As such they give rise to the familiarity of the world, its customs and habits of intercourse between men and things as well as between men and men. What consumer goods are for the life of man, use objects are for his world.[52]

The central charge against modern consumer societies is that while it issues in a world of abundance in use objects at the same time it reduces them to consumer goods that lack the durability or permanence of the objects of work. Though the objects of work will pass in the end, their passing is not the aim of production.[53] What is significant about consumer society is that the rate of use of objects is accelerated to the point that 'the objective difference between use and consumption, between the relative durability of use objects and the swift coming and going of consumer goods dwindles to insignificance'.[54] The durable common world of fabricated use objects gives way to a world of consumer goods: 'we must consume, devour, as it were, our houses and furniture and cars as though they were the "good things" of nature which spoil uselessly if they are not drawn into the never-ending cycle of man's metabolism with nature'.[55] The common stable and durable world of the worker disappears. With it is lost a common world that is shared across generations.

Arendt's republican theme is overdrawn. Her account of the ancient republican world is marked by some nostalgia. There are proper criticisms to be raised about her account and appraisal of labour and reproduction. However, in terms of the larger problem of the conditions for intergenerational citizenship I do want to defend two Arendtian claims. The first is an analytical point: that a distinction needs to be drawn between consumption and other relations to both the natural world and the world of human fabrication. We do consume items such as clean water, food and medication. It is part of the purpose of their production that they are used up as part of the metabolic processes of our biology. Other objects we use are also worn out from use and the processes of nature, but their being worn out is incidental to their function. Typical examples are buildings, vehicles for transport, furniture and clothing, each with different cycles of change and decay. We engage with or in other human performances such as music and theatre, but we do not properly consume at all. To treat all use of objects and performances as items of consumption is to conflate those different relations to the worlds in which we live and the social meanings they have for us. That conflation matters. While it is not itself a cause of the increasing rapidity in the cycles of use and waste of non-consumer goods, it does disguise the nature of those changes and the loss of the public world over generations in which at least some of these issue.

The second Arendtian point is that the existence of a material public world that crosses generations is of significance in creating a sense of citizenship over generations. Two remarks are in order about this claim. First, the problem of sustaining such a public world is not one of freezing the physical constitution of places in the manner of the heritage industry, which produces its own objects for tourist consumption. To freeze places is to block the possibility of a continued human narrative. The problem is rather of the continued maintenance and formation of publicly shared material objects and spaces in a way that allows them to constitute part of a coherent human narrative between generations. Second, Arendt's identification of a common world with the world of fabricated objects is too narrow. The ties of intergenerational community are also embodied in landscapes and familiar places shared across generations which, while they are transformed by human action, are not the results of intentional human artifice.[56] Correspondingly, a problem of nature conservation needs to be understood in similar terms to that of maintaining and transforming our cultural world. As Holland and Rawles put it, 'conservation is . . . . about preserving the future *as a realisation of the potential of the past* . . . . [it] is about negotiating the transition from past to future in such a way as to secure the transfer of. . .significance' (Holland and Rawles, 1994, p. 37).[57]

Finally, to make the point about the need for a sense of belonging to a human world that stretches into the future is to point to a deep paradox and dilemma in modern environmentalism. Environmentalists have quite properly recorded the threats to the biophysical conditions of a continuing world for human habitation, most notably, for example, climate change in which that which was solid literally melts before us as glaciers recede and the polar ice cap shrinks. However, in placing at the forefront the fragility and potential impermanence of the world they at the same time undermine conditions for a sense of identity over generations that relies on the perceived continued existence of a durable common world. To present our relation to the future as one of impending catastrophe can consequently have the effect of decreasing the sense of a longer time horizon required for a sense of community over generations. It can induce a temporal myopia that is inconsistent with intergenerational citizenship.

The classical republican problem of understanding and creating the conditions for intergenerational citizenship is one that deserves more prominence in political theory and practice than it has received. It is, I have suggested, not a particularly tractable problem. It raises long-standing questions in political theory about the conditions for sustaining individual autonomy with ties of community. It raises particular difficulties and paradoxes for environmentalists. I offer no answer here to those problems and difficulties, only a plea that they should be taken seriously as such. The problem with the recent return to Epicurus in recent hedonic theories of well-being is that they disappear from view.[58]

12

'Alternative Hedonism' and the Citizen-Consumer

Kate Soper

Consumerism and self-interest

The role of 'consumer' is today often contrasted with that of 'citizen' precisely by reason of its egoism. Individuals as consumers are frequently regarded as driven by self-interest alone and concerned only with private acquisition, utility, pleasure or advancement. It is only in their role as citizens that they supposedly look above the parapet of private needs and desires or could be said to have an eye to the public good. In this conception of human motivation, which is strongly influenced by neo-liberal economic and rational choice theory, if altruism enters at all into the picture of personal motivations it is certainly not at the level of consumption, where it is often assumed that considerations for the welfare of others (at least outside one's immediate circle) have little sway in determining private purchases. Critical discussions of recent attempts by government to reposition consumers of public services as if they were rights-bearing citizens have also, despite the indisputable justice of the criticism, continued to sustain the division between the 'selfish' consumer and the 'concerned' citizen, in their exposures of the purely rhetorical nature of these policy moves.[1] Indeed so powerful is the presumption that these roles are mutually exclusive, that it functions almost as an analytic truth in some theoretical approaches: if the consumer shows signs of being motivated by any but the most acquisitive and narrowly defined economic self-interest, then he or she is a 'bad' consumer or not acting in the properly consumerist role. In this conception, any more altruistic motivation is, by definition, ruled out as an attribute or aspect of the consuming self.[2] (An associated tendency to explain even the more 'green' and 'ethical' consumers as motivated primarily by a 'selfish' interest in status and self-distinction is discussed in more detail below.)

The theoretical paradigm of exclusively self-interested motivation underpinning this approach to consumption has, over the last decade or so, come in for some trenchant criticism ('the purely economic man is close to being a social moron', we have been told by one prominent critic),[3] and it no longer holds quite the sway it once did in economic and political argument. Other-oriented motives (for both good and ill, benevolent and malevolent) now occupy a more central role again in explanations of behaviour in social science. Nor did the extreme form of moral scepticism about altruism that sustained contemporary neo-classical economic and rational choice theory ever command much support among philosophers, who have over centuries questioned its ultimate coherence. Joseph Butler famously disputed the sup-posed egoism of all acts of apparent benevolence.[4] Hume, too, very clearly saw that if we insist on representing all acts, even those most seemingly altruistic, as essentially egoistic, then we opt for an entirely vacuous account of human motivation that will hardly help with exploring the difference between self-sacrificial and self-indulgent behaviour.[5] In his *Discourse on the Origin of Inequality* Rousseau insisted against Hobbes on the coexistence in human nature of compassion with self-love.[6] Other influential dissectors of human motives, such as Adam Smith, Voltaire and John Stuart Mill, likewise argued that self- and other interest are mutually bound up together, and none of them presented self-interest as the sole motive of human action.[7] More recently, Thomas Nagel has defended altruism on the purely rational grounds that to deny it would ultimately involve accepting that an individual could never view the self impersonally – in other words, never adopt the outlook of another person – and that this is something that is inconsistent with having a conception of oneself as a person in the first place.[8] (And much philosophy, of course, notably Hegel in his 'Master-Slave' dialectic in the *Phenomenology of Spirit*, has insisted on the importance of the other as the very condition of self-recognition. Daniel Miller also draws directly on Hegel's rejection in the *Philosophy of Right* of the ideal of a pure individual fulfilment in defending his 'dialectics of shopping'.)[9]

We should note, too, that the tradition of neo-classical economics from the eighteenth century into our own times has not always been as relentlessly anti-altruistic as some theorists of consumption have maintained. In the mid-nineteenth century, Ricardo, John Stuart Mill, Hobson and other English political economists had arguments that ran counter to the 'French school' of utility theorists whose emphasise on self-interest could be said to flow more smoothly into current neo-liberal thinking.[10] (Mill indeed was closer to Marx in seeking to dissociate the production of wealth from its seemingly indispensable capitalist and competitive integument.) Pearson and others have also pointed to the vein of altruism in Victorian and *fin de siècle* neo-classical economics, especially in the argument of Alfred Marshall, who con-sistently advanced altruism or the 'principle of sympathy' as a natural human response that confounded notions of 'economic man' as a bloodless egoist.[11] But the story is probably even more complex than these qualifications sug-gest; partly because what is adduced in support of the necessary role of altruism in economic life by at least some of this theory refers more to its presence as a form of mutual aid at the level of production (its contribution to what today we term 'corporate spirit') rather than to a benevolence motivating individual consumers;[12] and partly because the idea of a 'welfare'-oriented dimension of consumption in Marshall's argument appears to have its primary source in his well-meant paternalism rather than being self-evidently grounded in actual consumer attitudes or practice at the time. If the normal motives of economic man have always been presumed to include an unselfish desire to make provision for his family, then why, Marshall inquires, 'should they not include all other altruistic motives (...) There seems to be no reason.'[13] But, in fact, there are many reasons why altruism might not extend beyond the family, and Marshall's appeal here is almost entirely rhetorical. However, despite the various caveats or qualifications one might want to make, there can be little doubt that even in the argument of the economists, not to speak of that of moral philosophers and social and psychological theorists, the idea of the individual as exclusively driven by narrow self-interest has been regularly and powerfully challenged. As Pearson has put it,

> every economist has an indefeasible right to define the discipline's remit as he or she sees fit, but no definition that excludes altruistic motives can claim the mantle of historical continuity. By the same token, the growing number of theorists who acknowledge an altruistic motive are not exploring *terra incognita* so much as they are bringing modern tools and sensibilities back to exotic landscapes that a previous generation knew well.[14]

In short, economics in the more recent period has cut out all 'externalities', considerations of altruism included, in the interest of turning itself into rigorous calculus. But the abstraction it has thus become is precisely what lies behind the ire of the sociologists – for whom everything that makes up the actual consumer has fallen out of the frame of this perfectly egoistic *homo economicus*.[15] What has also been overlooked in the process is the complex history of the emergence of the 'consumer' as a distinct identity, and the extent to which this history gainsays any idea of a straightforward linear development in 'selfish' acquisitiveness from the period of Enlightenment through to the present day. According to Trentmann, the category of the 'consumer' is a relatively late arrival, and the initial attention it receives when it takes off in the 1890s is driven by a dialogue outside or at the margins of mainstream liberal economics. Much of the discussion, moreover, in that period is focussed on the ways in which consumption will contribute to public welfare through the sagacity of the 'conscientious' consumer, rather than on the consumer as an essentially egoistic being driven by private greed or irrational appetite.[16]

These sociological and historical reappraisals also raise a number of interesting conceptual issues. What, for example, are the implications of their repositioning of the consumer as in some sense 'distorted' in the picture offered by neo-classical and rational choice theory? Does this mean that where consumers *are* today caught up in their more insatiable, shopaholic, self-interested – 'consumerist' – modes of behaving they are in some sense given over to inauthentic or pathological practices? Does it imply that where consumption is indeed pursued in a way that takes no account of the welfare of others or of the environmental consequences (and those considerations do not figure as an influence in the formation of subjective choices), then what is going on is better described as an *avoidance* of, or *resistance* to, recognising the implications for others rather than as a form of 'rational' choice or 'natural' egoism?

There will be a range of responses on these issues.[17] But one might certainly claim that if the denial of altruism is indeed both ontologically incoherent and psychologically flawed then it implies that we block or evade rather than dispense altogether with any identification with the other. And this in turn implies that the inducements to the specific form of consumption ('consumerism') that expects and encourages us to ignore any but the most immediate economic and acquisitive interests of ourselves as supposedly autonomous individual consumers are colluding in a form of denial or repression rather than coinciding in some unproblematic way with primary human needs, desires and values. In short, it would seem that we are talking here of a distinctively consumerist form of self-interest (and profit-driven encouragement of that) rather than of a mode of consumption that can readily be justified or adequately understood by referring it to its roots in 'human nature'. Consumer culture is indeed a specifically cultural formation – and one, moreover, that might be better viewed as missing rather than meeting many human aspirations and hedonistic opportunities.

Many will dissent from an explicit formulation of this kind. Yet it is surely no accident that theorists of very differing complexion in other respects have so regularly arrived at the idea of 'consumerism' as compensatory for various forms of existential loss (of meaning, security, identity, etc.). And whatever, of course, is presented as compensatory is, at least implicitly, also being presented as a distortion or alienation or displacement of the system of gratifications that would have been more appropriate. Conversely, few, if any, theorists write about consumer culture as if it were the final and triumphant realisation of the human spirit: the fulfilment of a 'species-being' that had been long in the maturing and had now finally managed to flower to the benefit of all. When theorists insist on egoistic desire and its insatiability as the key features of consumerist culture, what they are therefore really directing attention to is its endless failure to gratify – and thus ultimately, one may argue, to its misdirection of human and ecological resources.[18]

'Alternative hedonism': A republican form of self-interest ?

What is more, even if this form of self-interest presides over most consumption choices in affluent societies at the present time, it is certainly not the case that all of them are made in obedience to it. Any theory of contemporary consumption that invokes only this motivation is therefore altogether too reductive and cannot accommodate the full range of influences that go into shaping a more critical and 'republican' perspective. It clearly cannot do justice to the more altruistic concerns for human and environmental well-being that motivate the ethical consumers. But it also cannot do justice to what I would describe as a specifically 'alternative hedonist' self-interest in consuming differently. The essential – and essentially abstract – distinction to which I am here referring is between attitudes and decisions that are primarily motivated by dispassionate concern for the social and environmental exploitation that sustains consumer culture, and attitudes towards, and decisions on, consumption that have been prompted primarily by the distraints on satisfaction incurred for consumers themselves. It is a rather different thing to go by bike rather than car because of the intrinsic pleasures of biking and the personal interest in avoiding long waits in traffic queues than it is to do so out of concern for dwindling fossil fuel reserves, or general pollution caused by car transport. It is one thing to avoid fast food because it tastes awful or is bad for one's health, another to do so out of concern for animal welfare, or agricultural malpractice or exploitation of the workers involved in the industry. It is one thing to change one's job in quest of a less personally stressed existence, another to do so because one no longer wants to lend oneself so directly to the unscrupulous environmental and social practices of one's employer. It is one thing to move to a rural location in search of a peaceful retreat, another to do with a view to becoming more self-sufficient and less dependant on market provision.

But it is also evident that these are strained oppositions and that the motives of actual consumers are unlikely to divide very precisely along these lines. A primarily egoistic rationale for changing consumption will very often be coloured by something more altruistic, and vice versa. The more selfishly motivated preference for cycling will be inseparable from a more collectively oriented concern to avoid contributing to car pollution and congestion, if only because the pleasures of cycling are themselves to a large extent (especially in more built-up areas) dependant on their reduction. Most regular cyclists, moreover – to judge by the Internet chat sites, friendly exchanges on the road, and cycling literature – take pleasure in other cyclists cycling, not only because it reduces car use, but because of the pleasure taken in the other cyclist's pleasure. Many who avoid fast food will do so for a complex of more or less self-interested motives since to be bothered about its impact on one's own health is usually also to be bothered about the processes of manufacture. In many cases, moreover, these pleasures are enhanced by the 'altruistic' or moral pleasure of knowing that one's consumption has contributed less than other alternatives to environmental destruction and social exploitation. There is clearly, then, a considerable overlap between these more specifically 'alternative hedonist' types of motivation and the altruism of the green or ethical consumer who is seeking to avoid the harm that ensues to others and the environment of certain forms of consumption. Indeed, in some cases, the difference here may merely be one of emphasis depending on whether one is dwelling on the aggregate social and environmental impact of consumerism or on its negative by-products at the level of individual gratification. We have already noted that part of the pleasure for the 'alternative hedonist' consumer may well be that of knowing he or she is finding pleasure in ways that are less socially and environmentally damaging than the alternatives. But the reverse is true, too, and the more altruistically motivated consumers will also very often take pleasure in avoiding collusion in exploitative consumption. What is here shared across the distinction we have drawn between more or less self-interested motives is a distinctively moral form of self-pleasuring or a self-interested form of altruism: that which takes pleasure in committing to a more socially accountable mode of consuming.

Two kinds of qualifications are in order here. In the first place, it may be said that this argument overlooks the extent to which ethical consumption is motivated by an interest in acquiring status and distinction rather than more altruistic concerns for the collective well-being. Engagement in ethical consumption has certainly been presented as involving forms of 'moral-selving', distinction and display in a number of recent commentaries.[19] Barnett *et al.* offer an analysis in which a Foucaultian exercise of self-cultivation, or 'governing of the consuming self', avails itself of ethical products and fair trade campaigning strategies in 'performative practices' of virtuous consumption. The arena for these, it is argued, may be home or workplace and will generally invite social distinction and provide a forum for a process in which 'caring for others is achieved through the cultivation of the care of the self'.[20] The sending of charity cards and involvement in fair trade special events is also cited as enabling similar forms of self-messaging and virtuous display.[21] The authors concede that ethical consumption is not always about such forms of self-display. Some governing will be aimed, as they put it, at a 'going-beyond the self, in a deliberate attempt to achieve degrees of selflessness in order to practice responsibilities to distant others'.[22] And at certain points, they also appear to argue for a more qualified approach in which pre-existing ethical commitments based on information are allowed a greater role.[23] Such concessions to a more humanist perspective might indeed seem necessary, since otherwise an account in terms of 'performative practices' can offer no compelling reason why only some people are co-opted into ethical consumption. On the other hand, the Foucaultian approach sits uneasily with any such concession, and the attempt to combine these contrary forms of thinking on subjectivity is liable to considerable strain.

I would definitely want to question myself whether an account in terms of practices of virtuous display and self-distinction can provide the whole of the story, in part because of an intuitive sense that those who turn to green and ethical consumption will be rather less likely than most to be interested in using consumption in a purely emulative mode; but also because, in many cases, the 'consumption' involved is a non-consumption, a matter of with-holding purchasing power, and leaves rather little clear material trace. The 'signifying' commodity is in this event noticeable, if it is at all, only in its absence. It also seems counter-intuitive to suppose that ethical consumers are in any sense jealous rather than pleased at the signs that others have joined them. In other words, to analyse the turn to green and ethical consumption primarily in terms of *amour propre* would arguably be to miss the real complex-ity and over-determined quality of the motives involved in these shifts. As we have seen, there are also some more philosophical reasons to be wary of explanations in consumption theory that tend to exclude any but motives of self-distinction. I have argued here not only that there are indeed genu-inely altruistic motives underlying the turn to ethical and green consump-tion (where 'genuine' means not cultivated for the sake of displaying them), but also that even in the case of the 'alternative hedonist' consumer, the element of self-pleasuring often extends to, and includes as a condition, an interest in the pleasures and well-being of others. Yet altruism of this kind would be ruled out by any explanation of ethical consumption entirely in terms of the purely emulative interest in personal distinction, or would figure in it only as the instrument of personal gratification (in the form of needing the other only as a source of admiration and esteem), and not therefore as genuinely altruistic in the moral sense.

Of course it is true – to turn now to the second line of objection – that the 'self-pleasuring' I have associated with the 'alternative hedonist' motive may not always include a concern for the well-being of others. The option against fast food or to move job or house may well be chosen without any concern other than to improve health, avoid stress and so on, and may do little or nothing to check an otherwise entirely consumerist lifestyle. It may even entail additional forms of damaging consumption, as is the case whenever the new 'rural' lifestyle involves a lot of domestic refurbishing or remains heavily dependant on the use of car and air flight. We must also acknowledge that there will be consumers who are very averse to some types of consumerist consumption (e.g. junk food) but have few qualms about indulging in others, and for whom this option is an eccentricity in the context of an otherwise untroubled consumerist lifestyle. But in these cases we also need to distin-guish between a simple (and essentially still 'consumerist') interest in con-suming differently (having a rural rather than, or in addition to, a city existence, for example eating organic rather than inorganic foods) and a more properly 'alternative hedonist' – and 'republican' – response, which will always involve some fairly consistent and consciously felt disenchant-ment with the consumer culture, and desire to avoid collusion in it, even though its main motives are self-interested. The 'alternative hedonist' con-sumer differs from the 'eccentrically' or 'occasionally' alternative or the merely downsizing or re-locating consumer in being sensitive to the 'tragedy

of the commons' factor in consumerism and keen to adjust individual consumption in the light of it. This is a 'citizen-consumer' who recognises the
impact of aggregate individual consumer decisions in stealing the personal
pleasure of each and everyone, and for that reason tries to avoid personally
contributing to the aggregate 'tragedy'.

Such consumers, one might add, are theorized as being sensitive not only to
the *compromisation* of the pleasures of affluence by their negative by-products,
but also to their *pre-emption* of other enjoyments. In one case the concern is
with the ways in which previously unquestioned forms of gratification such
as driving, air flight, eating certain foods, or using certain materials have now
been tainted by the congestion, pollution, noise, ill health and excessive
waste they cause. In the other case we are talking primarily of deprivation
rather than of compromisation: of a critical response that is troubled by an
intuition of the pleasures that are being directly occluded or denied by the
consumerist lifestyle. If one can speak of experienced displeasure here, it is in
the sense of loss or lack of gratification rather than an experience of gratification spoiled or distrained upon (of the desire the ancient Greeks referred to as
pothos rather than *himeros*, a yearning for what is not obtainable in the
present rather than a desire for that which is already available).[24] And here
the examples can be more or less tangible, more or less retrospective and
nostalgic, more or less utopian. It may be a nostalgia for certain kinds of
material, objects, practices, or forms of human interaction that no longer
figure in everyday life as they once did; it may be a case of missing the
experience of certain kinds of landscape, or spaces (to play, talk, loiter, meditate or commune with nature); it may be a sense that possibilities of erotic
contact or conviviality have been closed down that might otherwise have
opened up; or a sense that were it not for the dominance of the car, there
would be an altogether different system of provision for other modes of
transport, such as cycling, and both rural and city areas would look and feel
and smell and sound entirely different. Or it may just be a vague and rather
general malaise that descends in the shopping mall or supermarket: a sense of
a world too cluttered and encumbered by material objects and sunk in waste,
of priorities skewed through the focus on evermore extensive provision and
acquisition of things.

Consumption and political agency

Although I have noted and discussed here the quite extensive degree of
overlap between the altruistic and the self-regarding (or 'alternative hedonist') motives for resisting consumerism, I justify the special attention paid to
the latter in my research in part because of the reinforcement and over-
determining role it may come to play in promoting sustainable consumption.
For I believe that in the absence of a revised conception among the already
more affluent communities of their own needs, interests and pleasures, little

pressure is likely to be applied to secure the necessary policy changes. A changed perception of the 'good life' (an 'alternative hedonism') is in this sense an essential stimulant to any possible future curbing of consumerist culture and its more negative social and environmental impacts. The moral and material dissatisfactions generated by the affluent lifestyle – discontents that find their 'utopian' summons in a post-consumerist vision of the 'good life' – acquire in this sense a definite political dimension. Or to put the point slightly differently, it is not at all clear that other than at the level of consumption, and through the forms of consumer resistance generated by the disaffection with consumerism and its compromisation and pre-emption of pleasure, we can discover any potential actors for a democratically achieved process of change in the West today (and it would be absurd to suppose that it could be achieved by any other means). My argument then, in summary form, is that if we are to see any radical shift of political direction in the developed nations, its agents will be found not, or not only, in the traditional labour movement, but will come from a much broader trans-class body of concerned producers and consumers; that the pressure for change will be fuelled in large part by moral and material revulsions generated by the affluent lifestyle itself; and that it will discover its 'utopian' summons in a post-consumerist vision of the 'good life': a vision in which enjoyment and personal fulfilment are indissolubly linked to methods of production and modes of consumption that are socially just and environmentally protective. This is not to predict a process, only to hypothesise the likely form of its evolution *were* it to come about.

To present consumption as a potential site of political agency and influence for change of this kind will doubtless seem problematic to many who are otherwise in essential agreement about the need to counter the dominance of de-regulated corporate capitalism and to move to a more sustainable mode of production. Most radicals, especially those of Marxist formation, have regarded production as having more relevance politically since they see it as both the primary influence on consumption and the site where resistance to the capitalist order is most likely to be mobilised. On this view, it is the exploitations of the workplace that stimulate the political will for change, while consumption, being essentially determined and controlled by production, is regarded as exercising a placating influence: it is in their role as consumers that workers tend to be reconciled to the existing order rather than fired to resist it. Radicals need not deny the consumer politics involved in boycotts or campaigns waged over standards and prices. But they will not see these as having any really radical agenda or potential and, where they are primarily directed at improving standards and reducing costs, will treat them as fully consistent with rather than challenging market modes and values.

This emphasis on the structural 'primacy' of production and production relations is in many ways justified, and it is important not to lose sight of it in any attention directed to consumption as political agency. Or rather, what we always need to keep in mind is the interdependence of production and consumption, and the extent to which the specific character (and modes of exploitation) at the one level is responsible for what happens at the other. The expansion of the consumerist way of life is profoundly implicated in the work culture of modernity, and the 'work and spend' dynamic that has been set off in recent decades is precisely a consequence of this. But having acknowledged all this, there are still a number of factors that need to be borne in mind. In the first place, the emphasis of the radical left on worker struggles in the place of production belonged to a politics that was directed ultimately towards a transformation of the relationships of ownership and control over industrial production. It was about equalising access to consumer culture, not about revolutionising its culture and lifestyle. It was about expanding industrial production rather than re-directing it along sustainable lines. As Rudolf Bahro was putting the point in the early 1980s,

> Our customary idea of the transition to socialism is the abolition of the capitalist order within the basic conditions European civilisation has created in the field of techniques and technology – and not in Europe alone. Even in this century, a thinker as profound as Antonio Gramsci was still able to view technique, industrialism, Americanism, the Ford system in its existing form as by and large an inescapable necessity, and thus depict socialism as the genuine executor of human adaptation to modern machinery and technology. Marxists have so far rarely considered that humanity has not only to transform its relations of production, but must also fundamentally transform the entire character of its mode of production, i.e. the productive force, the so-called techno-structure. It must not see its perspective as bound up with any historically transmitted form of the development of needs and their satisfaction, or of the world of products designed for this purpose. The commodity world that we find around us is not in its present form a necessary condition for human existence. It does not have to look the way it does in order for human beings to develop both intellectually and emotionally as far as we would like.[25]

This is an argument that has been echoed in numerous critiques since, several of which have noted the implications for the inclusion of consumption and issues of lifestyle within the left-wing political agenda.[26] As Ryle put it, 'a green "politics of consumption" or lifestyle politics is developing, which calls on us to accept that "the consumer" (each one of us) is something more than a passive victim of the capitalist expansion of needs'.[27] What has also been widely commented on in the red–green literature is the success of capitalism in enhancing the material prosperity of the working class to a point where it makes little sense to continue theoretically to invoke it as the sole possible agent of political opposition to the existing economic order.[28] Indeed, if anything, it is those in the working class who have – often by reason of their dependency on jobs supplied through the automobile, defence and other less eco-friendly industries – been least likely to commit to any greening of the economy. Ulrich Beck and others have also theorised the shift that has taken place from a politics of class organised around provision for basic material needs to a mass politics of 'risk' organised round the fears of contemporary consumers (although Beck's tendency has been to emphasise our collective victimisation by industrial pollution rather than our collective implication in its creation).[29] In this situation, labour militancy and trade union activity have, by and large, been confined to protection of income and employees' rights within the existing structures of globalised capital, rather than directed at anything more transformative of the 'work and spend' dynamic of affluent cultures. It is not, one may therefore argue, at the level of production or through the agency of the traditional working class that any pressure of that kind is likely to arise in the immediate future. If it does, it is rather more likely to do so, I would hazard, in the form of consumption decisions to downsize, simplify and settle for a less materially encumbered and work-driven existence. This will involve decisions *not* to buy but to do without; decisions to boycott and bypass the brand articles of the hitherto all-powerful transnational providers; decisions to avoid supermarkets and shopping malls, and decisions to purchase and invest only in goods and services of proven ethical and green credentials. Such 'agency', needless to say, will no longer be class specific but altogether more diffusely exercised – though probably in the first instance most of the more rebellious consumers will come from the more affluent echelons.

There is, of course, no guarantee at all that consumer pressure of this kind will ever attain a sufficient momentum to exercise decisive political influence for a more sustainable mode of production. It is quite possible that it will not even seriously dint the profits of the multinationals or influence their invest-ment and marketing decisions. In short, I am not at all confident of the efficacy of the politics of the 'new consumption'. I am, at most, pointing to some signs or symptoms of a movement that may assume more political importance in the coming decades. But in support of the signalling, let us note in conclusion some indices of the more politicised role that consump-tion appears already to be assuming.

One of these is the ideological efforts now being made to reinforce the association between shopping and Western values. The moment in the after-math of 11th September when the West supposedly returned to some sort of normality was marked by an expedition to the New York shops. The celebrity shoppers, who had lunched on caviar and champagne, arrived in Concorde, to be greeted at Kennedy by Mayor Guiliani with an invitation to 'Spend ! Spend ! Spend !' As a signal of Western spiritual revival this seemed fairly bizarre, and its celebration of conspicuous consumption was hardly tactful in a global context where living standards in the world's 49 least-developed countries are now lower than they were 30 years ago, and the UN estimates that some 400 million will fall below the basic subsistence rate of a dollar a day over the next 15 years.[30] But there was little that was very surprising about that. What struck one as more unusual on this occasion was the deliberate staging of the event as a piece of political PR: one whose aim was to persuade the public that the newly launched 'war on terror' was to be fought not only by military means, but also in the malls and supermarkets, and that everyone therefore had a duty of 'patriotic' shopping. (In the United Kingdom, the *Telegraph* and other papers had headlines to this effect at the time.) Here, one felt, was a kind of tacit acknowledgement on behalf of the establishment and corporate capital that it is at the level of consumption rather than (or certainly as well as) that of production that the power to 'flick the switches' is now located, and the continued commitment to consumerist culture that therefore has to be now secured. The invitation to the public was to view consumption not just as a matter of private expenditure, self-styling and gratification, but as an act of political identification through which the 'patriotic' consumer signals support for the Western way of life. Calls of this kind are not unprecedented, and have been made before in wartime contexts.[31] But they have not been a prominent feature in recent times, and not surprisingly, given the contradiction between the collectivising pressure of a rhetorical summons of this kind and the promotion of a de-regularised global marketplace whose supposed virtue is to allow all individual consumers to exercise a choice untrammelled by any compulsion other than private desire. Of course, the tensions of the state's involvement in the 'day-to-day instrumentation of consumer obedience' have long been recognised, following as they do from the need to weaken citizenship and civil society while yet sustaining some sort of simulacrum of community through the loose attachments of consumer subjects.[32] But one may argue that the success of any such balancing act is immediately compromised by the promotion of the act of shopping, that bastion of private choice, as a civic 'duty'. For this is an act of contradictory 'interference' on the part of the neo-liberal state that cannot but signal its vulnerability.

But we must relate these new appeals to patriotic consumerism not only to the Twin Towers attack and its counter-terrorist aftermath, but also to the assessments of consumer power that have been voiced in recent times by the more anti-consumerist lobby. For if the world of corporate capitalism is now more openly acknowledging its reliance on continued consumer insatiability and logo-loyalty, it is doing so in the context of – and partly, one presumes, in response to – an oppositional invocation of the growing subversive potential of consumption. Introducing *No Logo*, Naomi Klein tells us that

> This book is hinged on a simple hypothesis: that as more people discover the brand-name secrets of the global logo web, their outrage will fuel the next big political movement, a vast wave of opposition squarely targeting trans-national corporations, particularly those with very high name-brand

recognition. (...) It's true that (...) this movement is coming, as all such movements do, from a minority, but it is an increasingly powerful minority. Simply put, anti-corporatism is the brand of politics capturing the imagination of the next generation of troublemakers and shit-disturbers, and we need only look to the student radicals of the 1960s and the ID warriors of the eighties and nineties to see the transformative impact such a shift can have.[33]

Similar claims have been voiced by the academic theorists of consumption. The IMF and political parties of right and left, Daniel Miller has insisted, 'are increasingly the agents not of international capitalists so much as international shopping', and in this sense, 'the tail of consumption decisions wags the dog of production activity'.[34] Miller views the economic power of First World consumers as mainly epitomised in the relatively impotent and denigrated 'housewife', since it is she, he claims, who in her role as canny and thrifty (rather than narcissistic and profligate) buyer for the household forces down prices in the supermarkets, and thus determines the activities of producers and retail managers. To place all the emphasis on relatively utilitarian supermarket shopping is arguably seriously to skew the overall picture since there is a lot more to consumerism than supermarket shopping, even if it is true that this is largely answerable to the bargain-dictates of his virtuous 'housewife'. It is, for example, to ignore some very burgeoning luxury forms of consumption (of cosmetics, computers, tourism, fashion, etc.) as well as the more collective forms of consumption such as sport and entertainment, and this is not to mention all those 'must-have Nike' purchases for which it is precisely brand name rather than economy that counts. Miller's position also tends to ignore the power of global capitalism in closing down other options for consumers. The supermarkets may instantiate the power of the housewife in their cheap goods and narrow profit margins and global impacts. But you have, usually, to be able to drive to them, and they come at the cost of other more local shops. All the same, Miller is surely right to direct attention to the global reach of First World consumer decisions, and the power that goes with that. Elsewhere, too, it should be said, he has also acknowledged the growing importance of the more reflexive and self-consciously political consumer constituencies. Thus he argues,

On the one hand, consumption appears as the key contemporary 'problem' responsible for massive suffering and inequality. At the same time it is the locus of any future 'solution' as a progressive movement in the world, by making the alimentary institutions of trade and government finally responsible to humanity for the consequences of their actions. (...) From the legacy of Ralph Nader in the United States, through consumer movements in Malaysia, to the consumer cooperatives of Japan, to the green movements of Western Europe, the politicized form of consumption concern has become increasingly fundamental to the formation of many branches of alternative politics. (...) Nevertheless, it is vital not to view consumption as simply important when it is politicized, but also to consider the implications of these movements for our imagination of politics.[35]

The green movement, moreover, he goes on to suggest, should be seen not so much as anti-consumerist but as the vanguard of new forms of consumption that are motivated by a 'global' version of the same ideology of thrift that underlies most forms of shopping:

> As it becomes a mass movement, its mystical relationship to a reified notion of nature becomes tempered by a more rationalistic concern with the defetishism of goods. This shows increasing awareness of the consequence of goods for peoples as well as for the planet's natural resources. In practice 'green' food choices seem to be more actualised by fear of consequences for the consumer's body than by abstract planetary health. Nevertheless this movement shows signs of transcending simple self-interest and at least re-conceptualising this linkage between the healthy and moral individual and healthy and moral world.[36]

These arguments chime with those voiced in Micheletti's more closely focussed work on 'virtuous shopping', where it is argued that recent consumer campaigns indicate the emergence of a rather different – 'political consumerist' – view of politics and its conduct:

> They show that there is a political connection between our daily consumer choices and important global issues of environmentalism, labour rights, human rights, and sustainable development. There is, in other words, a politics of consumer products which for growing numbers of people implies the need to think politically privately. This politicises what we have traditionally conceived as private consumer choice and erases the division between the political and economic spheres.[37]

Perhaps it is also worth recalling in this context a point made earlier about the general disinclination of the theorists of consumer culture, wherever they position themselves politically, to justify consumerism as the appropriate telos of Western civilisation. Even Miller, despite his criticism of the presumption of anti-consumerism that pre-capitalist societies had some direct relation to 'true' or basic needs, and consumed to satisfy them,[38] suggests that in an age of large-scale rationalisation and impersonal institutions, people use consumption to extract a specific humanity that negates the generality and alienatory scale of the institutions from which they received their goods and services.[39]

So although we are indeed speaking at present of minority movements and marginal, rather than mainstream, pressures, there is little doubt that the dependency of globalised capitalism on the continued preparedness of its consumers to remain forever unsated, forever fobbed off with compensatory forms of gratification, and forever nonchalant about the consequences of consumerism both socially and ecologically has now been recognised across the political spectrum as one of the more significant sources of dialectical tension of our times. Unorthodox as it therefore may seem in terms of standard left analysis, it is this, one might suggest, that is the new point of vulnerability for the de-regulated market, the site where shifting cultural perspectives and modes of representation might begin to have an impact. It is a tension, moreover, that in indicating the emergence of a rather more 'civic' role for consumption than has hitherto been the norm is problematising traditional views on consumption and citizenship.

Notes

1 Introduction

1. For example, B. Stråth, 'The State and its Critics', in Q. Skinner and B. Stråth (eds), *States and Citizens: History, Theory, Prospects* (Cambridge, 2003), p. 185. A rare exception is Paul Ginsborg, *The Politics of Everyday Life* (New Haven, CT, 2005). See also the special issue of the *Journal of Consumer Culture*, 7(2) (2007).
2. D. Hebdige, *Subculture: The Meaning of Style* (London, 1979); F. Mort, 'The Politics of Consumption', in S. Hall and M. Jacques (eds), *New Times: The Changing Face of Politics in the 1990s* (London, 1989), pp. 160–172; F. Mort, *Cultures of Consumption: Masculinities and Social Space in Late Twentieth-Century Britain* (London, 1996).
3. T. Blair, *The Courage of Our Convictions: Why Reform of the Public Services is the Route to Social Justice* (London, 2002); C. Needham, *Citizen-Consumers: New Labour's Marketplace Democracy* (London, 2004); D. Marquand, *Decline of the Public* (Cambridge, 2004).
4. J. Davidson, *Courtesans and Fishcakes: The Consuming Passions of Classical Athens* (New York, 1999).
5. D. Horowitz, *The Morality of Spending: Attitudes Towards the Consumer Society in America, 1875–1940* (Chicago, 1992).
6. Q. Skinner, *Liberty before Liberalism* (Cambridge, 1998).
7. A. de Tocqueville, *Democracy in America* (1835, 1840), cit. in Horowitz, *Morality of Spending*, pp. 6f.
8. M. Sandel, *Democracy's Discontent: America in Search of a Public Philosophy* (Cambridge, MA, 1996).
9. For this, see J. Clarke, J. Newman, N. Smith, E. Vidler, and L. Westmarland, *Creating Citizen-Consumers: Changing Identities in the Remaking of Public Services* (London, 2006), and the special issue 'Consumerism and Social Policy', *European Societies*, 8(3) (2006).
10. V. A. Zelizer, *The Purchase of Intimacy* (Princeton, NJ, 2005).
11. D. Miller, *The Dialectics of Shopping* (Chicago, 2001); D. Miller, P. Jackson, N. Thrift, B. Holbrook, and M. Rowlands (eds), *Shopping, Place and Identity* (London, 1998); S. Zukin, *Point of Purchase: How Shopping Changed American Culture* (New York, 2004).
12. For a critical overview, see J. Keane, *European Citizenship? Historical Foundations, New Departures* (London and WZB Berlin, 2005).
13. C. Calhoun (ed.), *Habermas and the Transformation of the Public Sphere* (Cambridge, MA, 1992); B. Cowan, *The Social Life of Coffee: The Emergence of the British Coffeehouse* (New Haven, CT, 2005).

14. For case studies and further literature, see E. F. Biagini (ed.), *Citizenship and Community: Liberals, Radicals, and Collective Identities in the British Isles, 1865–1931* (Cambridge, 1996).

15. F. Trentmann, 'The Modern Genealogy of the Consumer: Meanings, Knowledge, and Identities', in J. Brewer and F. Trentmann (eds), *Consuming Cultures, Global Perspectives: Historical Trajectories, Transnational Exchanges* (Oxford and New York, 2006), pp. 19–69; E. D. Rappaport, *Shopping for Pleasure: Women and the Making of London's West End* (Princeton NJ, 2000); K. K. Sklar, 'The Consumers' White Label Campaign of the National Consumers' League, 1898–1918', in S. Strasser, C. McGovern and M. Judt (eds), *Getting and Spending: European and American Consumer Societies in the Twentieth Century* (Cambridge, 1998); G. Scott, *Feminism and the Politics of Working Women: The Women's Co-operative Guild, 1880s to the Second World War* (London, 1998); P. Maclachlan and F. Trentmann, 'Civilising Markets: Traditions of Consumer Politics in Twentieth-Century Britain, Japan, and the United States', in M. Bevir and F. Trentmann (eds), *Markets in Historical Contexts: Ideas and Politics in the Modern World* (Cambridge, 2004), pp. 170–201; F. Trentmann (ed.), *The Making of the Consumer: Knowledge, Power and Identity in the Modern World* (Oxford and New York, 2006); L. Cohen, *A Consumer's Republic: The Politics of Mass Consumption in Postwar America* (New York, 2003); M. Jacobs, *Pocketbook Politics: Economic Citizenship in Twentieth-Century America* (Princeton, 2005).

16. M. Bevir and F. Trentmann, Chapter 2, in this volume.

17. R. Levett, *A Better Choice of Choice: Quality of Life, Consumption and Economic Growth* (London, 2003). A. Offer, *The Challenge of Affluence: Self-Control and Well-Being in the United States and Britain since 1950* (Oxford, 2006).

18. K. Gerth, Chapter 3, in this volume.

19. F. Hammer, Chapter 4, in this volume.

20. R. H. Frank, *Luxury Fever: Money and Happiness in an Era of Excess* (Princeton, NJ, 1999).

21. A. Smith, *An Inquiry into the Nature and Causes of The Wealth of Nations* (1776), Book III.

22. J. Gronow and A. Warde (eds), *Ordinary Consumption* (London, 2001); E. Shove, *Comfort, Cleanliness and Convenience: The Social Organisation of Normality* (Oxford, 2003); A. Warde, 'Consumption and Theories of Practice', *Journal of Consumer Culture* 5(2) (2005), pp. 131–153; Theodore R. Schatzki, Karin Knorr-Cetina and Eike von Savigny (eds), *The Practice Turn in Contemporary Theory* (London, 2001).

23. R. D. Putnam, *Bowling Alone: The Collapse and Revival of American Community* (New York, 2000); for critiques, see *American Prospect* (March/April 1996). S. Johnson, *Everything Bad is Good for You: How Popular Culture is Making Us Smarter* (London, 2005).

24. N. Couldry, Sonia Livingstone, and Tim Markham, Chapter 7, in this volume.

25. T. H. Breen, *The Marketplace of Revolution: How Consumer Politics Shaped American Independence* (New York, 2004); M. Daunton and M. Hilton (eds), *The Politics of Consumption: Material Culture and Citizenship in Europe and America* (Oxford, 2001); F. Trentmann, *Free Trade Nation: Consumption, Commerce, and Civil Society in Modern Britain* (Oxford, 2007); Cohen, *Consumers' Republic*; Jacob, *Pocketbook Politics*.

26. B. Morgan and F. Trentmann (eds), 'The Politics of Necessity', special issue for *Journal of Consumer Policy* 29(4) (2006).

27. M. Hilton, Chapter 6, in this volume.

28. M. Micheletti, Chapter 8, in this volume.

29. See now also D. N. McCloskey, *The Bourgeois Virtues: Ethics for an Age of Commerce* (Chicago, Ill., 2006).

30. A. Porter, 'Trusteeship, Anti-Slavery, and Humanitarianism', in A. Porter (ed.), *The Oxford History of the British Empire: The Nineteenth Century* (Oxford and New York,

1999), pp. 198–221; F. Trentmann, 'Before "Fair Trade": Empire, Free Trade, and the Moral Economies of Food in the Modern World', *Environment and Planning D: Society and Space* 35 (2007).

31. Cf. I. M. Young, 'Responsibility and Global Justice: A Social Connection Model', *Social Philosophy and Policy* 23 (2006), pp. 107–130; 'Responsibility and Global Labor Justice', *The Journal of Political Philosophy* 12(4) (2004), pp. 365–388.
32. B. Morgan, Chapter 5, in this volume.
33. M. Everson and C. Joerges, Chapter 10, in this volume.
34. J. O'Neill, Chapter 11, in this volume; K. Soper, Chapter 12, in this volume.
35. R. Layard, *Happiness: Lessons for a New Science* (London, 2005); N. Donovan and D. Halpbern, *Life Satisfaction: The State of Knowledge and Implications for Government* (London, 2002). Cf. J. Porritt, *Redefining Prosperity* (London, 2003).

2 Civic Choices: Retrieving Perspectives on Rationality, Consumption, and Citizenship

1. T. Blair, *The Courage of Our Convictions: Why Reform of the Public Services is the Route to Social Justice* (London, 2002); C. Needham, *Citizen-Consumers: New Labour's Marketplace Democracy* (London, 2004); D. Marquand, *Decline of the Public: The Hollowing-out of Citizenship* (Cambridge, 2004); N. Rose, *Powers of Freedom: Reframing Political Thought* (Cambridge, 1999). J. Clarke, J. Newman, N. Smith, E. Vidler, and L. Westmarland, *Creating Citizen-Consumers: Changing Publics and Changing Public Services* (London, 2007).
2. L. Cohen, *A Consumer's Republic: The Politics of Mass Consumption in Postwar America* (New York, 2003); F. Trentmann (ed.), *The Making of the Consumer: Knowledge, Power and Identity in the Modern World* (Oxford and New York, 2006); A. Chatriot, M.-E. Chessel, and M. Hilton (eds), *Au Nom du Consommateur: Consommation et politique en Europe et aux États-Unis au XX Siècle* (Paris, 2004); D. Miller, *The Dialectics of Shopping* (Chicago, 2001); M. Douglas and B. Isherwood, *The World of Goods: Towards an Anthropology of Consumerism* (London, 1996); V. Zelizer, 'Culture and Consumption', in N. J. Smelser and R. Swedberg (eds), *The Handbook of Economic Sociology* (Princeton, N.J., 2005); J. Gronow and A. Warde (eds), *Ordinary Consumption* (London, 2001); E. Shove, *Comfort, Cleanliness and Convenience: The Social Organisation of Normality* (Oxford, 2003).
3. A. Marshall, *Principles of Economics*, Vol. 1 (London, 1890).
4. D. Winch, 'The Problematic Status of the Consumer in Orthodox Economic Thought', in Trentmann (ed.), *The Making of the Consumer* (Oxford, 2006) pp. 31–51; H. Pearson, 'Economics and Altruism a the Fin de Siècle', in M. Daunton and F. Trentmann (eds), *Worlds of Political Economy: Knowledge and Power in the Nineteenth and Twentieth Centuries* (Basingstoke and New York, 2004), pp. 24–46.
5. F. Trentmann, 'The Modern Genealogy of the Consumer: Meanings, Knowledge, and Identities', in J. Brewer and F. Trentmann (eds), *Consuming Cultures, Global Perspectives: Historical Trajectories, Transnational Exchanges* (Oxford and New York, 2006), pp. 19–69.
6. Cited in Winch, 'Problematic Status', p. 42.
7. J. K. Galbraith, *The Affluent Society* (London, 1958).
8. Douglas and Isherwood, *World of Goods*.
9. G. M. Peter Swann, 'Marshall's Consumer as an Innovator', in S. C. Dow and P. E. Earl (eds), *Economic Organization and Economic Knowledge*, I (Cheltenham, 1999), pp. 98–118.

10. A. Warde, 'Consumption and Theories of Practice', *Journal of Consumer Culture* 5(2) (2005), pp. 131–153; E. Shove and M. Pantzar, 'Consumers, Producers and Practices: Understanding the Invention and Reinvention of Nordic Walking', *Journal of Consumer Culture* 5(1) (2005), pp. 43–64.

11. J. Vincent, 'L' économie morale du consommateur britannique en 1900', in Chatriot, Chessel, and Hilton (eds), *Au Nom du Consommateur*, esp. pp. 237–240.

12. H. Kyrk, *Economic Problems of the Family* (New York, 1929).

13. Cohen, *A Consumer's Republic*; M. Jacobs, '"How About Some Meat": The Office of Price Administration, Consumption Politics, and State Building from the Bottom up, 1941–1946', *The Journal of American History* 84(3) (1997), pp. 910–941; M. Jacobs, *Pocketbook Politics: Economic Citizenship in Twentieth-Century America* (Princeton, 2005).

14. H. Kyrk, *Theory of Consumption* (London, 1923).

15. J. Dewey, *Human Nature and Conduct: An Introduction to Social Psychology* (New York, 1922), pp. 199f.

16. Ibid., p. 207.

17. Ibid., p. 208.

18. Kahneman and Tversky, *Choices, Values, and Frames* (Cambridge, 2002). For a rare discussion using Dewey's work in this direction, see S. Modarres-Mousavi, *Methodological Foundations for Bounded Rationality as a Primary Framework* (2002).

19. H. A. Simon, *Models of Bounded Rationality* (Cambridge, 1982).

20. M. Bevir, *The Logic of the History of Ideas* (Cambridge, 1999); M. Bevir and F. Trentmann, 'Markets in Historical Contexts: Ideas, Practices and Governance', in M. Bevir and F. Trentmann (eds), *Markets in Historical Contexts: Ideas and Politics in the Modern World* (Cambridge, 2004), pp. 1–24.

21. Consider, to mention just a few prominent examples, A. Etzioni, *The Spirit of Community: Rights, Responsibilities, and the Communitarian Agenda* (New York, 1993); R. Putnam, *Bowling Alone: The Collapse and Revival of American Community* (New York, 2000); and M. Sandel, *Democracy's Discontent* (Cambridge, MA., 1996). For historical accounts, see D. Horowitz, *The Anxieties of Affluence: Critiques of American Consumer Culture* (Amherst, 2004); and A. Schäfer, 'German Historicism, Progressive Social Thought, and the Interventionist State in the US since the 1880s', in M. Bevir and F. Trentmann (eds), *Markets in Historical Contexts* (Cambridge, 2004).

22. See J. March and J. Olsen, *Rediscovering Institutions: The Organizational Basis of Politics* (New York, 1989). Governmentality theorists too neglect situated agency and local reasoning. They present the consumer as a passive subject-position. Consumers are merely acting out a role given to them by a discourse or a regime of power/knowledge. See P. Miller and N. Rose, 'Mobilizing the Consumer: Assembling the Subject of Consumption', *Theory, Culture and Society* 14 (1997), pp. 1–36. Indeed, while governmentality theorists adopt a critical tone when discussing social norms or social reason, they sometimes rely, like the other sociologists we have discussed, on modernist modes of knowing (synchronic analysis of the relations between signs within discourse) and a hostility to a modern capitalism that they conceive as totalising.

23. Examples include M. Featherstone, *Consumer Culture and Postmodernism* (London, 1991); and A. Giddens, *Modernity and Self-Identity* (Cambridge, 1991).

24. Rose, *Power of Freedom*.

25. Brewer and Trentmann, *Consuming Cultures, Global Perspectives*.

26. See the studies in M. Bevir and F. Trentmann (eds), *Governance, Consumers, and Citizens: Agency and Resistance in Contemporary Politics* (Basingstoke, 2007).

27. Compare Wittgenstein's argument about the open-ended nature of rule-following in L. Wittgenstein, *Philosophical Investigations*, trans. G. Anscombe (Oxford, 1972), pp. 143–242.
28. F. Trentmann, 'Before "Fair Trade": Empire, Free Trade, and the Moral Economies of Food in the Modern World', *Environment and Planning D: Society and Space* 35 (2007).
29. See K. Gerth, 'Consumption and Politics in Twentieth-Century China', Chapter 3, in this volume.
30. See J. Harris, 'Society and State in Twentieth-century Britain', in F. Thompson (ed.), *The Cambridge Social History of Britain 1750–1950*, Vol. 3: *Social Agencies and Institutions* (Cambridge, 1990); J. Harris (ed.), *Civil Society in British History: Ideas, Identities, Institutions* (Oxford, 2003); J. Hall and F. Trentmann, *Civil Society: A Reader in History, Theory and Global Politics* (Basingstoke, 2004); M. Glasius, D. Lewis, and H. Seckinelgin (eds), *Exploring Civil Society: Political and Cultural Contexts* (London and New York, 2004).
31. G. J. Holyoake, inaugural address delivered at the 19th annual Co-operative Congress at Carlisle, 30 May–1 June 1887, Manchester 1887, pp. 11f.
32. S. J. Wiesen, 'Creating the Nazi Marketplace: Public Relations and Consumer Citizenship in the Third Reich', in G. Eley and J. Palmowski (eds), *Citizenship and National Identity in Twentieth-Century Germany* (Stanford, forthcoming).

3   Consumption and Politics in Twentieth-Century China

1. T. H. Marshall, *Citizenship and Social Class* (Cambridge, 1950); *Class, Citizenship, and Social Development* (New York, 1964).
2. M. Goldman, *From Comrade to Citizen: The Struggle for Political Rights in China* (Cambridge and London, 2005), p. 6.
3. M. Goldman and E. Perry, 'Introduction: Political Citizenship in Modern China,' in M. Goldman and E. Perry (eds), *Changing Meanings of Citizenship in Modern China* (Cambridge, MA, 2002).
4. Goldman, *From Comrade to Citizen*, p. 6.
5. S. Ogden, *Inklings of Democracy in China* (Cambridge, MA, 2002).
6. W. T. Rowe, *Hankow: Conflict and Community in a Chinese City, 1796–1895* (Stanford, 1989); M. Rankin, 'State and Society in Early Republican Politics,' *The China Quarterly* 150 (June 1997).
7. B. Dickson, 'Do Good Businessmen Make Good Citizens? An Emerging Collective Identity Among China's Private Entrepreneurs,' in Goldman and Perry (eds), *Changing Meanings of Citizenship in Modern China* (Cambridge, MA, 2002), p. 286.
8. R. Thompson, *China's Local Councils in the Age of Constitutional Reform, 1898–1911* (Cambridge, MA, 1995).
9. R. B. Wong, *China Transformed: Historical Change and the Limits of European Experience* (Ithaca, 2000).
10. J. A. Fogel and P. G. Zarrow (eds), *Imagining the People: Chinese Intellectuals and the Concept of Citizenship, 1890–1920* (Armonk, NY, 1997).
11. See K. O'Brien, 'Villagers, Elections, and Citizenship,' in Goldman and Perry (eds), *Changing Meanings of Citizenship in Modern China* (Cambridge, MA, 2002).
12. This is the conclusion of a study by Tsinghua University law professor Chen Jianmin. See 'Chinese Consumers' Rights Only on Paper,' UPI, 16 March 2006.

13. For a more complete examination, see Gerth, *China Made: Consumer Culture and the Creation of the Nation* (Cambridge, MA, 2004).

14. J. Townsend, 'Chinese Nationalism,' in J. Unger (ed.), *Chinese Nationalism* (Armonk, NY, 1996), pp. 1–30.

15. Z. Yougui, *Woguo guanshui zizhu hou jinkou shuilü shuizhun zhi bianqian* (Guidelines for import duties since our country recovered tariff autonomy) (Changsha, 1939), p. 12.

16. G. S. Cross, *An All-Consuming Century: Why Commercialism Won in Modern America* (New York, 2000), p. 1.

17. N. McKendrick, J. Brewer, and J. H. Plumb, *The Birth of a Consumer Society: The Commercialization of Eighteenth-Century England* (Bloomington, 1982).

18. For the classic statement of this position, see M. Friedman and R. D. Friedman, *Capitalism and Freedom* (Chicago, 1982), esp. pp. 7–21.

19. Z. Bauman, *Freedom* (Minneapolis, 1988), pp. 7–8.

20. Movement literature explicitly drew such equations. See, for example, 'Guohuo he guomin' [national products and national people], *Shenbao*, 1 January 1933; 'Zhongguo huo xianyao Zhongguoren ziji yong qilai' [Chinese should buy first the Chinese products], *Shenbao*, 12 August 1935. On the introduction of and connections between the concepts of citizenship and nationality by journalists, see J. Judge, *Print and Politics: 'Shibao' and the Culture of Reform in Late Qing China* (Stanford, 1996), esp. pp. 83–99.

21. For a survey of 'Buy American' campaigns since the Revolution, see D. Frank, *Buy American: The Untold Story of Economic Nationalism* (Boston, 1999).

22. The terms applied to the histories of other countries that overlap with the term 'nationalizing consumer culture,' as I use it here, include 'indigenization,' 'indigenism,' 'domestication,' 'import-substitution,' 'decolonization,' 'autarky,' and 'de-foreignization.' For a survey of the various approaches to 'indigenization' taken throughout Africa, see A. Adedeji (ed.), *Indigenization of African Economies* (New York, 1981). On South America, see B. S. Orlove (ed.), *The Allure of the Foreign: Imported Goods in Postcolonial Latin America* (Ann Arbor, 1997). On Southeast Asia, see F. H. Golay, R. Anspach, M. R. Pfanner and E. B. Ayal (eds), *Underdevelopment and Economic Nationalism in Southeast Asia* (Ithaca, 1969).

23. See, for example, 'Aiyong guohuo fengqi zhi puji' [The spread of an atmosphere of cherishing national products], *Shangye zazhi* 5(10) (February 1932), p. 2.

24. See S. Sarkar, *The Swadeshi Movement in Bengal, 1903–1908* (Cambridge, 1973); B. Chandra, *The Rise and Growth of Economic Nationalism in India: Economic Policies of Indian National Leadership, 1880–1905* (New Delhi, 1966), pp. 122–141. On Gandhi's ties, see J. M. Brown, *Gandhi: Prisoner of Hope* (New Haven, 1989), pp. 89–90, 163–64, and 203–205; and S. S. Bean, 'Gandhi and Khadi, the Fabric of Indian Independence,' in A. B. Weiner and J. Schneider (eds), *Cloth and the Human Experience* (Washington, 1989), pp. 355–376. A brief lecture by a prominent subaltern scholar, however, emphasizes the coercive component of the *swadeshi* movement; see R. Guha, *A Disciplinary Aspect of Indian Nationalism* (Santa Cruz, 1991), pp. 1–18. For a subtle introduction to the origins of *swadeshi*, see C. A. Bayly, 'The Origins of Swadeshi (Home Industry): Cloth and Indian Society, 1700–1930,' in A. Appadurai (ed.), *The Social Life of Things: Commodities in Cultural Perspective* (Cambridge, 1986), pp. 285–321. As in the Chinese case, literature provides the most morally complex portrait of the participants. In 1919, the Nobel Prize–winning Indian writer Rabindranath Tagore captured the coercive side of the *swadeshi* movement in his novel *Ghare baire* (The Home and the World).

25. For an overview of the anti-materialistic emphasis in Gandhi's ideas, see O. P. Misra, *Economic Thought of Gandhi and Nehru: A Comparative Analysis* (New Delhi, 1995). Despite Gandhi's emphasis on limiting material desires and creating self-sufficient villages, his ideas did overlap with the movement on one fundamental issue. Both rejected a simple embrace of capitalist relations that privileged price over provenance. Criticizing those who argued that the use of home-spun was costlier than mill-made cloth, Gandhi said that if expense were the most important issue, then, by the same logic, we should kill our aged parents and children 'whom we have to maintain without getting anything in return' (quoted in Misra, *Economic Thought*, p. 35).

26. See, for example, A. D. Smith, *Nationalism and Modernism: A Critical Survey of Recent Theories of Nations and Nationalism* (New York, 1998).

27. Moreover, some studies recognize 'nationality' as a significant category of consumption without explaining the historical origins. For instance, Joseph Tobin notes that 'in Japan, before a food, an article of clothing, or a piece of furniture is evaluated as good or bad, expensive or cheap, it is identified as either foreign or Japanese' ('Introduction: Domesticating the West,' in Tobin (ed.), *Re-Made in Japan: Everyday Life and Consumer Taste in a Changing Society* [New Haven, 1992], pp. 25–26).

28. For example, L. Cohen, *Making a New Deal: Industrial Workers in Chicago, 1919–1939* (Cambridge, 1990).

29. Early influential studies include D. J. Boorstin, *The Americans: The Democratic Experience* (New York, 1973), pp. 89–164; S. Ewan and E. Ewan, *Channels of Desire* (New York, 1982); and R. W. Fox and T. J. Lears, *The Culture of Consumption: Critical Essays in American History, 1880–1980* (New York, 1983).

30. C. Crow, *Four Hundred Million Customers* (New York, 1937), pp. 17–18.

31. B. S. Orlove and A. J. Bauer, 'Giving Importance to Imports,' in Orlove, *The Allure of the Foreign*, p. 13.

32. On the problem of determining 'nationality,' see Anthony DePalma, 'It Isn't So Simple to Be Canadian: Tough Rules Protecting the Culture Make for Confusion and Surprises,' *New York Times*, 14 July 1999.

33. K. Marx, *Capital: A Critique of Political Economy*, 3 vols (New York, 1967), Vol. 1, p. 71.

34. See S. Jhally, *The Codes of Advertising: Fetishism and the Political Economy of Meaning in the Consumer Society* (New York, 1990), pp. 24–63.

35. See M. Friedman, *Consumer Boycotts: Effecting Change Through the Marketplace and the Media* (New York, 1999).

36. J. K. Galbraith, *A Tenured Professor: A Novel* (Boston, 1990).

37. M. M. Pearson, *Joint Ventures in the People's Republic of China: The Control of Foreign Direct Investment Under Socialism* (Princeton, 1991), esp. Chapter 2.

38. S. Qiang, Z. Zangzang, and Q. Bian, *Zhongguo keyi shuo bu* (China can also say no) (Beijing, 1996); see also W. Xiaodong, F. Ning, and S. Qiang (eds), *Quanqiuhua yinyingxia de Zhongguo zhilu* [China's road under the shadow of globalization] (Beijing, 1999).

39. On the well-known battle between Kentucky Fried Chicken and local businesses in Beijing over the fast-food market, see Y. Yan, 'Of Hamburgers and Social Space: Consuming McDonald's in Beijing,' in D. Davis (ed.), *The Consumer Revolution in Urban China* (Berkeley, 2000), pp. 201–225, and the essays collected in Z. Feng (ed.), *Guohuo, yanghuo ni ai shei* [National products or foreign products: which do you cherish?] (Tianjin, 1994). In 'Changyong guohuo gai bu gai' [Should national products be promoted?], a Chinese author once again browbeats fellow Chinese for their unpatriotic consumption, citing patriotic South Korean consumers as

models to emulate. The author states that even while academics debate the merits of fully opening China to foreign products, and even if imports are widely available, 'every Chinese person' has the responsibility to favor Chinese products (Z. Feng, *Guohuo*, p. 171).

40. For an example from the late 1990s, see Y. Zhao, 'State, Children, and the Wahala Group of Hangzhou,' in J. Jun (ed.), *Feeding China's Little Emperors: Food, Children, and Social Change* (Stanford, 2000), pp. 185–198. Zhao's case study also reveals the ongoing ambivalent relationship between Chinese consumers and imports: 'The Wahaha Group's decision to emphasize its drink's indigenous character was followed by the company's determination to depict itself as a staunch defender of the domestic food and beverage industry against what Wahaha's executives called an 'unhealthy tendency' in mass consumption: the public's fascination with Western and Japanese consumer goods' (p. 189).

41. J. Fewsmith, 'The Political and Social Implications of China's Accession to the WTO,' *The China Quarterly* 167 (2001), pp. 573–591.

42. J. Bo, 'Imported Movies: Entertainment or Hegemony?' *China Daily*, 8 April 2002.

43. E. Rosenthal, 'Chinese Students Are Caught up by Nationalism,' *New York Times*, 12 May 1999.

44. J. Watson, 'China's Big Mac Attack,' *Foreign Affairs*, May/June 2000.

4 Sartorial Manoeuvres in the Dusk: Blue Jeans in Socialist Hungary

1. The research consists of analyses of (i) archival materials, newspaper articles, books, television reports and movies; (ii) interviews; (iii) secondary literature; and (iv) about 100 stories that I received after I placed adverts in newspapers and Internet bulletin boards asking for stories of their first pair of jeans.

2. János Kádár was the first secretary of the Hungarian Socialist Workers' Party (HSWP) between 1956 and 1988.

3. 'Between 1958 and 1962 the number of television subscribers increased by twenty times, to 325 thousand. Between 1960 and 1970 the number of car-owners increased by more than 11 times. At the same time, the question of quality of life became a permanent feature in the Politbüro's work. At the Seventh Party Congress in 1959, János Kádár himself described how many orders for washing machines, refrigerators, motorcycles and cars the party had made decisions on. This explosive spread of consumer durables would not have been possible without the doubling of real wages between 1960 and 1975.' F. Hammer and T. Dessewffy, 'A fogyasztás kísértete' [The Spectre Of Consumption], *Replika*, 26 (1997), pp. 31–46.

4. M. Szabó, Politikai kultúra Magyarországon [Political culture in Hungary] (Budapest, 1989).

5. Picture made in Budapest, published in *Time Magazine* in 1950. The author and publisher have made attempt to contact copyright holders. If any have overlooked, the publisher will be pleased to make the appropriate arrangements at the first opportunity.

6. 'Barbaric Culture', *Time Magazine*, October 23, 1950. http://www.time.com/time/archive/preview/0,10987,813599,00.html.

7. Somewhat similar to the Soviet *stiliagi*, the *zoot suiters* in the 1940s and the *Teddy Boys* in the 1950s, the German *Halbstarke*, the French *Blousons Noirs*, the Austrian *Schlurf*, the Czechoslovak *pásek* or the Polish *bikiniarze*. These groups, however,

cannot regarded as sheer cultural synonyms, though all present a certain counter-
ing of mainstream culture through consumption and choice of outfit. L. Flint,
'Unzipping the USSR: Jeans as a Symbol of the Struggle between Consumerism and
Consumption in the Brezhnev Era'. (Unpublished M.A. thesis submitted to the
History Department of the Central European University, 1997). S. Horváth,
'Huligánok, jampecek, galerik' [Hooligans, jampecs, gangs], in Rainer (ed.),
Hatvanas évek' Magyarországon [The 'sixties' in Hungary] (Budapest, 2000), p. 164.
1956s Intézet. T. W. Ryback, *Rock Around the Bloc* (Oxford, 1990).

8. Calefato's note on the zoot suiters' Second World War performance in the Untied
States suggests a curious parallel between them and the fate of the jampec in the
1950s. Referring to Polhemus, she argues that wartime regulations over fabric
production drastically curtailed the use of wool, thus making it practically illegal,
or in any case unpatriotic, to wear the eccentric and costly zoot suit, whose wide
jackets and trousers required enormous amounts of fabric. P. Calefato, *The Clothed
Body* (Oxford, 2004).

9. L. Burget and S. Kovácsvölgyi, *Hogyan viselkedjünk?* [How To Behave?] (Budapest,
1962), p. 46.

10. Unpublished interview with N. Ádám by Ryan Mehan.

11. Story from H. István (born: 1945).

12. Story from H. János (born: 1953).

13. Something similar can be said about the blunt material concessions the state
provided. Opportunities for choice were growing year by year, but in this external
case material constraints turned out to be nearly catastrophic. State socialism has
turned out to be a timid giant. It has never had the courage to introduce such
measures that subsequent, democratically elected governments introduced in
order to stabilize the economy. As a result of this economic policy, Hungary was
the most indebted country in Eastern Europe in the late 1980s.

14. M. Haraszti, *A cenzúra esztétikája* [The Velvet Prison] (Budapest, 1985/1991), p. 79
(my translation).

15. A popular German–Caribbean disco band in the 1980s. Hungarian radio played
most of their songs except for 'Rasputin' ('Russia's greatest love machine').

16. Story from M. György (born: 1952).

17. The name of a Hungarian brand.

18. The Hungarian Pioneer's Organization was the Party's youth organization for
children between 10 and 14.

19. Interview with N. Ádám conducted by Ryan Mehan, 13 May 2003.

20. R. Ungváry, 1959, in *Beszélő évek 1957–1968* (Budapest, 2000), p. 113.

21. 'From the very fragmentary available information on the early hippies, it appears
that they were mostly in their late teens, and the children of well-to-do and
intellectual families; in Moscow, hippies still come disproportionately from
the elite central districts. They claimed to have deliberately dropped out of mainstream Soviet society', J. Bushnell, *Moscow Graffiti: Language and Subculture* (Boston,
1990), p. 115.

22. I have found no Western parallel for the 1960s craze for this particular garment: it
was basically a light waterproof plastic coat. Kálmán Kecskeméti writes in his
memoir on the year of 1960, 'Everyone in the city wore plastic raincoats
smuggled from Austria. The authorities caught every day reckless smuggler
gangs, but in vain: from the construction worker to the university professor
everybody was wearing it.' K. Kecskeméti, 1960, in *Beszélő évek 1957–1968*
(Budapest, 2000), p. 164.

23. *Ifjúsági Magazin* [Youth Magazine], 3.5. (1967) May, p. 58.
24. Personal information from linguist Dr Géza Balázs.
25. J. Kádár, *Hazafiság és internacionalizmus* [Patriotism and internationalism] (Budapest, 1968), p. 188.
26. M. Balázs, 'Az Ifipark' [The Youth Park], *Budapesti Negyed*, 3(1) (1994), pp. 23–46.
27. I find Kádár's blurb on outfit a bit puzzling. Kádár's personal taste, his relationship to elite culture, his everyday gestures and his talk reflected his working-class background. Considering that most people of his age (and many who were younger) strictly dismissed men's long hair and jeans in the late 1960s, it is curious that this basically rather conservative man opted to say yes to jeans and long hair. Was he seeking popularity among the youth; was he advised so to speak; or maybe he did not really care about jeans and long hair? We shall never know.
28. 'Lapunk elé' [Foreword], *Beszélő*, 1.1 (1981), p. 11.

5   Consuming Without Paying: Stealing or Campaigning? The Civic Implications of Civil Disobedience Around Access to Water

1. Interview with Shanta Reddy, solicitor, Durban, September 2003. See B. Morgan, 'Global Business, Local Constraints: The Case of Water in South Africa', in N. Woods (ed.), *Making Corporate Self-Regulation Effective in Developing Countries* (Oxford, 2007) for a more detailed account of the South African narrative. This and other research cited in this article by Morgan is based on research funded by a joint ESRC–AHRC Research Grant 143-25-0031 under the Research Programme Cultures of Consumption, whose support is gratefully acknowledged.
2. See B. Morgan, 'Emerging Global Water Welfarism: Access to Water, Unruly Consumers and Transnational Governance', in J. Brewer and F. Trentmann (eds), *Consuming Cultures, Global Perspectives: Historical Trajectories, Transnational Exchanges* (Oxford, 2006) for a more detailed account with more context of the New Zealand story.
3. M. Hilton, Chapter 6 in this volume.
4. M. Micheletti, Chapter 8 in this volume.
5. B. Page, 'Paying for Water and the Geography of Commodities', *Transactions of the Institute of British Geographers* (2005), pp. 293–306.
6. The designations employed and the presentation of material do not imply the expression of any opinion whatsoever on the part of UNESCO concerning the legal status of any country, territory, city or area or of its authorities, or concerning its frontiers or boundaries.
7. See Morgan, *Consumer Cultures, Global Perspectives* for a more detailed account with more context of the New Zealand story.
8. *Metrowater* vs. *Gladwin et al.*, High Court of New Zealand, 17 December 1999, unreported judgement of Salmon, J.
9. When Metrowater bills a customer for wastewater treatment it states that it is passing on charges it pays to the bulk supplier (Watercare) for this service and charges a volumetric fee calculated at 75% of the water used that month. The dispute letter claims that this is misleading the customer in breach of the Consumer Guarantees Act because Watercare actually charges Metrowater a *fixed*, and not a volumetric, charge for wastewater treatment.

10. Para 27 of the General Comment No. 15 by the UN Committee on Economic, Social and Cultural Rights, asserting that 'Equity demands that poorer households should not be disproportionately burdened with water expenses as compared to richer households.'

11. The occupant of the house refused to comply and was charged with contempt of court. He continued to refuse to comply and was jailed for 18 days. The Auckland City Council moved for a withdrawal of the contempt order in embarrassment at the publicity it was receiving on the issue.

12. *Bright v. Mulholland* [2002] DCR 196.

13. Interview, Penny Bright, Water Pressure Group, January 2004.

14. *Local Government Act*, 2002 (NZ), Sections 130–137: the effect is to prohibit local governments from divesting themselves of water supply and wastewater services within their areas, unless it is to another local government authority. Contracting out of water services operations is limited to a maximum of 15 years, and it is illegal to delegate control over water pricing, water services management and the development of water policy. These restrictions prohibit some types of public–private partnerships and significantly dilute the commercial scope and attractiveness of other types.

15. *Residents of Bon Vista Mansions v Southern Metropolitan Local Council*, 2002 (6) BCLR 625. In July 2006 a case was filed in Johannesburg by residents of Phiri, Soweto, challenging the constitutionality of pre-paid metres as forms of 'self-disconnection' lacking the procedural protections required by the *Bon Vista* case. The outcome was unknown at the time of publication.

16. F. Trentmann and V. Taylor, 'From Users to Consumers: Water Politics in Nineteenth Century London', in F. Trentmann (ed.), *The Making of the Consumer: Knowledge, Power and Identity in the Modern World* (Oxford, 2006).

17. ESRC-AHRC Research Grant 143-25-0031 Bolivian protestors sustained a powerful praxis of political agency without any connection to judicial or quasi-judicial actions, largely because the issue of access to water engaged a far broader cross section of social groups there than in any of the other case studies. The Chilean case also illustrated an absence of judicial or quasi-judicial action but for the opposite reason: its protest movement was highly muted, engaged only upon the terrain of consumer identities and did not engage in civil disobedience.

18. B. Morgan, 'Turning Off the Tap, Urban Water Service Delivery and the Social Construction of Global Administrative Law', *European Journal of International Law* 17 (2006), pp. 215–247.

19. Morgan, *Consumer Cultures, Global Perspectives*.

20. Micheletti, Chapter 8 in this volume.

21. A. Malpass, C. Barnett, N. Clarke and P. Cloke, 'Problematising Choice: Responsible Consumers and Sceptical Citizens', in M. Bevir and F. Trentmann (ed), *Governance, Citizens and Consumers: Agency and Resistance in Contemporary Politics* (Basingstoke, 2007).

22. B. Morgan, 'The North–South Politics of Necessity: Rights, Markets and Consumers Between National and International Levels', special issue, 'The Politics of Necessity', for *Journal of Consumer Policy*, 29(4) (2006).

23. Morgan, *European Journal of International Law*.

24. B. Morgan, 'Water: Frontier Markets and Cosmopolitan Activism', *Soundings: A Journal of Politics and Culture*, 27 (2004), pp. 10–24.

25. Interview with Carlos Crespo, lecturer, the University of San Simón, The Bolivian School of Planning, Cochabamba, Bolivia, 3 March 2004.

26. D. Jacobson, 'If England was what England seems', revised version of the Alan Marre Maccabeans Centenary Lecture, University College London, November 2004, reprinted in the *Times Literary Supplement*, 11 March 2005, pp. 11–12.

27. M. McCann, *Rights at Work: Pay Equity Reform and the Politics of Legal Mobilisation* (Chicago, 1994); H. Silverstein, *Unleashing Rights: Law, Meaning and the Animal Rights Movement* (Ann Arbor, MI, 1996); D. Engel and F. W. Munger, *Rights of Inclusion: Law and Identity in the Life Stories of Americans with Disabilities* (Chicago, 2003); P. Ewick and S. Silbey, *The Common Place of Law: Stories from Everyday Life* (Chicago 1998); J. Brigham, 'Right, Rage, and Remedy: Forms of Law in Political Discourse', *Studies in American Political Development*, 2 (1988), pp. 303–316.

6 The Banality of Consumption

1. M. Horkheimer and T. W. Adorno, *Dialectic of Enlightenment* (London, 1973), p. 137.

2. T. W. Adorno, *The Culture Industry: Selected Essays on Mass Culture* (London, 1991), p. 89.

3. H. Marcuse, *One-Dimensional Man: The Ideology of Industrial Society* (London, 1994); J. Habermas, *The Structural Transformation of the Public Sphere: An Inquiry into a Category of Bourgeois Society* (Cambridge, 1989).

4. M. Hilton, 'The Legacy of Luxury: Moralities of Consumption since the Eighteenth Century', *Journal of Consumer Culture*, 4(1) 2004, pp. 101–123.

5. G. Debord, *Society of the Spectacle* (Detroit, 1970), Ch. 7, section 168.

6. J. Baudrillard, *The Consumer Society: Myths and Structures* (London, 1998).

7. J. Baudrillard, *America* (London, 1988), p. 102.

8. J. Baudrillard, *Dust Breeding*, 2001, read from www.egs.edu/faculty/baudrillard October 2005.

9. M. Morris, 'Banality in Cultural Studies', *Discourse*, 10(2) (1988), pp. 3–29.

10. D. Hebdige, 'Banalarama, or Can Pop Save Us All?', *New Statesman & Society*, 1(27) (9 December 1988), pp. 29–32.

11. D. Hebdige, 'Object as Image: The Italian Scooter Cycle', *Block*, 5 (1981), pp. 44–64; D. Hebdige, *Subculture: The Meaning of Style* (London, 1979); S. Hall and T. Jefferson (eds), *Resistance Through Rituals: Youth Subcultures in Post-War Britain* (London, 1976).

12. J. Baudrillard, 'For a Critique of the Political Economy of the Sign', in M. Poster (ed.), *Jean Baudrillard: Selected Writings* (Cambridge, 1988), pp. 64–75.

13. Morris, 'Banality in Cultural Studies'.

14. S. Deshpande, 'Hegemonic Spatial Strategies: The Nation-Space and Hindu Communalism in Twentieth-century India', *Public Culture*, 10(2) (1998), pp. 249–283, 270.

15. D. Harvey, 'Cosmopolitanism and the Banality of Geographic Evils', *Public Culture*, 12(2) (2000), pp. 529–564, 555.

16. H. Keum, N. Devenathan, S. Deshpande, M. R. Nelson and D. V. Shah, 'The Citizen-Consumer: Media Effects at the Intersection of Consumer and Civil Culture', *Political Communication*, 21 (2004), pp. 369–391, 384.

17. D. Roche, *Histoire des choses banales. Naissance de la consommation, XVIIe-XIXe siècle* (Paris, 1997), p. 10, translated as *A History of Everyday Things: The Birth of Consumption in France, 1600–1800* (Cambridge, 2000), p. 2.

18. J. Gronow and A. Warde, 'Epilogue: Conventional Consumption', in J. Gronow and A. Warde (eds), *Ordinary Consumption* (London, 2001).

19. P. Bourdieu, *Distinction: A Social Critique of the Judgement of Taste* (London, 1986).

20. P. Bourdieu, *The Logic of Practice* (Cambridge, 1990), p. 108.
21. P. Bourdieu, *In Other Words: Essays Towards a Reflexive Sociology* (Cambridge, 1994), p. 9.
22. A. Warde, 'Consumption and Theories of Practice, *Journal of Consumer Culture*, 5(2) (2005), pp. 131–153, 144.
23. Ibid., p. 145.
24. G. Eley, *Forging Democracy: The History of the Left in Europe, 1850–2000* (Oxford, 2002).
25. L. Cohen, *A Consumers' Republic: The Politics of Mass Consumption in Postwar America* (New York, 2003); G. Cross, *An All-Consuming Century: Why Commercialism Won in Modern America* (New York, 2000); V. de Grazia, *Irresistible Empire: America's Advance Through Twentieth-Century Europe* (Cambridge, MA, 2005).
26. N. C. Smith, *Morality and the Market: Consumer Pressure for Corporate Accountability* (London, 1990), pp. 299–309; M. Friedman, *Consumer Boycotts: Effecting Change through the Marketplace and the Media* (London, 1999).
27. R. Harrison, T. Newholm and D. Shaw (eds), *The Ethical Consumer* (London, 2005); M. Micheletti, A. Follesdal and D. Stolle (eds), *Politics, Products and Markets: Exploring Political Consumerism Past and Present* (London, 2004).
28. A. Nicholls and C. Opal, *Fair Trade: Market-Driven Ethical Consumerism* (London, 2005).
29. D. Miller, 'Consumption as the Vanguard of History: A Polemic by Way of an Introduction', in D. Miller (ed.), *Acknowledging Consumption: a Review of New Studies* (London, 1995), pp. 1–57.
30. J. Bové and F. Dufour, *The World is Not for Sale: Farmers Against Junk Food* (London, 2001).
31. P. Kingsnorth, *One No, Many Yeses: A Journey to the Heart of the Global Resistance Movement* (London, 2003); N. Klein, *Fences and Windows: Dispatches from the Front Lines of the Globalisation Debate* (London, 2002); J. Heath and A. Potter, *Nation of Rebels: Why Counterculture Became Consumer Culture* (New York, 2004).
32. D. Donherty and A. Etzioni (eds), *Voluntary Simplicity: Responding to Consumer Culture* (Oxford, 2003).
33. T. H. Breen, *The Marketplace of Revolution: How Consumer Politics Shaped American Independence* (Oxford, 2004); D. Frank, *Buy American: The Untold Story of Economic Nationalism* (Boston, MA, 1999).
34. K. Gerth, *China Made: Consumer Culture and the Creation of the Nation* (Cambridge, MA, 2003); M. E. Robinson, *Cultural Nationalism in Colinial Korea, 1920–1925* (Seattle, 1988); L. C. Nelson, *Status, Gender and Consumer Nationalism in South Korea* (New York, 2000); C. A. Bayly, 'The Origins of Swadeshi (Home Industry): Cloth and Indian Society, 1700–1930', in A. Appadurai (ed.), *The Social Life of Things: Commodities in Cultural Perspective* (Cambridge, 1986).
35. B. J. Davis, *Home Fires Burning: Food, Politics and Everyday Life in World War I Berlin* (Chapel Hill, NC, 2000); M. Hilton, *Consumerism in Twentieth-Century Britain: The Search for a Historical Movement* (Cambridge, 2003).
36. P. Gurney, *Co-operative Culture and the Politics of Consumption in England, c. 1870–1930* (Manchester, 1996); S. Yeo (ed.), *New Views of Co-operation* (London, 1988).
37. Cross, *An All-Consuming Century*.
38. Certainly, this is the view held by many within the consumer movement: interview with Rhoda Karpatkin, 19 February 2005; interview with Julian Edwards, 8 September 2004.
39. F. G. Sim, *IOCU on Record: A Documentary History of the International Organisation of Consumers Unions, 1960–1990* (New York, 1991); S. Brobeck, R. N. Mayer and

R. O. Herrmann (eds), *Encyclopaedia of the Consumer Movement* (Santa Barbara, CA, 1997).

40. Cited in Consumers' Association (CA), *Annual Report, 1979–1980* (London, 1980), p. 13.
41. D. Sanford, *Me & Ralph: Is Nader Unsafe for America?* (Washington, D.C., 1976); J. Martin, *Nader: Crusader, Spoiler, Icon* (Cambridge, MA, 2002); P. C. Marcello, *Ralph Nader: A Biography* (Westport, CO, 2004); Capital Legal Foundation, *Abuse of Trust: A Report on Ralph Nader's Network* (Chicago, 1982).
42. S. Lazarus, *The Genteel Populists* (New York, 1974); R. D. Holsworth, *Public Interest Liberalism and the Crisis of Affluence: Reflections on Nader, Environmentalism, and the Politics of a Sustainable Society* (Cambridge, MA, 1980).
43. http://www.rightlivelihood.org; P. Ekins, *A New World Order: Grassroots Movements for Global Change* (London, 1992); J. Seabrook, *Pioneers of Change: Experiments in Creating a New Society* (London, 1993); T. Woodhouse (ed.), *People and Planet: The Right Livelihood Award Speeches* (London, 1987).
44. H. Arendt, *Eichmann in Jerusalem: A Report on the Banality of Evil* (1963; Harmondsworth, 1976), p. 252.

7 'Public Connection' and the Uncertain Norms of Media Consumption

1. C. Campbell, 'The Sociology of Consumption', in D. Miller (ed.), *Acknowledging Consumption* (London, 1995), pp. 109–110.
2. His particular target was R. Silverstone and E. Hirsch (eds), *Consuming Technologies* (London, 1992), which discussed domestic information and communication technologies.
3. B. Longhurst, G. Bagnall and M. Savage, 'Ordinary Consumption and Personal identity: Radio and the Middle classes in the North West of England', in J. Gronow and A. Warde (eds), *Ordinary Consumption* (London, 2001), pp. 125–142.
4. P. du Gay, S. Hall, L. James, H. Mackay and K. Negus, *Doing Cultural Studies: The Story of the Sony Walkman* (London, 1996).
5. See also generally D. Miller, *Material Culture and Mass Consumption* (Oxford, 1987); H. Mackay (ed.), *Consumption and Everyday Life* (London, 1997); G. Murdock, 'Public Broadcasting and Democratic Culture: Consumers, Citizens, and Communards', in J. Wasko (ed.), *A Companion to Television* (Malden, 2005), pp. 174–198.
6. R. Silverstone, *Television and Everyday Life* (London, 1994).
7. *Democracy and Education* (quoted J. Carey, *Communication as Culture* [Boston, 1989], p. 22.)
8. R. Williams, *The Long Revolution* (Harmondsworth, 1961); Carey, *Communication as Culture*.
9. M. Hilton and M. Daunton, 'Material Politics: An Introduction', in M. Daunton and M. Hilton (eds), *The Politics of Consumption: Material Culture and Citizenship in Europe and America* (Oxford, 2001), p. 12.
10. P. Scannell, *Radio Television and Modern Life* (Oxford, 1996).
11. Yet the grounds for regulatory intervention in this market are often framed in terms of citizen interests – universal service obligation, broadcasting codes, journalists ethics, and so forth (S. Livingstone, P. Lunt and L. Miller, 'Citizens and Consumers: Discursive debates during and after the Communications Act 2003', *Media, Culture & Society*, 29(4) (2007), pp. 613–638.

12. See N. Couldry, 'Communicative Entitlements and Democracy: The Future of the Digital Divide Debate', in R. Mansell, C. Avgerou, D. Quah and R. Silverstone (eds), *Oxford Handbook on ICTs* (Oxford 2007).
13. Though this is a difficult distinction to maintain, see Corner's distinction between the scholarly analysis of 'public knowledge and that of popular culture': (J. Corner, Meaning, Genre and Context: The Problematics of 'Public Knowledge' in the New Audience Studies, in J. Curran and M. Gurevitch (eds), *Mass Media and Society* (London, 1991). For further discussion, see S. Livingstone, 'The Changing Nature of Audiences: From the Mass Audience to the Interactive Media User', in A. Valdivia (ed.), *The Blackwell Companion to Media Research* (Oxford, 2003), pp. 337–359.
14. See especially J. Corner and D. Pels (eds), *Media and the Restyling of Politics* (London, 2003).
15. October 2003–March 2006, funded under the ESRC/AHRC Cultures of Consumption programme (grant number RES-143-25-0011), whose financial support is gratefully acknowledged.
16. A. Touraine, *Can We Live Together?* (Cambridge, 2000), pp. 5–6.
17. This point is fully argued in N. Couldry, S. Livingstone and T. Markham, *Media Consumption and Public Engagement: Beyond the Presumption of Attention* (Basingstoke, 2007), chapters 1 and 2.
18. R. Putnam *Bowling Alone* (New York, 2000).
19. The word 'public' is notoriously difficult, since it has a range of conflicting meanings. J. Weintraub and K. Kumar (eds), *Public and Private in Thought and Practice* (Chicago, 1997). See also Couldry, Livingstone, and Markham, *Media Consumption and Public Engagement*, chapter 1; S. Livingstone, 'On the Relation between Audiences and Publics', in S. Livingstone (ed.), *Audiences and Publics: When Cultural Engagement Matters for the Public Sphere* (Bristol, 2005), pp. 17–42; cf. R. Geuss, *Public Goods Private Goods* (Princeton, 2001), and J. Elshtain, 'The Displacement of Politics', in J. Weintraub and K. Kumar (eds), *Public and Private in Thought and Practice* (Chicago, 1997), pp. 103–132.
20. L. Bennett, 'The Uncivic Culture: Communication, Identity, and the Rise of Lifestyle Politics', *PS: Political Science and Politics* 31(4) (1998), pp. 740–761.
21. For details of our diary and survey samples, see Couldry, Livingstone and Markham, *Media Consumption and Public Engagement*, appendices 1 A and 2B.
22. A. Reckwitz, 'Toward a Theory of Social Practices', *European Journal of Social Theory*, 5(2) (2002), p. 249.
23. Ibid., p. 255.
24. T. Schatzki, *Social Practices: A Wittgensteinian Approach to Human Activity and the Social* (Cambridge, 1996), p. 89.
25. Cf. N. Couldry and A. Langer, 'Media Consumption and Public Connection: Towards a Typology of the Dispersed Citizen', *The Communication Review* (8) (2005), pp. 237–257, discussing a pilot for the Public Connection project.
26. For an extension of these ideas to media research, see N. Couldry, 'Theorising Media as Practice', *Social Semiotics* 14(2) (2004), pp. 115–132. This was in part inspired by Alan Warde's presentation to a methodology seminar of the Cultures of Consumption programme, Birkbeck College, October 2003: see now A. Warde, 'Consumption and Theories of Practice', *Journal of Consumer Culture* 5(2) (2005), pp. 131–153.
27. G. Almond and S. Verba, *The Civic Culture* (Princeton, 1963).
28. P. Dahlgren, 'Reconfiguring Civic Culture in the New Media Milieu', in J. Corner and D. Pels (eds), *Media and the Restyling of Politics* (London, 2003), pp. 151–170.

29. P. Dahlgren, 'The Internet, Public Spheres, and Political Communication: Dispersion and Deliberation', *Political Communication* 22(2) (2005), pp. 147–162.

30. Cf. Z. Bauman, *In Search of Politics* (Cambridge, 1999).

31. Internet use and access still remains highly socially stratified according to our survey (and indeed most other research).

32. See www.statistics.gov.uk/cci/nugget_print.asp?ID=8. Of those 60%, 86% said they accessed the Internet at home, suggesting a lower figure for home Internet access.

33. www.statistics.gov.uk/cci/nugget_print.asp?ID=1367.

34. This contrasts with a recent US survey in which 24% of people name the Internet as a principal news source. See Pew report 'Public More Critical of Press, But Goodwill Persists', June 2005 (http://people-press.org/reports).

35. In our survey we found that social expectation to keep up to date with 'what's going on in the world' was important in predicting news engagement, itself a factor in predicting political interest: see N. Couldry, S. Livingstone and T. Markham, *Media Consumption and the Future of Public Connection*. Report, 20 March 2006, pp. 55–56, downloadable from www.publicconnection.org.

36. Silverstone and Hirsch, *Consuming Technologies*; Silverstone, *Television and Everyday Life*.

37. T. Benn, 'Collective Campaign for Real Politics', *Times Higher Education Supplement*, 24 March 2006, p. 16.

38. J. Katz and R. Rice, *Social Consequences of the Internet* (Cambridge, MA, 2002), p. 150.

39. H. Rheingold, *The Virtual Community* (London, 1994).

40. O. Gandy, 'The Real Digital Divide: Citizens Versus Consumers', in L. Lievrouw and S. Livingstone (eds), *The Handbook of New Media* (London, 2002), p. 452.

41. L. Boltanski, *Distant Suffering* (Cambridge, 1999).

42. For more detailed analysis of Kylie's situation as an example of the contradictions of the mediated public sphere, see N. Couldry, S. Livingstone and T. Markham, 'Connection or Disconnection? Tracking the Mediated Public Sphere in Everyday Life', in R. Butsch (ed.), *Media and the Public Sphere* (New York, 2006).

43. Our survey was conducted in the period 3–5 June 2005, and the Iraq conflict was the single most-named issue by our survey population (13%), compared with the second highest (crime) at 12%. It is clear that the last 3 years in Britain have been relatively exceptional in this respect, and this must be taken into account in interpreting the overall 38% who said their issue was an international one.

44. S. Pharr and R. Putnam (eds), *Disaffected Democracies* (Cambridge, MA, 2000).

45. Some argue (R. Dalton, 'Value Change and Democracy', in S. Pharr and R. Putnam (eds), *Disaffected Democracies* [Cambridge, MA, 2000], pp. 252–269) that mistrust per se is a positive sign of more critical and sophisticated engagement with politics.

46. This project, nearing completion, by Andrea Press and Bruce Williams of the University of Illinois at Urbana-Champaign, was funded by the National Science Foundation; it adopted our methodology but, unlike our study, was locally focused in central Illinois. More detailed comparative work will be published by us jointly in due course: for now, see B. Williams, A. Press, E. Moore and C. Johnson-Yale, 'Comparative Issues in the Study of Media and Public Connection', paper presented to the annual International Communication Association conference, Dresden, June 2006.

47. For more detail, see Couldry, Livingstone and Markham, *Media Consumption and Public Engagement*, chapter 5.

48. Couldry, Livingstone, and Markham, *Media Consumption and Public Engagement*, chapter 8.

49. This requires a link between discussion and effective decision making (J. Cohen, 'Deliberation and Democratic Legitimacy' in J. Bohman and W. Rehg (eds), *Deliberative Democracy* [Cambridge, MA, 1997], pp. 67–92). The basic threshold of deliberative democracy is that 'each citizen [is] able to initiate deliberation and participate effectively in it' (ibid., p. 333). Compare Cohen and Arato's account of civil society as the space 'in which individuals speak, assemble, associate and reason together on matters of public concern and act in concert in order to influence political society and, indirectly, decision-making' (J. Cohen and A. Arato, *Civil Society and Political Theory* [Cambridge, MA, 1992], p. 564).

50. C. Pattie, P. Seyd and P. Whitely, *Citizenship in Britain: Values, Participation and Democracy* (Cambridge, 2004), p. 278.

51. Our survey found some traces of consumer action: when asked which of a long list of possible actions the respondents had taken on an issue they had named as of importance to them, 11% said they had made a 'personal protest' (defined to include boycotting a product) (Couldry, Livingstone and Markham, *Media Consumption and the Future of Public Connection*, p. 45).

52. Here, following our earlier discussion of the term 'public', we distinguish between 'public' action (actions in relation to potentially contentious issues) and civic action (where nothing contentious need be involved).

53. Cf. G. Mulgan, 'Central reservations', *Guardian*, society section, 1 March, 10, 2006.

54. For the class-based distribution of opportunities to do voluntary work see N. Burns, K. Schlozman and S. Verba, *The Private Roots of Public Action* (Cambridge, MA, 2001).

55. Power, *The Report of Power: An independent Inquiry into Britain's Democracy* (London, 2006). Downloadable from www.powerinquiry.org/report/index.php.

56. The latter including an exercise in citizen involvement in budget-setting (Power Report, *The Report of Power: An independent Inquiry into Britain's Democracy* (London, 2006). Downloadable from www.powerinquiry.org/report/index.php, chapter 7.

57. See Kim Schrøder, 'The Everyday Construction of Mediated Citizenship: People's Use of News Media in Denmark', and Peter Dahlgren, 'Young Activists, Civic Practices and Net Use: Beyond the Deliberative Democracy Model', both papers presented at the annual International Communication Association conference, Dresden, June 2006.

58. For the ambiguities of the hyphenated 'citizen-consumer' couplet in current UK debates on media and communications regulation, see Livingstone, Lunt and Miller, 'Citizens and Consumers'.

59. See C. Taylor, *Modern Social Imaginaries* (Durham, NC, 2004), chapters 6 and 7 on 'public' issues as those requiring collective resolution.

60. J. Elster, 'The Market and the Forum', in J. Bohman and W. Rehg (eds), *Deliberative Democracy* (Cambridge, MA, 1997), pp. 10–11.

61. See D. Morley, 'Finding About the World from Television News: Some Difficulties', in J. Gripsrud (ed.), *Television and Common Knowledge* (London, 1999), pp. 136–158.

62. J. Dewey, The Public and its Problems (Chicago, 1946), p. 43.

8   The Moral Force of Consumption and Capitalism: Anti-slavery and Anti-sweatshop

1. This chapter is part of a research project on political consumerism funding by the Swedish Council of Research.

2. F. Klingberg, *The Anti-Slavery Movement in England: A Study in English Humanitarianism* (New Haven, 1926), p. vii.

3. T. Haskell, 'Capitalism and the Origins of the Humanitarian Sensibility, Part 1,' in T. Bender (ed.), *The Antislavery Debate: Capitalism and Abolitionism as a Problem in Historical Interpretation* (Berkeley, 1992), p. 107.
4. A. Hochschild, 'Against All Odds,' *Mother Jones* January/February 2004; A. Hochschild, *Bury the Chains: Prophets and Rebels in the Fight to Free an Empire's Slaves* (New York, 2005).
5. For example, I. M. Young, 'Responsibility and Global Justice: A Social Connection Model,' *Social Philosophy and Policy* 23(1) (2006), pp. 102–130; W. L. Bennett, 'Communicating Global Activism: Strengths and Vulnerabilities of Networked Politics,' *Information, Communication & Society* 6(2), pp. 143–168; R. Goodin, 'Globalizing Justice' in D. Held and M. Koenig-Archibugi (eds), *Taming Globalization: Frontiers of Governance* (Oxford, 2003).
6. Cf. D. Bender and R. Greenwald, *Sweatshop USA: The American Sweatshop in Historical and Global Perspective* (London, 2003); R. Ross, *Slaves to Fashion: Poverty and Abuse in the New Sweatshops* (Ann Arbor, 2004); A. Ross (ed.), *No Sweat: Fashion, Free Trade, and the Rights of Garment Workers* (New York, 1997); and R. Shaw, *Reclaiming America: Nike, Clean Air, and the New National Activism* (Berkeley, 1999).
7. D. B. Davis, 'Reflections on Abolitionism and Ideological Hegemony,' in T. Bender (ed.) and T. Bender, 'Introduction' in Bender (ed.), *The Antislavery Debate* (Berkeley, CA, 1992), pp. 4–5.
8. J. Ashworth, 'Capitalism, Class, and Antislavery,' in Bender (ed.), *The Antislavery Debate* (Berkeley, CA, 1992), p. 274.
9. Ibid., and diagrams on p. 275.
10. Bender, *The Antislavery Debate*, Infoplease, 'The Antislavery Movement, Encyclopedia. Online' (online at infoplease.com/ce6/bus/A08661125.html, accessed 21 January 2006).
11. For a general discussion on this spillover effect from private to public virtues see M. Micheletti, *Political Virtue and Shopping: Individuals, Consumerism, and Collective Action* (New York, 2003), chapter 1.
12. Bender, *The Antislavery Debate*, p. 7.
13. Temperely as quoted in Haskell, 'Capitalism and the Origins of the Humanitarian Sensibility,' Part 1, p. 109.
14. T. Haskell, 'Capitalism and the Origins of the Humanitarian Sensibility,' Part 2, in Bender (ed.), *The Antislavery Debate*, p. 141.
15. Ross, *No Sweat*; Clean Clothes Campaign, *Frequently Asked Questions* (online at cleanclothes.org, accessed January 21, 2006), United Students Against Sweatshops, *Students Across the US Launch the NEW Sweat-Free Campus Campaign!* (online at studentsagainstsweatshops.org, accessed January 21, 2006), Global Unions, home page (online at global-unions.org/default.asp?Language=EN, accessed 21 January 2006).
16. Information on globally integrated enterprises and the quotation come from S. Palmisano, 'The Globally Integrated Enterprise,' *Foreign Affairs* 85(3) (2006), pp. 127–136, p. 129. On new consumers and buyer-driven corporations see M. Korthals, 'Taking Consumers Seriously: Two Concepts of Consumer Sovereignty,' *Journal of Agricultural and Environmental Ethics* 14 (2001), pp. 201–215; M. Lee (ed.), *Consumer Society Reader* (Oxford, 2000); J. Schor and D. Holt, *Consumer Society Reader* (New York, 2002); G. Gereffi, 'Beyond the Producer-driven/Buyer-driven Dichotomy: The Evolution of Global Value Chains in the Internet Era,' *IDS Bulletin* 32(3) (2001), pp. 30–40.
17. M. Ward, 'Fashion as a Culture Industry,' in Ross (ed), *No Sweat*.

18. G. Howells and S. Weatherill, *Consumer Protection Law* (Aldershot, 2005).
19. See the interesting court case *Kasky* vs. *Nike* (2003, Issue brief available online at sustainability.com/insight/issue-brief.asp?id= 61, accessed February. 2006), talk by H. Lindholm from the Fair Trade Center, Stockholm, Sweden at the open seminar 'Shopping och de mänskliga rättigheterna' (Karlstad University, 2 March 2005), Clean Clothes Campaign, *Looking for a Quick Fix: How Weak Social Auditing is Keeping Workers in Sweatshops* (online at cleanclothes.org/pub.htm, accessed January 21, 2006).
20. Gereffi, 'Beyond the Producer-driven/Buyer-driven Dichotomy: The Evolution of Global Value Chains in the Internet Era.'
21. N. Klein, *No Logo* (New York, 2000); G. Knight and J. Greenberg, 'Promotionalism and Subpolitics: Nike and Its Labor Critics,' *Management Communication Quarterly* 15(4) (2002), pp. 541–570; B. Edvardsson, B. Enquist, and B. Johnston, 'Co-Creating Customer Value through Hyperrelaity in the Pre-purchase Service Experience,' *Journal of Service Research* 8(2) (2005), pp. 149–161.
22. R. deWinter, 'The Anti-Sweatshop Movement: Constructing Corporate Moral Agency in the Global Apparel Industry,' *Ethics & International Affairs* 15(2) (2003), pp. 99–115, p. 108.
23. S. Krasner, 'Power Politics, Institutions, and Transnational Relations,' in T. Risse-Kappen (ed.), *Bringing Transnational Relations Back In: Non-State Actions, Domestic Structures and International Institutions* (Cambridge, 2003).
24. Young, 'Responsibility and Global Justice'; I. Marion Young, 'Responsibility and Global Labor Justice,' *The Journal of Political Philosophy* 12(4) (2004), pp. 365–388.
25. Young, 'Responsibility and Global Justice, p. 106.
26. C. Sabel, A. Fung, and D. O'Rourke, 'Ratcheting Labour Standards: How Open Competition Can Save Ethical Sourcing,' *Financial Times Op-Ed*, no date (online http://www2.law.columbia.edu/sabel/papers/fintimes.pdf, accessed 21 January 2006); A. Fung, D. O'Rourke, and C. Sabel, *Can We Put An End to Sweatshops?* (Beacon, 2001).
27. R. H. Turner quoted in D. Snow, 'Framing Processes, Ideology, and Discursive Fields,' in D. Snow, S. Soule, and H. Kriesi (eds), *The Blackwell Companion to Social Movements* (Oxford, 2004), p. 392. See also Hochschild, *Bury the Chains*, p. 5.
28. Davis, 'Reflections on Abolitionism and Ideological Hegemony'.
29. M. Keck and K. Sikkink, *Activists Beyond Borders: Advocacy Networks in International Politics* (Cornell, 1998).
30. Davis, 'Reflections on Abolitionism and Ideological Hegemony'; J. Oldfield, *British Anti-Slavery* (BBC History, 1 January 2001, online at bbc.co.uk/history/society_culture/protest_reform/antilsvery_print.html, accessed January 21, 2006); G. Duquella, P. Hassell, C. Jackson, E. Marmesh, and M. Saldaña, *Quakers in the Anti-Slavery Movement* (no date, online at http://cghs.dade.k12.fl.us/slavery/anti-slavery_movement/quakers.htm. Accessed 21 January 2006).
31. M. Young, 'A Revolution of the Soul: Transformative Experience and Immediate Abolition,' in J. Goodwin, J. Japser, and F. Polletta (eds), *Passionate Politics: Emotions and Social Movements* (Chicago, 2001), p. 99.
32. A. Burton, *Burdens of History: British Feminists, Indian Women, and Imperial Culture, 1865–1915* (Chapel Hill, 1994); C. Sussman, *Consuming Anxieties: Consumer Protest, Gender and British Slavery, 1713–1833* (Stanford, 2000).
33. M. Young, 'A Revolution of the Soul: Transformative Experience and Immediate Abolition'; Hochschild, *Bury the Chains*.
34. As used to summarize William Lloyd Garrison's anti-slavery activism, online at http://www.infoplease.com/ce6/people/A0820261.html, accessed August 2, 2007.

35. Culture jamming is changes in the meaning of corporate advertising through artistic techniques that alter corporate logos visually and by giving marketing slogans new meaning.

36. J. Whittier, *The Branded Hand* (*ca.* 1845).

37. Garrison as quoted in J. McKivigan, 'A Brief History of the American Abolitionist Movement' (no date, online at americanabolitionist.liberalarts.iupui.edu/briefl.htm, accessed January 21, 2006).

38. See Micheletti, *Political Virtue and Shopping*, chapters 2 and 3.

39. Hochschild, 'Against All Odds,' and Hochschild, *Bury the Chains*, p. 193.

40. Burton, *Burdens of History*, p. 77; A. Orleck, '"What are that Mythical Thing Called the Public"': Militant Housewives during the Great Depression,' *Feminist Studies* 19 (1993), pp. 147–172; Micheletti, *Political Virtue and Shopping*, chapter 2; D. Stolle and M. Micheletti, 'The Gender Gap Reversed: Political Consumerism as a Women-Friendly Form of Civic and Political Engagement,' in B. O'Neil and E. Digengil (eds), *Gender and Social Capital* (London, 2005).

41. J. Oldfield, *Popular Politics and British Anti-Slavery: Mobilisation of Public Opinion Against the Slave Trade, 1787–1807* (Manchester, 1995), p. 156.

42. Ibid., p. 179.

43. Ibid.; Hochschild, *Bury the Chains*.

44. See, for example, the discussion in J. Mandle, 'The Student Anti-Sweatshop Movement: Limits and Potential', *The Annals of the American Academy of Political and Social Science* 570(1) (2000), pp. 92–103.

45. International Labor Organization, *A Fair Globalization: Creating Opportunities for All. World Commission on the Social Dimension of Globalization* (2004, online at ilo.org/public/english/wcsdg/docs/report.pdf, accessed 14 February 2006); International Labor Organization, *Decent Work: The Heart of Social Progress* (online at ilo.org/public/english/decent.htm, accessed 14 February 2006); Trade Justice Movement, *Right Corporate Wrongs – New Laws for Trade Justice* (online at tjm.org.uk, accessed 14 February 2006).

46. M. Micheletti and D. Stolle, 'Mobilizing Consumers for Global Social Justice Responsibility-Taking', *American Annals of Political and Social Science* 611 (2007): pp. 157–175.

47. L. Featherstone, 'The New Student Movement', *The Nation* (May 15, 2000) (online version available at nationarchive.com), L. Featherstone and USAS, *Students against Sweatshops* (New York, 2002).

48. B. Bullert, *Strategic Public Relations, Sweatshops ad the Making of a Global Movement* (Seattle, 2000).

49. Global Unions, home page.

50. Clean Clothes Campaign, *Frequently Asked Questions*.

51. Examples are Blackspot Shoes, Shoes with Souls, No Sweat, and American Apparel.

52. Clean Clothes Campaign, *Frequently Asked Questions*; United Students Against Sweatshops, *Students Across the US Launch the NEW Sweat-Free Campus Campaign!* (online at studentsagainstsweatshops.org, accessed 25 February 2006).

53. M. Micheletti, 'Just Clothes? Discursive Political Consumerism and Political Participation,' paper for the European Consortium of Political Research Joint Sessions, Uppsala, 2004(Unpublished).

54. Activist information communicated to Micheletti, Spring 2005.

55. Fair play at the Olympics Campaign 2005 (online fairolympics.org, 2005, accessed 26 February 2006), Play Fair, *Respect Workers' Rights in the Sportswear Industry* (online at fairolympics.org/en/index.htm, no date, accessed 2 March 2006).

56. For instance, *The Consumer and Sweatshops, November 1999* (survey online at marymount.edu/news/garmentstudy/overview.html, accessed 17 March 2006), Treehugger, *Instant Survey: Clothes* (online at treehugger.com/files/2005/09/treehugger_know.php, 2005, accessed 17 March 2006), and G. Trudeau, *Doonesbury Nike Comic Strips 1997* (online at geocities.com/athens/acropolis/5232/comicmay97.htm, accessed 2 March 2005). Data on newspaper reporting is from D. Stolle and M. Micheletti's forthcoming book on political consumerism and the rise of global responsibility-taking. See also J. Greenberg and G. Knight, 'Framing Sweatshops: Nike, Global Production, and the American News Media,' *Communication and Critical/Cultural Studies* 1 (2) (2004), pp. 151–175.

57. J. Peretti with M. Micheletti, 'The Nike Sweatshop Email: Political Consumerism, Internet, and Culture Jamming,' in M. Micheletti, A. Follesdal and D. Stolle (eds), *Politics, Products, and Markets: Exploring Political Consumerism Past and Present* (New Brunswick, 2003); D. Stolle and M. Micheletti with L. Nishikawa and research assistance from M. Wright. 'A Case of Discursive Political Consumerism: The Nike Email Exchange,' *Political Consumerism: Its Motivations, Power, and Conditions in the Nordic Countries and Elsewhere* (TemaNord 2005), p. 517.

58. For information on the online communication for customized and personalized customer service and the received award, see *Critical Mass wins Grand Prix at Cyber Lions in Cannes* (online at ciw-online.org/slavery.html http://www.criticalmass.com/about/news/view.do?article=nike_062001_p&year=2001, accessed 4 February 2006).

59. H. Temperley, 'Capitalism, Slavery and Ideology,' *Past and Present* 75 (1977), pp. 94–118.

60. A-J. Zwierlein, 'Who Bids Abstain?' On Boycott and Empowerment,' *The Review of Communication* 2(3) (2002), pp. 312–317.

61. For an interesting discussion on the hopelessness of complete reliance on public virtues see S. Burtt, 'The Politics of Virtue Today: A Critique and a Proposal,' *American Political Science Review* 87 (1993), pp. 360–368.

62. S. Alinsky, 'Proxies for People: A Vehicle for Involvement. An Interview with Saul Alinsky,' *Yale Review of Law and Social Action* 1(Spring) (1971), pp. 64–69, p. 64.

63. K. Sklar, 'The Consumers' While Label Campaign of the National Consumers' League 1898–1919,' in S. Strasser, C. McGovern, and M. Judt (eds), *Getting and Spending: European and American Consumer Societies in the 20th Century* (Cambridge, 1998); D. Frank, *Purchasing Power: Consumer Organizing, Gender, and the Seattle Labor Movement 1919–1929* (Cambridge, 1994); Smithsonian Institution, *Between Rock and Hard Place: A History of American Sweatshops 1820 to the Present* (online at americanhistory.si.edu/sweatshops, accessed 2 August 2006); Bender and Greenwald, *Sweatshop USA*.

64. O. O'Neill, 'Agents of Justice,' in T. Pogge (ed.), *Global Justice* (Oxford, 2001), pp. 199–201.

65. Probably the best example here is the boycott against South Africa that occurred during Apartheid. For a listing see M. Friedman, *Consumer Boycotts: Effecting Change through the Marketplace and the Media* (New York, 1999).

66. From the Buy Blue web site at buyblue.org, accessed 4 August 2006.

67. B. Cashore, G. Auld, and D. Newson, *Governing through Markets: Forest Certification and the Emergence of Non-State Authority* (New Haven, 2004); A. Jordan, R. Wurzel, and A. Zito (eds), *'New' Instruments of Environmental Governance? National Experiences and Prospects* (London, 2003); Micheletti, *Political Virtue and Shopping*, chapter 3.

68. Micheletti, 'Just Clothes.'
69. D. Zwick, J. Denegri-Knott and J. E. Schroeder, '*The Social Pedagogy of Wall Street: Stock Trading as Political Activism?*, Special issue 'Shopping for Human Rights' edited by M. Micheletti and A. Follsesdal, *Journal of Consumer Policy* 30(3) (2007), pp. 177–199.
70. For an interesting discussion on this point see A. Segerberg, *Thinking Doing. The Politicisation of Thoughtless Action* (Elanders Gotab, 2006).

9 Exit *Homo Politicus*, Enter *Homo Consumens*

1. See F. Furedi, 'Consuming Democracy: Activism, Elitism and Political Apathy', www.geser.net/furedi.html.
2. See www.politics.co.uk of 1 March 2005.
3. T. Deluca, *Two Forms of Political Apathy* (Philadelphia, 2005).
4. B. Berelson, P. Lazarsfeld, and W. McPhee, *Voting* (Chicago, 1954).
5. Furedi, 'Consuming Democracy'.
6. Ibid.
7. M. Lawson, *Dare More Democracy* (London, 2005), p. 18.
8. T. Frank, *Marché de droit divin: capitalisme sauvage et populisme de marché*, Agone (Marseille, 2003).
9. I. Ramonet, *La Tyrannie de la communication* (Paris, 1999), p. 184.
10. T. H. Eriksen, *Tyranny of the Moment* (London and Sterling, 2001), p. 92.
11. Ibid., p. 17.
12. J. Dean, 'Communicative Capitalism: Circulation and the Foreclosure of Politics', *Cultural Politics* (March 2005), pp. 51–73.
13. All following quotations come from *The Future of an Illusion* and *Civilization and Its Discontents*, in James Strachey's translation , The Penguin Freud Library, Vol. 12, *Civilization, Society and Religion* (London, 1991), pp. 179–341.
14. S. Kracauer, *History: The Last Things before the Last* (Oxford and New York, 1969), p. 24.
15. R. Rorty, 'The End of Leninism and History as Comic Frame', in A. M. Melzer, J. Weinberger and M. R. Zinman (eds), *History and the Idea of Progress* (New York, 1995), p. 218.
16. T. Mathiesen, *Silently Silenced: Essays on the Creation of Acquiescence in Modern Society* (Winchester, 2004), p. 15.

10 Consumer Citizenship in Post-national Constellations?

1. J. Q. Whitman, 'Consumerism versus Producerism: On the Golbal Menace of "Consumerism" and the Mission of Comparative Law', Yale Law School, Yale Law School Faculty Scholarship Series, Year 2006, Paper 6.
2. J. Habermas, 'The Postnational Constellation and the Future of Democracy', *The Postnational Constellation: Political Essays* (Cambridge-Oxford, 2001), pp. 58–112.
3. European Communities – Measures affecting the approval and marketing of biotech products' (DS291, DS292 and DS293). Findings and conclusions: http://www.wto.org/english/tratop_e/dispu_e/291r_conc_e.pdf. Full panel report: http://www.wto.org/english/news_e/news06_e/291r_e.htm.
4. See Max Weber, J. Winckelmann (ed.), *Rechtssoziologie* (Neuwied-Berlin, 2nd edn, 1967).
5. Ch. Joerges, *Verbraucherschutz als Rechtsproblem* (Heidelberg, 1981).

6. Whitmann, 'Consumerism versus Producerism and Comparative Law' (note 1).
7. Whitmann, 'Consumerism, Producerism and Comparative Law', Footnotes 2 and 4.
8. See, *Public Papers of the U.S., John F. Kennedy*, Containing the Public Messages, Speeches and Statements of the President, 1 January–31 December 1962, pp. 235–243.
9. D. Bollier and J. Claybrook, *Freedom from Harm* (Washington, D.C., 1986), p. 31.
10. M. Everson, 'Legal Constructions of the Consumer', in F. Trentmann (ed.), *The Making of the Consumer Knowledge, Power and Identity in the Modern World* (Oxford, 2006).
11. See, for example, Ch. Joerges, 'Quality Regulation in Consumer Goods Markets: Theoretical Concepts and Practical Examples', in T. Daintith and G. Teubner (eds), *Contract and Organization* (Berlin, 1986), pp. 142–163.
12. K. Polanyi, *The Great Transformation: The Political and Economic Origins of Our Time (1944)* (Boston, 1992), esp. at pp. 45–58, 71–80.
13. Ch. Joerges, 'What is left of the European Economic Constitution? A Melancholic Eulogy', *European Law Review* 30 (2005), pp. 461–489.
14. See J. Pelkmans, *Market Integration in the European Community* (Den Haag, 1984).
15. F. W. Scharpf, 'The European Social Model: Coping with the Challenges of Diversity', *Journal of Common Market Studies* 40 (2002), pp. 645, 646.
16. OJ 1975 C 92/1. This initiative was inspired by President John F. Kennedy's famous sentiments (see Note 8).
17. Everson, 'Legal Constructions of the Consumer' (note 10).
18. European Commission, 'Commission White Paper to the European Council on Completion of the Internal Market', COM(85) 310 final of 14 June 1985.
19. For an impressively comprehensive though dated account, see V. Eichener, *Entscheidungsprozesse in der regulativen Politik der Europäischen Union* (Opladen, 1997).
20. Commission of the European Communities, 'European Governance. A White Paper', COM(2001) 428 final of 25 July 2001.
21. See, Ch. Joerges, 'Law, Science and the Management of Risks to Health at the National, European and International Level – Stories on Baby Dummies, Mad Cows and Hormones in Beef', *Columbia Journal of European Law* 7 (2000), pp. 1–19 at 6ff.
22. Communication from the Commission. A More Coherent European Contract Law: An Action Plan, COM (2003) 68 final of 12 February 2003.
23. First Annual Progress Report on European Contract Law and the Acquis Review, COM (2005) 456 final of 23 September 2005.
24. OJ L 148, 22 of 11 June 2005.
25. Recent examples include Case C-481/99, *Heininger*, ECR 2001, I-234 (unfair contract terms).
26. Regulation 178/2002 (OJ 2002 L 31/16).
27. Ch. Joerges and E.-U. Petersmann (eds), *Constitutionalism, Multilevel Trade Governance and Social Regulation* (Oxford, 2006).
28. S. Zarrilli, 'International Trade in GMOs: Legal Frameworks and Developing Country Concerns', in Italienerin in F. Francioni and T. Scovazzi (eds), *Biotechnology and International Law* (Oxford, 2006), pp. 231–254.
29. W. van den Daele, 'Legal Framework and Political Strategy in dealing with the Risks of New Technology — The Two Faces of the Precautionary Principle', in J. Somsen (ed.), *Regulating Biotechnology* (Cheltenham, 2007).
30. On this controversy see, P. H. Sand, 'Labelling Genetically Modified Food: The Right to Know', *Review of European Community & International Environmental Law* 15(2) (2006), pp. 185–192.

31. 'Europeans and Biotechnology in 2005: Patterns and trends', *Eurobarometer* 64(3) (2006).
32. P. Dabrowska, *Hybrid Solution for Hybrid Products? EU Governance of GMOs*, Ph.D Thesis, EUI Florence (2006), p. 200ff.
33. 'European Communities — Measures Affecting the Approval and Marketing of Biotech Products', DS291, DS292 and DS293.
34. G. C. Shaffer and M. A. Pollack, 'Reconciling (or Failing to Reconcile) Regulatory Differences: The Ongoing Transatlantic Dispute over the Regulation of Biotechnology', in D. Andrews, M. A. Pollack, G. C. Shaffer and H. Wallace (eds), *The New Transatlantic Agenda and the Future of Transatlantic Economic Governance* (Florence, 2005), pp. 167–229.
35. Ch. Joerges, 'Scientific Expertise in Social Regulation and the European Court of Justice: Legal Frameworks for Denationalized Governance Structures', in Ch. Joerges, K.-H. Ladeur and E. Vos (eds), *Integrating Scientific Expertise into Regulatory Decision-Making: National Traditions and European Innovations* (Baden-Baden, 1997), pp. 295–324.
36. A.W. Gouldner, 'Cosmopolitans and Locals: Towards an Analysis of Latent Social Roles', *Administrative Science Quarterly* (1957), pp. 281–306, and (1958), pp. 444–480.
37. 'Members shall ensure that any sanitary or phytosanitary measure is . . . is based on scientific principles and is not maintained without sufficient scientific evidence . . . (Art. 2 (2)).' 'In cases where relevant scientific evidence is insufficient, a Member may provisionally adopt sanitary or phytosanitary measures on the basis of available pertinent information, including that from the relevant international organizations as well as from sanitary or phytosanitary measures applied by other Members. In such circumstances, Members shall seek to obtain the additional information necessary for a more objective assessment of risk and review the sanitary or phytosanitary measure accordingly within a reasonable period of time (Art. 5 (7)).'
38. Most prominently ECJ, Case C-236/01, *Monsanto* v. *Italy* [2003], ECR I-8105.
39. WTO Appellate Body Report, *European Communities – Measures Concerning Meat and Meat Products (Hormones)* ('EC - Hormones'), WT/DS26/AB/R and WT/DS48/AB/R, adopted 13 February 1998.
40. Case C-236/01, *Monsanto* v. *Italy* [2003], ECR I-8105, paras. 106 and 107.
41. A. Herwig, 'The Precautionary Principle in Support of Practical Reason: An Argument Against Formalistic Interpretations of the Precautionary Principle', in Joerges and Petersmann, *Constitutionalism, Multilevel Trade Governance and Social Regulation* (Oxford, 2006), pp. 301–326.
42. For details, see Dabrowska, *Hybrid Solution for Hybrid Products?*, pp. 177–372.
43. Case C-236/01, *Monsanto* vs. *Italy* [2003], ECR I-8105, para. 109.
44. Dabrowska, *Hybrid Solution for Hybrid Products?* chapter 2.1, p. 43.
45. Instructive, van den Daele, 'Legal Framework and Political Strategy in dealing with the Risks of New Technology'.
46. See, http://www.euractiv.com/en/trade/eu-accepts-trade-ruling-gmos/article-159918.

11 Sustainability, Well-Being and Consumption: The Limits of Hedonic Approaches

1. J. Porritt, *Redefining Sustainablity* (London, 2003), p. 4.
2. Ibid., p. 4.

3. N. Donovan and D. Halpbern, *Life Satisfaction: The State of Knowledge and Implications for Government* (London, 2002), p. 17.
4. Porritt, *Redefining Sustainablity*, p. 18.
5. Ibid., p. 18.
6. Ibid., p. 6.
7. B. Frey and A. Stutzer, *Happiness and Economics* (Princeton, 2002), chapters 7–9.
8. D. Kahneman, P. Wakker and R. Sarin, 'Back to Bentham? Explorations of Experienced Utility', *The Quarterly Journal of Economics* 112 (1997), pp. 375–405; R. Layard, *Happiness: Lessons for a New Science* (London, 2005).
9. Epicurus, *Principal Doctrines* 15, in B. Inwood and L. Gerson (eds), *Hellenistic Philosophy* (Indianapolis, 1988), p. 27.
10. Aristotle, *Politics*, E. Barker trans. (Clarendon Press, 1948), Book 1, chapter 8.
11. D. Kahneman, E. Diener and N. Schwarz (eds), *Well-Being: Foundations of Hedonic Psychology* (New York, 1999), p. ix.
12. Kahneman, Wakker and Sarin, 'Back to Bentham?'
13. B. Frey and A. Stutzer, 'What can Economists Learn from Happiness Research?' *Journal of Economic Literature*' 40 (2002), pp. 402–435, p. 405.
14. Layard, *Happiness*, pp. 242–243.
15. R. Kraut, 'Two Conceptions of Happiness', *Philosophical Review* 88 (1979), pp. 167–197.
16. A. Sen, *Development as Freedom* (Oxford, 1999), p. 75.
17. D. Kahneman, 'Objective Happiness', in Kahneman, Diener and Schwarz (eds), *Well-Being* (New York, 1999), pp. 3–27.
18. Ibid., p. 8.
19. B. Kahneman, B. Fredrickson, C. Schreiber and D. Redelmeier, 'When More Pain is Preferred to Less: Adding a Better End', *Psychological Science* 4 (1993), pp. 401–405.
20. Sen, *Development as Freedom*, p. 62.
21. Cf. Kahneman, 'Objective Happiness', pp. 13–15.
22. J. Elster, *Nuts and Bolts for the Social Sciences* (Cambridge, 1989), pp. 65–67.
23. Kahneman, 'Objective Happiness', p. 15.
24. Porritt, *Redefining Sustainablity*, p. 18, my emphasis.
25. D. Wiggins, 'The Claims of Need', *Needs, Values, Truth*, 3rd edition (Oxford, 1998).
26. Aristotle, *Politics*, 1236b 31.
27. F. Hirsch, *Social Limits to Growth* (London, 1977).
28. Layard, *Happiness*, pp. 41–48.
29. J. O'Neill, *The Market: Ethics, Knowledge and Politics* (London, 1998), chapter 4.
30. See R. Lane, *The Loss of Happiness in Market Democracies* (New Haven, 2001); and Layard, *Happiness*.
31. Porritt, *Redefining Sustainablity*, p. 16.
32. Consider, for example, Martha Nussbaum's list of the central human functional capabilities in *Women and Human Development* (Cambridge, 2000), pp. 78–80.
33. Layard, *Happiness*, pp. 112–114.
34. Kahneman, Wakker and Sarin, 'Back to Bentham?', p. 397.
35. R. Nozick, *Anarchy, State and Utopia* (Oxford, 1980), p. 43.
36. Lucretius, *On Nature*, R. Greer trans. (Indianapolis, 1965), Book 3, pp. 967–971.
37. Lucretius, *On Nature*, Book 3, pp. 972–975.
38. F. Ramsey, 'A Mathematical Theory of Saving', *The Economic Journal* 38 (1928), pp. 543–559.
39. Cf. D. Read, 2004, 'Utility theory from Jeremy Bentham to Daniel Kahneman', London School of Economics Working Paper No: LSEOR 04-64 2004, p. 7.

40. J. O'Neill, *Ecology, Policy and Politics: Human Well-Being and the Natural World* (London, 1993), pp. 53–54.

41. Aristotle, *Nicomachean Ethics*, T. Irwin trans. (Indianapolis, 1985), Book I, chapters 10 and 11.

42. T. S. Eliot, 'Tradition and Individual Talent', *Selected Essays* (London, 1951), p. 15.

43. J. Pocock, *The Machiavellian Moment* (Princeton, 1975), p. 458.

44. K. Polanyi, *The Great Transformation* (Boston, 1957), p. 73.

45. Ibid., p. 184.

46. Ibid., p. 185ff.

47. W. Morris, 'Useful Labour versus Useless Toil', in A. Morton (ed.), *Political Writings of William Morris* (London, 1973), p. 88.

48. S. Weil, *The Need for Roots* (London, 1952), p. 96.

49. J. O'Neill, *Ecology, Policy and Politics*, chapter 3; *Markets, Deliberation and Environment* (London, 2007), Chapter 5.

50. G. A. Cohen, 'Marx's Dialectic of Labour', *Philosophy and Public Affairs*, 3 (1974), pp. 235–261; K. Marx, *German Ideology* (London, 1970), pp. 70–71; and *Grundrisse* (London, 1973), pp. 162–164, 487–489.

51. H. Arendt, *The Human Condition* (Chicago, 1958), p. 55.

52. Ibid., p. 94.

53. Ibid., p. 137.

54. Ibid., p. 125.

55. Ibid., p. 126.

56. Arendt in discussing cultivation appears to suggest the opposite in discussing the possibility that the cultivation of land could be understood as both work and labour: 'This seems so because tilling the soil, its close relation to the biological cycle and its utter dependence upon the larger cycle of nature notwithstanding, leaves some product behind which outlasts its own activity and forms a durable addition to the human artifice: the same task, performed year in and year out, will eventually transform the wilderness into cultivated land. The example figures prominently in all ancient and modern theories of labouring precisely for this reason' (Ibid., p. 138). Arendt responds as follows: 'The cultivated land is not, properly speaking, a use object, which is there in its own durability and requires for its permanence no more than ordinary care in preservation; the tilled soil, if it is to remain cultivated, needs to be laboured upon time and again. A true reification, in other words, in which the produced thing in its existence is secured once and for all, has never come to pass; it needs to be reproduced again and again in order to remain within the human world at all' (Ibid., pp. 138–139). As noted above, I am not convinced by her accounts of labour and reproduction. But leaving this aside taken as a general criticism of landscape and place as parts of the common human world the response misses their mark. Tilling forms but part of the activities that create a human landscape which include a deal more from stone wall and cleared land to coppiced woodland and hedgerow. That their maintenance requires human labour to sustain them does not render the landscape itself something outside the common human world. Labour is just as central to sustaining the urban landscape that clearly does belong to the common world.

57. A. Holland and K. Rawles, *The Ethics of Conservation* (Report presented to The Countryside Council for Wales, Thingmount paper: Lancaster, 1994), p. 37.

58. This chapter draws on material in J. O'Neill, 'Citizenship, Well-Being and Sustainability: Epicurus or Aristotle?', *Analyse & Kritik* 28(2) (2006), pp. 158–172.

12   'Alternative Hedonism' and the Citizen-Consumer

1. Cf. J. Clarke, 'Unstable Connections: Citizen-Consumers and Public Services', paper presented at Seminar on 'Consumers as Citizens', HM Treasury, London, 22 April 2004, p. 8; R. Keat, N. Whiteley and N. Abercrombie (eds), *The Authority of the Consumer* (London and New York, 1994), p. 15; K. Walsh, 'Citizens, Charters and Contracts', in Keat, Whiteley and Abercrombie (eds), *The Authority*, pp. 189–206; N. Fairclough, 'Conversationalization of Public Discourse and the Authority of the Consumer', in Keats, Whiteley and Abercrombie (eds), *The Authority*, pp. 253–268.

2. Cf. K. Soper, 'Re-thinking the "Good Life": The Citizenship Dimension of Consumer Disaffection with Consumerism', *Journal of Consumer Culture* 7(2) (2007). This, of course, is by no means the whole of the story, if only because what is missed out here is the history of the 'making' of the consumer and consumer politics, and the involvement of consumers in cooperative organisations and campaigns to protect their interests against manufacturing monopolies and unscrupulous retailers. Cf. P. Maclachlan and F. Trentmann, 'Civilising Markets: Traditions of Consumer Politics in Twentieth-century Britain, Japan and the United States', in M. Bevir and F. Trentmann (eds), *Markets in Historical Contexts* (Cambridge, 2004); F. Trentmann (ed.), *The Making of the Consumer: Knowledge, Power and Identity in the Modern World* (Oxford and New York, 2006); F. Trentmann, 'The Modern Genealogy of the Consumer: Meanings, Knowledge, and Identities', in J. Brewer and F. Trentmann (eds), *Consuming Cultures, Global Perspectives: Historical Trajectories, Transnational Exchanges* (Oxford and New York, 2006), pp. 19–69. It could be argued, however, that wherever such collective activity is directed at acquiring cheaper and better goods, it is still observing the fundamental rule of the self-interested consumer, and therefore a matter of collective representation of those private interests rather than directed to any more suprapersonal objectives. Certainly such campaigns differ from those mounted on environmental grounds. However, the issues are more complex than can be done justice to here.

3. A. Sen, 'Rational Fools', in J. J. Mansbridge (ed.), *Beyond Self-Interest* (Chicago, 1990), p. 37.

4. J. Butler, *Fifteen Sermons Preached at the Rolls Chapel*, W. R. Mathews (ed.) (London, [1726] (1949)).

5. D. Hume, *Enquiries concerning Human Understanding and concerning the Principles of Morals*, L.A. Selby-Bigge (ed.) (Oxford [1748, 1751] 1966), pp. 296–298.

6. J.-J. Rousseau, 'Discourse on the Origin of Inequality', in V.Gourevitch (ed. and trans.), *The First and Second Discourses Together with Replies to Critics; and an Essay on the Origin of Languages* (New York and London [1750] (1986)).

7. S. Holmes, 'The Secret History of Self-Interest', in Mansbridge (ed.), *Beyond Self-Interest* (Chicago, 1990), pp. 267–286, esp. 282–283. See also C. Jencks, 'Varieties of Altruism', in Mansbridge (ed.), *Beyond Self-Interest*, pp. 53–67; J. A. W. Gunn, '"Interest will not Lie": A Seventeenth-Century Political Maxim', *Journal of the History of Ideas* 29 (1968); H. Pearson, 'Economics and Altruism at the *Fin de Siècle*', in M. Daunton and F. Trentmann (eds), *Worlds of Political Economy: Knowledge and Power in the Nineteenth and Twentieth Centuries* (Basingstoke, 2004), pp. 24–46.

8. T. Nagel, *The Possibility of Altruism* (Princeton, 1970), esp. Part III.

9. D. Miller, *The Dialectics of Shopping* (London and Chicago, 2001), pp. 111–148.

10. D. Winch, 'The Problematic Status of the Consumer in Orthodox Economic thought', in Trentmann (ed.), *The Making of the Consumer*, pp. 31–52.
11. Cf. Pearson, 'Economics and Altruism in the *Fin de Siècle*', pp. 24–46, esp. 34–37; Winch, 'The Problematic Status of the Consumer in Orthodox Economic Thought', pp. 38–42; Trentmann, *Consuming Cultures, Global Perspectives*.
12. Pearson, 'Economics and Altruism in the *Fin de Siècle*', pp. 25–28.
13. A. Marshall *Principles of Economics*, 1st edn. (London, 1890), p. vi; Ibid., pp. 36–37.
14. Marshall, *Principles of Economics*, p. 39.
15. B. Fine and E. Leopold, *The World of Consumption* (London, 1993); G. M. Hodgson and E. Screpanti, *Rethinking Economics: Markets, Technology and Economic Evolution* (Aldershot, 1991); R. E. Lane, *The Market Experience* (Cambridge, 1991); D. Slater, *Consumer Culture and Modernity* (Cambridge, 1997), pp. 42–62.
16. Trentmann, 'The Modern Genealogy of the Consumer', in Brewer and Trentmann (eds), *Consuming Cultures, Global Perspectives*, pp. 19–69.
17. These are issues, one might add, that also bear, at least indirectly, on the current engagements with the so-called 'banality' of consumption, where we arguably need a clearer distinction between the ordinary or 'banal' consumption that consists in the routine satisfaction of everyday consumer needs, and the 'banality' of the recourse to consumer gratifications as substitution or displacement or compensation for loss of other pleasures and forms of self-realisation. Matthew Hilton arguably misreads (see Chapter 6 in this volume) the position of the Frankfurt School theorists on this issue: for Adorno the use of spectacular consumption (of fashion, etc.) for status and identity is indeed banal because it is a form of displacement or sublimation. 'Political' or counter-consumerist campaigns are in this sense not so much avoiding or disregarding the banality of consumption but directly addressing it. They are pointing, in other words, to the trivialising and homogenising pressures of consumer culture today, and to the ways in which it might be better viewed as missing rather than meeting many human aspirations and hedonistic opportunities.
18. For a fuller treatment of this theme, see K. Soper and L. Thomas, ' "Alternative Hedonism" and the Critique of Consumerism', Working Paper submitted in Phase 2 of the ESRC/AHRC-funded 'Cultures of Consumption' Programme.
19. N. Gregson and L. Crewe, 'Possession and Performance: Rethinking the Act of Purchase in the Space of the Car Boot Sale', *Journal of Material Culture* 2 (1997), pp. 241–263; C. Barnett, P. Cafaro and T. Newholm, 'Philosophy and Ethical Consumption', in R. Harrison, T. Newholm and D. Shaw (eds), *The Ethical Consumer* (London, 2005); C. Barnett, P. Cloke, N. Clarke and A. Malpass, 'Consuming Ethics: Articulating the Subjects and Spaces of Ethical Consumption', *Antipode* 37(1) (2005), pp. 23–45
20. Barnett *et al.*, 'Consuming Ethics', p. 39, cf. p. 36.
21. Ibid., p. 39
22. Ibid., p. 31.
23. Ibid., p. 32.
24. On the difference see Plato, *Cratylus* 420a-b. Cf. J.-P. Vernant, *Mortals and Immortals* (London, 1991), p. 101.
25. R. Bahro, *Socialism and Survival* (London, 1982), p. 27.
26. R. Williams, *Towards 2000* (London, 1983); M. Ryle, *Ecology and Socialism* (London, 1988); T. Benton, 'The Malthusian Challenge: Ecology, Natural Limits and Human Emancipation', in P. Osborne (ed.), *Socialism and the Limits of Liberalism* (London, 1991); K. Soper, 'Greening Prometheus', in Osborne (ed.), *Socialism and the Limits of*

Liberalism, pp. 271–293; M. Redclift and G. Woodgate (eds), *The Sociology of the Environment* Vol. 1. (Aldershot, 1995), pp. 253–606; J. O'Connor, *Natural Causes: Essays in Ecological Marxism* (London, 1998).

27. Ryle, *Ecology and Socialism*, pp. 90–91.
28. A. Giddens, *Beyond Left and Right: The Future of Radical Politics* (Cambridge, 1994); see also M. Crozier and P. Murphy (eds), *Left in Search of a Center* (Illinois, 1996), pp. 1–30, esp. pp. 23–24; B. Smart, 'From Rationalization to Reflexivity', *Left in Search of a Center*, pp. 43–63.
29. U. Beck, *The Risk Society: Towards a New Modernity* (London, 1992); cf. A. Giddens, *Modernity and Self-Identity: Self and Society in the Late Modern Age* (Cambridge, 1991), pp. 109–143.
30. See report in the *Guardian*, 19 June 2002 (annual income per capita for these countries is 287 dollars compared with 27,402 for the developed market economies). And this is not to speak of the 2 billion injured or made homeless in the last decade through disasters triggered by global warming, which has more than doubled since the 1970s. (How right Adorno has proved in thinking some 50 years ago that it would prove utopian enough to hope that no one should go hungry any more? *Minima Moralia*, trans. E. F. N. Jephcott (London, 1974), p. 156).
31. E. Ewen and S. Ewen, *Channels of Desire, Mass Images in the Shaping of American Consciousness* (New York, 1982), pp. 265–267; W. Benjamin, *Illuminations*, trans. H. Zohn (ed.) (New York, 1968), pp. 243–244. On the more general politicisation of consumers in the past, see J. Winward, 'The Organised Consumer and Consumer Information Co-operatives', in Keats, Whitely and Abercrombie (eds), *The Authority of the Consumer*, pp. 72–90; J. Brewer, 'The Error of our Ways: Historians and the Birth of Consumer Society', public lecture in the Cultures of Consumption Programme, ESRC/AHRB, at the Royal Society, London, 23 September 2003; Trentmann, 'The Modern Genealogy of the Consumer', in Brewer and Trentmann (eds), *Consuming Cultures, Global Perspectives*, pp. 19–69.
32. Cf. Retort (I. Boal, T.J. Clark, J. Mathews and M. Watts), *Afflicted Powers* (London, 2005), p. 21.
33. N. Klein, *No Logo* (London, 2000).
34. D. Miller, 'Consumption as the Vanguard of History', in D. Miller (ed.), *Acknowledging Consumption* (London, 1995), pp. 8–9.
35. Ibid., p. 31; cf. 40–41.
36. Ibid., p. 47; cf. *The Dialectics of Shopping*, pp. 111–148.
37. M. Micheletti, *Political Virtue and Shopping* (New York, 2003), p. 2; M. Micheletti and J. Peretti, 'The Nike Sweatshop Email: Political Consumerism, Internet and Cultural Jamming', in M. Micheletti, A. Føllesdal and D. Stolle (eds), *Politics, Products and Markets: Exploring Political Consumerism Past and Present* (New Brunswick, NJ, 2003); M. Scammell, 'The Internet and Civil Engagements: The Age of the Citizen-Consumer', *Political Communication* 17 (2000).
38. Miller, 'Consumption as the Vanguard of History', p. 24.
39. Ibid., p. 31.

Index